Joshua A. Berman, Ph. D. (2002) is a lecturer
in the Department of Bible at Bar–Ilan University, Israel. His scholarly focuses are upon
the literary analysis of biblical narrative with
a penchant for interdisciplinary approaches
to the biblical text. He has published several
articles and is also the author of *The Temple:
Its Symbolism and Meaning Then and Now*
(Jason Aronson, 1995).

SUPPLEMENTS

TO

VETUS TESTAMENTUM

VOLUME CIII

NARRATIVE ANALOGY IN THE HEBREW BIBLE

Battle Stories and

Their Equivalent Non-battle Narratives

BY

JOSHUA A. BERMAN

BRILL

LEIDEN · BOSTON

2004

This book is printed on acid-free paper.

Library of Congress Cataloging-in-Publication Data

Berman, Joshua.
  Narrative analogy in the Hebrew Bible : battle stories and their equivalent non-battle narratives / by Joshua A. Berman.
    p. cm. – (Supplements to Vetus Testamentum, ISSN 0083-5889 ; v. 103.)
    Includes bibliographical references and index.
    ISBN 90-04-13119-1 (alk. paper)
    1. Military history in the Bible. 2. Bible. O.T.–Criticism, Narrative. I. Title. II. Series.

BS410.V452 vol. 103
[BS1199.M47]
221 s–dc22
[222'.066]

                                                                    2004040657

ISSN   0083-5889
ISBN   90 04 13119 1

PRINTED IN THE NETHERLANDS

To Michal
אשת חיל

CONTENTS

ACKNOWLEDGMENTS

It is with awe and wonder that I thank the Almighty for having granted me the opportunity to draw from the wisdom of teachers both from the great world of classical rabbinic learning and from the modern academy. The impetus to seek out vast networks of subtle connections between disparate biblical passages was a consciousness bestowed to me during my eight years of study at Yeshivat Har-Etzion under the inspired guidance of Rabbi Aaron Lichtenstein and Rabbi Yehuda Amital. This consciousness was further refined through the rigor and discipline afforded me in doctoral studies in the department of Bible at Bar-Ilan University.

The present study is a revised version of my doctoral dissertation conducted under the supervision of Professor Edward L. Greenstein and Professor Rimon Kasher. Each had very valid reasons with which they could have politely asked me to turn elsewhere for sponsorship. Each has gone above and beyond the normal call of duty in order to take on mentorship of my doctoral work. Conventional wisdom states that a doctoral student should avoid taking on two advisors, as the demands of one may differ from the demands of the other. In this case, I have been blessed to receive their combined wisdom and perspective and close friendship. I pray that I may be able to give to my students what they have given me.

I am indebted to the Council of Higher Education of the Ministry of Education of the State of Israel for the support of a Rotenstreich Fellowship and to the Memorial Foundation for Jewish Culture for their support over the final three years of my work. I would also like to recognize the Scholarship Committee of Bar-Ilan University and Mrs. Fanya Heller of New York City for their generous support during the first two years of my doctoral study.

Significant portions of chapter 5 of this study originally appeared as an article in the Journal of Biblical Literature ("Hadassah bat Abihail: From Object to Subject in the Character of Esther," *JBL* 120:4 [2001] 647-69) and I thank its editors for their permission to reprint that material here.

I would also like to acknowledge the assistance granted me over the years by the Department of Bible at Bar-Ilan University, by its chairmen during this time, Profs. Shmuel Vargon, Yitschak Tzefati, Ya'akov Klein and Amos Frisch and by its office staff, Hedva Kaplan and Chenya Spungin. My thanks as well to Ivo Romein and to Mattie Kuiper of the Brill editorial staff for their cheerful assistance as they guided me through the various stages of the editorial process. My father, George Berman of Boca Raton, Florida instilled within me a zest for learning and for writing and lovingly copyedited the manuscript, a process that reminds me of how much more I have to learn from him.

ABBREVIATIONS

AB	Anchor Bible
ABD	*Anchor Bible Dictionary* (6 vols., New York, 1992), ed. David Noel Freedman
ANET	*Ancient Near Eastern Texts Relating to the Old Testament* (3rd ed., Princeton, 1969), ed. J.B. Pritchard
BASOR	*Bulletin of the American School of Oriental Research*
BBB	Bonner Biblische Beiträge
BDB	*Hebrew and English Lexicon of the Old Testament* (Oxford, 1980) ed. F. Brown, S.R. Driver and C.A. Briggs
BJS	Brown Judaic Studies
BKAT	Biblischer Kommentar: Altes Testament
BZAW	Beihefte zur Zeitschrift für die alttestamentliche Wissenschaft
CBC	Cambridge Bible Commentary
CBQ	*Catholic Biblical Quarterly*
EB	*Encyclopedia Biblica*, 9 vols. (Jerusalem, 1950-1988), eds. E. Sukenik, M.D. Casutto, B. Mazar, H. Tadmor, S. Ahituv
EJ	*Encyclopedia Judaica*, 16 vols. (Jerusalem, 1972), ed. Cecil Roth
FRLANT	Forschungen zur Religion und Literatur des Alten und Neuen Testaments
HAT	Handbuch zum Alten Testament
HSM	Harvard Semitic Monographs
IB	*Interpreter's Bible*, 12 vols. (Nashville, 1952-1955), ed. G.A. Buttrick
ICC	International Critical Commentary
IDB	*Interpreter's Dictionary of the Bible*, 4 vols. (Nashville, 1962), ed. G.A. Buttrick
IEJ	*Israel Exploration Journal*
ITC	International Theological Commentary
JANES	*Journal of the Ancient Near Eastern Society*
JBL	*Journal of Biblical Literature*
JNSL	*Journal of Northwest Semitic Languages*
JPS	Jewish Publication Society
JSNTSup	Journal for the Study of the New Testament—Supplement Series

JSOT	*Journal for the Study of the Old Testament*
JSOTSup	Journal for the Study of the Old Testament—Supplement Series
KAT	Kommentar zum Alten Testament
KBL	*Lexicon in Veteris Testamenti Libros*, (Leiden, 1953), eds. L. Koehler and W. Baumgartner
LD	Lectio divina
MGWJ	Monatsschrift für Geschichte und Wissenschaft des Judentums
NCBC	New Century Bible Commentary
NICOT	New International Commentary on the Old Testament
NIDOTTE	*New International Dictionary of Old Testament Theology and Exegesis*, 5 vols. (Grand Rapids, 1997), ed. Willem A. Van Gemeren
OTL	Old Testament Library
SBLDiss	Society of Biblical Literature Dissertation Series
TDOT	*Theological Dictionary of the Old Testament*, 8 vols. (Grand Rapids, 1974-) , eds. G.J. Botterweck and H. Ringgren. Trans. J.T. Willis, G.W. Bromiley, and D.E. Green
THAT	*Theologisches Handwörterbuch zum Alten Testament*, 2 vols. (Stuttgart, 1971-1976), eds. E. Jenni and C. Westermann
TWAT	*Theologisches Wörterbuch zum Alten Testament* (Stuttgart, 1970-), eds. G.J. Botterweck and H. Ringgren
VT	*Vetus Testamentum*
WBC	Word Biblical Commentary
ZAW	*Zeitschrift für die Alttestamentliche Wissenschaft*
ZDPV	*Zeitschrift des Deutschen Palästina-Vereins*

CHAPTER ONE

INTRODUCTION: NARRATIVE ANALOGY AND THE METAPHOR PLOT

In her recent study of the doubled narrative and its role in the formation of critical method over the past three centuries, Aulikki Nahkola succinctly illustrates the lack of uniformity in the language we use to describe biblical narratives that bear a strong resemblance to one another.[1] She draws our attention to the nomenclature employed by scholars to describe the doubling of the Hagar stories of Genesis 16 and 21. For Astruc and Cassuto, the stories are referred to as "repetitions"; for Gunkel they are "variants"; for the followers of Wellhausen they are "doublets," while for Alter they represent a "type-scene."

This study focuses upon one type of doubled narrative, what Robert Alter[2] has termed *narrative analogy* or what Moshe Garsiel[3] calls *narrative duplication*. Because the terms themselves reflect a degree of "duplication," a working definition is in order. Sternberg defines an analogy as:

> An essentially spatial pattern, composed of at least two elements (two characters, events, strands of action, etc.) between which there is at least one point of similarity and one of dissimilarity: the similarity affords the basis for the spatial linkage and confrontation of the analogical elements, whereas the dissimilarity makes for their mutual illumination, qualification, or simply concretization.[4]

What distinguishes *narrative analogy* from *analogy* is primarily a quantitative issue. An analogy, within Sternberg's definition, contains at least one element of similarity and one of dissimilarity. Whole narratives may be considered as analogous, however, as Garsiel writes, only "when the points of resemblance between narrative units are both

---

[1] Aulikki Nahkola, *Double Narratives in the Old Testament: The Foundation of Method in Biblical Criticism* (BZAW 290; Berlin and New York: Walter de Gruyter, 2001) 164.

[2] Robert Alter, *The Art of Biblical Narrative* (New York: Basic Books, 1981) 21.

[3] Moshe Garsiel *The First Book of Samuel: A Literary Study of Comparative Structures, Analogies and Parallels* (Hebrew original; Ramat Gan: Revivim, 1985) 28.

[4] Meir Sternberg, *The Poetics of Biblical Narrative* (Bloomington: Indiana University Press, 1985) 365.

numerous (my italics) and evident."[5] This is the definition of narrative analogy that we have in mind, even as we save for a later point in the discussion just what resemblances we will regard as "evident" ones.

In biblical studies, only two full-length works can be found devoted to the topic of narrative analogy. The first to appear was Moshe Garsiel's 1983 work, *The First Book of Samuel: A Literary Study of Comparative Structures, Analogies and Parallels.*[6] The second work, *Through the Looking Glass: Reflection Stories in the Bible*, was written by Yair Zakovitch in 1995.[7] Of the two, only Garsiel's pioneering work addresses methodological issues in a systematic fashion.[8] In his introduction, Garsiel considers the various functions of narrative duplication and the means by which narrative analogy may be identified and based. Zakovitch's premises can only be deduced from the examples in his book as the introduction attends to these issues in only brief fashion. In order to place the insights of these scholars into a broader context and to properly lay the groundwork for my own foray into the domain of narrative analogy, I wish to turn to an earlier and extensive body of literature on the subject that has developed surrounding another literary genre: English Renaissance Drama. It is within the plays of the Elizabethan period that one discovers the most extensive use of narrative analogy via the double-plot anywhere in modern English literature.[9]

---

[5] Garsiel, *First Book*, 28.

[6] The book was first published in Hebrew (Ramat Gan: Revivim, 1983). An English edition appeared in 1985 (Ramat Gan: Revivim, 1985). All citations are from the English edition. Garsiel's work expands upon guidelines originally laid down by Meir Sternberg in his article, "The Structure of Repetition in Biblical Narrative: Strategies of Informational Redundancy," *Hasifrut* 25 (1977) 109-50 (Hebrew), later adapted into an English translation in a chapter by the same name in idem, *Poetics* 365-440. The material most germane to the study of narrative analogy is found on pp. 365-66.

[7] Yair Zakovitch, *Through the Looking Glass: Reflection Stories in the Bible* (Tel Aviv: Hakibbutz Hameuchad, 1995) (Hebrew).

[8] While Nahkola (*Double Narratives*, 71, 162) underscores the need for criteria to determine what kind and degree of doubling is necessary for us to recognize two pericopes as doubled narratives, she seems to be unfamiliar with the work of Sternberg and Garsiel in this regard.

[9] See Richard Levin, *The Multiple Plot in English Renaissance Drama* (Chicago: University of Chicago Press, 1971). For the phenomenon of the double plot within the plays of Shakespeare, see: Herbert R. Coursen, "A Spacious Mirror: Shakespeare and the Play Within," Ph.D. dissertation, University of Connecticut, 1966; Christopher F. Givan, "Thematic Doubling in Shakespeare's Plays," Ph.D. dissertation Stanford University, 1971; Joan Hartwig, *Shakespeare's Analogical Scene: Parody as Structural Syntax*

Narrative Analogy vs. Metaphor Plots

Levin, in his study of multiple plots in English Renaissance drama, defines the primary modality through which two plots are made to resemble one another during this period:

> In almost all the plays, the formal analogy joins two or more actions concerned with the same area of human experience... love, marriage, friendship, manners, war, class conflict... or a "nuclear parallel"—two fathers misjudging their children, two wives tempted to commit adultery... pairs of lovers thwarted by parental opposition... the basis of connection is immediately apparent in the common subject matter.[10]

Thus, in the plays of Shakespeare, one finds almost as a staple contrasted parent-child relationships along the lines of the contrasted relationships in *King Lear*, of Lear with his children and Gloucester with his.[11]

Scholars have seen the prevalence of narrative doubling in this period as an outgrowth of the regnant cosmology. Pythagorean cosmology, whereby the whole cosmos was regarded as being structured, was a mainstay of the school of Plato, and later the Stoics, St. Augustine, and ultimately adopted by the Renaissance.[12] All facets of existence ultimately bear a deep interrelationship of interior organization, with a single pattern of order subsisting throughout all levels of creation.[13] For renaissance artists this meant that art should reflect the "sempiternal beauty of the divine order," and for writers this was to reflect itself not only in the content of their works but in the very poetics with which they styled those works. This principle of analogy concern-

---

Lincoln: University of Nebraska Press, 1983); Ann Thompson, "Who Sees Double in the Double Plot?," in Malcolm Bradbury and David Palmer, (eds.), *Shakespearean Tragedy* (New York: Holmes & Meier, 1984); Karen S. Henry, "The Shattering of Resemblance: The Mirror in Shakespeare," Ph.D dissertation, Tufts University, 1989.

[10] Levin, *The Multiple Plot*, 148.

[11] Thompson, "Who Sees Double," 51; Levin, *The Multiple Plot*, 12.

[12] S. K. Heninger, *Touches of Sweet Harmony: Pythagorean Cosmology and Renaissance Poetics* (San Marino: Huntington Library, 1974) 16; Herbert Grabes, *The Mutable Glass: Mirror-Imagery in Titles and Texts of the Middle-Ages and English Renaissance* (Cambridge: Cambridge University Press, 1982) 228. Analogical thinking during the Renaissance period is explored in S. K. Heninger, *Touches of Sweet Harmony* (San Marino: Huntington Library, 1974); Joseph Mazzeo, "Universal Analogy and the Culture of the Renaissance," *Journal of the History of Ideas* 14 (1953) 221-34; the roots of Renaissance thought in Pythagorean cosmology are further explored in Ernst Cassirer, *Individuum und Kosmos in der Philosophie der Renaissance* (Leipzig: B.G. Teubner, 1927).

[13] Heninger, *Touches of Sweet Harmony*, 357.

ing the universe resulted in a cardinal element of English literature from the 1590's to the 1650's of "a poetry of correspondences."[14] The mirror, or looking glass emerges as the dominant image in the titles of hundreds of works from this period. Within this doctrine of metaphor, the poet does not merely employ or create metaphors in his work; through their use he discovers and reveals the various analogous planes of God's creation through the use of metaphor, including the double plot, in his work.

By the late seventeenth century, the use of the double plot wanes considerably. Newtonian physics belied the inherent relationships in nature and explained them as empirically determined; the skepticism of Hume eroded overarching theories of cause and effect between disparate entities;[15] artistic interest shifts toward a less symmetrical and more Baroque aesthetic.[16]

In biblical studies this phenomenon of doubled narratives surrounding common subject or plot matter has been referred to by Miscall, following Alter, as narrative analogy.[17] Similarities in the life trajectories of Joseph and Jacob make the stories of each narrative analogous; Saul's vow on the eve of battle ultimately leading to complications with his child (1 Samuel 14) finds a narrative analogy in the similarity of circumstances surrounding Jephthah's vow (Judges 11).[18]

Sternberg has given one accounting of the prevalence of narrative doubling within biblical prose that strikes a resonant note with Renaissance cosmology as outlined before. For Sternberg, God's omnipotence is a factor that shapes the Bible's poetics in that:

> In a God-ordered world, analogical linkage reveals the shape of history past and to come with the same authority as it governs the contours of the plot in fiction. Having traced the rhythm of Genesis, for example, we can predict future developments which the agents in their short-sightedness can only yearn for or still hope to block: that Rachel too will be delivered from sterility, say, or that Joseph will get into trouble, but finally prevail. The foreknowledge gained from the structure often leads to evaluative as well as informational contrast in viewpoint. As

---

[14] Grabes, *The Mutable Glass*, 228.

[15] Heninger, *Touches of Sweet Harmony*, 16.

[16] Givan, "Thematic Doubling," 357.

[17] See also Garsiel, *First Book*, 19-21.

[18] For an examination of narrative doubling in the Joseph stories see, James S. Ackerman, "Joseph, Judah, and Jacob," in Kenneth R.R. Gros Louis and James Ackerman, (eds.), *Literary Interpretations of Biblical Narratives* (2 vols.; Nashville: Abingdon, 1982) 2.85-113.

one cycle follows another throughout the period of the judges, the Israelites thus stand condemned for their failure to read the lessons of history: the moral coherence of the series luminously shows the hand of a divine serializer.[19]

Like the world-view of the Renaissance, that of the Bible, according to Sternberg, posits an inherent order of events in the world, which is embodied in a poetics of analogy and metaphor. [20]

Within his work on multiple plots in English Renaissance drama, Levin establishes a distinction between categories of double-plots that is crucial for our poetics in this study. Most double plots compare common subject matter. Yet, within Elizabethan drama there are also plays whose multiple plots contrast seemingly dissimilar areas of human endeavor.[21] With analogies unavailable between them on the level of plot elements or subject matter, the primary modalities of comparison emerge in the realm of form. He refers to this class of analogies as *equivalence plots*. An early Beaumont and Fletcher comedy titled *The Woman Hater* (1606) typifies this class of analogy.[22] In one plot the primary figure displays efforts to avoid all women while the subplot focuses on the efforts of another figure to hunt down a choice morsel of fish. Levin asserts that an analogous relationship exists between them not solely on the basis of the continuous juxtaposition of the two plots, which is typical of Elizabethan drama, but by virtue of the common semantic fields established between the two plots. Alimentary terms such as "appetite," "stomach," "taste," "meat," and "flesh" frequently become the bearers of sexual connotations.

In similar fashion, says Levin, an analogy is created between the main plot and subplot of *A Fair Quarrel* (1615-17), by Thomas Middleton

---

[19] Sternberg, *Poetics*, 114.

[20] While Sternberg sees narrative analogy as a rhetorical medium reflective of ideology, Muriel Bradbrook attributes the penchant for doubling in the plays of Shakespeare to aesthetics, "the feeling of allegory which categorizes Shakespeare's audiences." See idem., *Themes and Conventions of Elizabethan Tragedy* (Cambridge: The University Press, 1935) 43. Whereas Sternberg suggests that the Bible revels in analogical links, Damrosch adopts a much more understated position, speaking of the Bible's "tolerance" for narrative doubling. See David Damrosch, *The Narrative Covenant* (San Francisco: Harper & Row, 1987) 234. Zakovitch (*Through the Looking Glass*, 12) offers the phenomenon a diachronic explanation of intertextuality: "the corpus of biblical literature evolved layer by layer, in a process whereby later works were composed in conversation with earlier ones that had become stock features of the culture."

[21] Levin, *The Multiple Plot*, 148.

[22] Ibid., 151.

and William Rowley, between the semantic field of courage on the
battlefield and the semantic field of chastity.[23] Again, the equivalence
between the two plots rests heavily on common diction, such that
various terms for the central concept of each plot, ("honor," "fame,"
"good name," "worth") are respectively applied to each of these values. Levin cites another instance where the two plots of a drama
draw a comparison between lust and murder[24] and in another drama,
between debate and wrestling[25] as well as between love and war in
Shakespeare's *Troilus and Cressida*.[26]

While these examples illuminate Levin's choice of nomenclature
for the phenomenon—*equivalence plot*—the present writer finds the
term somewhat unsatisfactory. Any two stories that stand in analogy bear some degree of "equivalence" between them and thus the
term *equivalence* plot does not convey the distinct nature of analogous
narratives or plots that stand in figurative analogy to one another,
in contradistinction to analogies between stories that share common
subject matter. I shall therefore refer to the narratives brought into
analogy in this fashion as *metaphor* plots.

Levin laments that his search for a literary source for this kind of
combination was "not very fruitful" and that he finds no precedent
for it in classical drama.[27] It may be suggested that the Elizabethans
were inspired in this regard by biblical poetics. Shuger reminds us
that as the central cultural text in Renaissance England, the Bible
served as "a primary locus for synthetic, speculative, and symbolic
production."[28] While the dependence of Elizabethan writers upon
the Bible is suggested speculatively, we may say, at the very least, that
within the Bible we see a precedent for what Levin has documented
in Elizabethan drama as the *equivalence*, or what I have termed the
metaphor analogy.

The present study is interested exclusively in the metaphor plot and
not in standard narrative analogy as illustrated by Alter and Miscall,
where both stories contain common subject matter. To bring cohesion
to our case studies, we will focus upon the ways in which six battle

---

[23] Ibid., 153.
[24] Ibid., 156.
[25] Ibid., 148.
[26] Ibid., 160-62.
[27] Ibid., 149.
[28] Debora Kuller Shuger, *The Renaissance Bible: Scholarship, Sacrifice and Subjectivity*
(Berkeley: University of California Press, 1994) 3.

stories stand in metaphoric analogy to a corresponding non-battle narrative. We will see battle narratives paralleled with, among other things, a trial (the second battle of Ha-Ai [Joshua 8] with the trial of Achan [Joshua 7]); a rape (the victory over the tribe of Benjamin [Judges 20] with the rape of the concubine [Judges 19]); a court debate (the battle at Ramot Gilead [2 Chronicles 18] and the diplomacy that precedes it); and a feast (two days of battle in Esther 8 with two days of feasting in Esther 5).

The metaphor plot, or narrative, has not been independently identified and isolated in works on narrative doubling in the Bible. To be sure, individual instances of the metaphor analogy have been documented, even if not identified as such.[29] Yet in terms of critical theory and Biblical poetics, the rhetorical tool of the metaphor analogy has yet to be distinguished from other forms analogical linkage between two passages. I maintain that it is necessary to see the metaphor analogy as a subspecies of the larger set of doubling strategies subsumed within the general heading of narrative analogy. As a subset of narrative analogy, the metaphor analogy will share some functional and formal aspects common to all forms of analogical doubling as will be demonstrated later in this chapter. Nonetheless, there are three aspects in which the metaphor analogy deserves special notice:

1) In the standard narrative analogy subtleties may abound but the issue of what to compare is usually straightforward; the analogies set up between the taking of the wives by foreign kings in Genesis presents questions that stem immediately from circumstances common to all three narratives: has the patriarch compromised his morality? Which king is the wickedest of the three? How does God interact with the patriarch? The answers we provide may vary, but the question of what to compare is straightforward. In the metaphor analogy, however, the central conceptual field of comparison is not always clear. Toward what end has the artist contrasted these two disparate areas of human endeavor? Are the central values contrasted in *Troilus and Cressida* "love" and "war" as Empson argued,[30] or "love" and "honor," as claimed

---

[29] E.g.: Edward L. Greenstein, "The Riddle of Samson," *Prooftexts* 1 (1981) 237-260; Joshua Berman, "'He Who Re-enacts the Creation in His Goodness': Parallels Between Genesis 1 and Genesis 8," *Megadim* 9 (5750) 9-14 (Hebrew).

[30] William Empson, *Some Versions of Pastoral* (London: Chatto & Windus, 1935) 34-42.

by Levin?[31] To properly draw the comparison will perforce require
a higher degree of abstraction in the metaphor analogy than in the
standard narrative analogy of common subject matter.[32]

2) Analogous narratives can be analyzed from a rhetorical, or literary perspective, as is typical of the works of Alter, Sternberg, Garsiel
and others. Alternatively, form criticism also claims to explain the
similarities between annunciation scenes, theophany scenes, and the
like, in an attempt to classify the genre at hand and locate its *Sitz im
Leben*. Yet, the establishment of fixed forms is predicated on the identification of basic common plot elements. The metaphor analogy, by
definition being the contrast of different areas of human endeavor,
cannot be analyzed within a form critical approach.

3) Because the establishment of the metaphor analogy rests so heavily on formal elements of comparison, particularly semantic ones, the
poetics of this vehicle deserves special attention. We turn, therefore, to
explore the formal rules guiding the establishment of narrative analogy
in general and the metaphor analogy in particular.

The Compositional Elements of Narrative Analogy

The poetics that guides the composition of narrative analogies and
within them metaphor analogies have found their most extensive exposition in Moshe Garsiel's pioneering work, *The First Book of Samuel: A
Literary Study of Comparative Structures, Analogies and Parallels*. The basis,
says Garsiel, for the formation of an analogy between two narratives
is a relationship between them: narratives about two characters in a
story; different actions or stages in a character's life; prophecy and
fulfillment; dream and realization. The elements of the analogy need
not be restricted to plot elements, or subject matter, but may also be
found in similarities of sound, language, imagery, style.[33] Significantly,
he adds that a stylistic anomaly may be introduced into a text to bring
a particular component into closer alignment with its corresponding
element in the parallel.[34] With the basic guidelines for substantiating

---

[31] Levin, *The Multiple Plot*, 160-68.

[32] In a similar vein regarding the equivalence plot in Elizabethan drama, see
Ibid., 149.

[33] Garsiel, *First Book*, 22-23.

[34] Garsiel, *First Book*, 27. Similar guidelines for the establishment of an analogical
relationship between two narratives are set forth in Sternberg, *Poetics*, 365-67.

analogous links already well established by Garsiel, I wish now to discuss two far-reaching issues concerning the establishment of narrative analogy that in my mind require clarification or expansion.

The first stems from methodological issues raised by Vladimir Propp in his study of the Russian folktale. In his 1928 work, *Morphology of the Folktale*, Propp outlined his theory that all Russian wonder-tales could be boiled down to a common sequence of 31 "functions," where a function is defined as a noun expressing an action defined by its place in the narration and its significance for the course of the action.[35] Not all wonder-tales will contain all 31 functions but the functions that are contained will uniformly appear in the same sequence.[36] In a later work, *Theory and History of Folklore*,[37] Propp expanded on the criteria necessary for an action to be considered a "function" within his schema of the Russian wonder-tale. The action may be considered "segmentable" as a function only if it always plays the same role in each tale. The fact that in numerous stories the hero is given a magic tool—say, a magic horse or a magic pipe—is yet insufficient, according to Propp, to establish that there is a standard function of the hero receiving a magic tool. It emerges as a segmentable unit only if it may be shown that it plays the same role in each narrative—such as to overcome a foe.[38] Propp searches for links across tales that are not only associative but functional as well.

Propp's poetics here can be extrapolated and applied to a particularly thorny issue concerning the poetics of narrative analogy. One of the primary modalities through which narrative analogy generally and the metaphor analogy in particular is established, is through shared lexical terms. When the terms are relatively uncommon, or when they have been used in either narrative in an unconventional way, the basis for viewing them as part of the analogical base is strong. Yet, when we are seeking to establish the base of a narrative analogy between two stories, what are we to make of shared lexical terms that are highly common terms and are employed in each narrative in a manner that is fully conventional? Can we rightfully assert that these terms, too,

---

[35] Vladimir I. Propp, *Morphology of the Folktale* (trans. Laurence Scott; Austin: University of Texas Press, 1968) 21.

[36] Ibid., 22.

[37] Vladimir Iakolevich Propp, *Theory and History of Folklore* (trans. Ariadna Y. Martin, Richard P. Martin, et al.; Manchester: University of Manchester Press, 1984).

[38] Propp, *Theory and History*, 73-74; see also the introductory essay to Propp's *Theory and History of Folklore* by Anatoly Liberman, xxix.

contribute to the analogical base when their appearance in each narrative may be attributed to happenstance?

Drawing upon Propp's insistence that segmentable units be defined on functional as well as associative grounds, we may establish a criterion that allows us to determine when shared frequent terms may rightfully be deemed part of the analogical base. My proposition is that lexical terms shared between two texts should be included in the base of a proposed analogy only if they serve the same function in each text. To illustrate the principle involved I would like to consider the analogical base that supports the flagship example from the introduction of Garsiel's book on First Samuel. The graphic reproduction below is faithful to the original, and the visual effect itself is very much part of the issue at hand:

The Affair of Adonijah and Abishag (1 Kings 1-2)		The Rebuke of the Ewe Lamb (2 Samuel 12)	
והמלך דוד זקן בא בימים...	1:1	שני אנשים היו בעיר אחת...	1
ויכסוהו בבגדים ולא יחם לו		ולרש אין כל	3
ויאמרו לו עבדיו	2	כי אם כבשה <u>אחת קטנה</u>...	
יבקשו לאדני המלך נערה בתולה		ויחיה ותגדל עמו ועם בניו יחדו	
ועמדה לפני המלך		מפתו תאכל ומכוסו תשתה	
<u>ותהי לו</u> סכנת		<u>ובחיקו תשכב</u>	
<u>ושכבה בחיקך</u>		<u>ותהי לו</u> כבת...	
וחם לאדני המלך...		ויחר אף דוד באיש מאד...	5
ויבא אדניהו בן חגית	2:13	<u>חי יהוה כי בן מות</u>	
אל בת-שבע...		האיש העושה זאת	
ועתה שאלה <u>אחת</u>	16	ואת הכבשה ישלם ארבעתיים	6
אנכי שואל מאתך...		עקב אשר עשה את הדבר הזה...	
ותבא בת-שבע אל המלך שלמה...	19	ויאמר נתן אל דוד...	7
ותאמר: שאלה <u>אחת קטנה</u>	20	ולקחתי את נשיך לעיניך	11
אנכי שואלת מאתך...		ונתתי לרעיך...	
יותן את אבישג השונמית לאדניהו...	21	כי אתה עשית בסתר	12
וישבע המלך שלמה ביהוה לאמר	23	ואני אעשה <u>את הדבר הזה</u>	
כה יעשה לי אלהים וכה יוסיף		נגד כל ישראל ונגד השמש...	
כי בנפשו דבר אדניהו		ויאמר נתן אל דוד...	13
<u>את הדבר הזה</u>		אפס כי נאץ נעצת	14
ועתה חי יהוה...	24	את אויבי יהוה <u>בדבר הזה</u>...	
כי היום יומת אדניהו			

Let us examine Garsiel's handling of shared terms. Note that graphically Garsiel has arranged the two texts so as to focus attention upon their common lexical terms. As Garsiel maintains,[39] Adonijah's attempt

---

[39] Garsiel, *First Book*, 25.

at taking Abishag represents the finale of the sentence meted out to David for taking Bath-sheba. The parallel, suggests Garsiel, demonstrates that Adonijah's infraction is of a scale equal to David's as evidenced by the semantic fields common to the parable of the ewe and to the account of 1 Kgs 1-2. Taken cumulatively, the common terms unquestionably buttress the analogy and guide the reader to the proper conclusion. I would maintain, however, that each term individually must contribute to the rhetorical coherence of the overall message, and pass what I would call the *criterion of congruence*: each of the common lexical terms in the first narrative must be used in a *matching* and *equivalent* fashion in the other. Propp insisted that a unit could be segmentable as a "function" of the wonder-tale, only if it consistently plays the same role in the narrative. In like fashion, I would suggest that we should consider like terms part of the analogical base only if they serve the same function, only if they operate in a *congruent* manner in both narratives.

Most of the common terms highlighted here pass this test. The ewe, now an allegory for Abishag within the narrative of 1 Kgs 1-2, is the referent of the phrase ותהי לו and lies in the bosom of his master, in a manner paralleled by Abishag. Solomon's invective, חי יהוה, and call for Adonijah's death, correspond to David's pronouncements concerning the rich man in the parable. Even the use of the term אחת קטנה passes the test. While referring to the ewe in 2 Sam 12, it refers to Bath-sheba's question in 1 Kgs 2. But since the import of Bath-Sheba's "one small question" is Abishag, the congruence of the analogy is preserved, for the ewe here represents Abishag. The highlighting of the word אחת in v. 16 of 1 Kgs 2 is likewise justified. Though a thoroughly routine word in the Bible, and with no direct reference in the narrative of 2 Sam 12, it receives its valence from the same phrase of אחת קטנה in 2 Sam 12, and likewise refers to Abishag. A lexical component in one narrative may have several matching components in the analogical narrative. There is no requirement that all the narratival elements line up in a one-to one correspondence. But there is a requirement that the elements that do appear each bear equivalent meanings.

It is on this account that the element of את הדבר הזה emerges as problematic. Referred to once in 1 Kgs 2 (v. 23) it has three parallel occurrences in 2 Sam 12– vv. 6, 12, and 14. In 1 Kgs 2:23, the reference is to Adonijah's contrivance, his evil act. The reference to הדבר הזה in 2 Sam 12:14 passes the congruence test, for it, too refers to the evil act—that of David, who throughout the analogy stands in equivalence with Adonijah. In like fashion, the occurrence in v. 6 would also pass the congruence test, as there it also refers to an evil act—that of the rich man in the parable, who also stands in equivalence with Adonijah (and also utilizes all three words of the phrase את הדבר הזה which appears in the Bible 47 times, in contrast with the pairing of הדבר הזה alone as in v. 14, which appears 85 times). Yet, the occurrence in v. 12 fails this test, for here the phrase refers not to the act of the offender, but to the divine punishment to be meted out. It is true that the semantic elements of a narrative analogy can bear contrasting meanings. Indeed, the occurrence of את הדבר הזה in v. 12 of 2 Sam 12, may stand in direct contrast to its occurrence in v. 6; the rich man (David)'s injustice will be matched in contrast with God's justice. But to infuse this contrasted meaning into the phrase in 1 Kgs 2:23 seems tenuous.

I must immediately, however, qualify my argument. For the question of whether to include the occurrence in v. 12 on the list of elements that contribute to the establishment of the analogy between the two passages is a question of hermeneutics, where it would appear that Garsiel has adopted one position, while I have taken another. In his opening words of analysis concerning this analogy he reminds us that most scholars see the two stories as having originated from the same literary complex and that this contributes to the appearance of common terms in the two narratives. It provides a compelling explanation of the appearance of like terms in the two narratives, including the common term את הדבר הזה in 2 Sam 12:12 and 1 Kgs 2:23.

Moreover, Garsiel[40] posits in his introduction that these narratives have their roots in processes of oral transmission and cites the work of Culley and Gunn, which underscore that the choice of language employed in a text may be the consequence of habitual borrowing that takes place from the general traditional stock.[41] Within such an approach a lexical repetition may be viewed as an empty formal pattern whose meaning is infused anew with each usage.[42]

---

[40] Ibid., 23.

[41] Ibid., 28-29. David Damrosch sees the roots of such doubling in oral traditions and attempts to trace the evolution of this phenomenon through its later literary stages where oral variants were later understood to bear potential as powerful literary tools. See Damrosch, *The Narrative Covenant*, 234-38, and particularly 234 n. 29 for bibliographic sources on the subject.

[42] Others however, maintain that formulaic narrative is the process of the adapta-

But this argumentation constitutes, to borrow Sternberg's terms, an argument from *source*, not from *discourse*.[43] This study aims toward a synchronic interpretation of the text, viewed as a whole from a formalist and structural point of view. Rhetorical coherence, then, is the measure of admissibility for claims of analogical linkage. Arguments for linkage from premises about source, while valid from a critical standpoint, will not be entered into our analysis, which focuses on discourse.

This standard of rhetorical congruence, moreover, is crucial for the present study in which we explore the battle report as a metaphor analogy. The metaphor analogy lacks associative elements on the level of plot and subject matter. Since its basis rests more fully upon common elements of form, a more rigorous standard by which to establish semantic linkage must be employed.

The criterion of rhetorical congruence and the problem of shared common words between the two narratives lead us immediately to a second, and intimately related issue in the establishment of narrative analogy. This concerns the relationship between the process of identifying common terms that form the base of the analogy and the process of ascribing meaning to the elements found. In the introduction to his work on analogies and parallel structures in 1 Samuel, Garsiel describes the process by which such analogies are identified and construed:

> Comparative structure can be divided into two parts. The first of these is the stage of linkage, in which connections are established between different members of the comparison. Highly varied strategies of linkage... enable the author to direct attention to the connection invited between separate items so that they may be placed side by side for a shared examination. Second comes the stage of comparison, in which the reader sets linked items together, makes a thoroughgoing comparison between them, and delves into the meaning which emerges from that comparison... the first stage may be described metaphorically as the foundation on which a building is to be raised, and the second as the superstructure upon that foundation.[44]

---

tion of an ideal-typical pattern of form and meaning. These differing approaches are surveyed in Susan Wittig, "Theories of Formulaic Narrative," *Semeia* 5 (1976) 65-91. The entirety of *Semeia* 5 is devoted to the application of theories of oral transmission from folklore studies to biblical studies.

[43] Sternberg, *Poetics*, 15.

[44] Garsiel, *First Book*, 17-18.

According to this theory the process of identifying the elements that establish an analogical link and the process of interpretation are not only distinct but, by definition, sequential. Only once the foundation of identifying common elements has been laid may the interpretive process of building meaning commence.

The present writer, in his own method of research and here in the presentation of his findings, wishes to propose an alternative to this theory. To be sure, the very notion of discovering analogical linkage between two narratives can only begin with the initial identification of elements of resemblance between the two passages. But the present writer has found that even once initial elements of analogy are noticed the process of interpretation perforce begins concomitantly, even as the two narratives are further scoured in search of additional elements that substantiate the analogy. From the moment that common elements are initially identified between two narratives the processes of establishing meaning and of discovering further common elements become highly interdependent. On the one hand, the identification of the initial elements of analogy immediately begs an interpretation. This interpretation, in turn, helps identify, categorize, rank, and potentially even discount altogether, other potential elements of the analogical base.

That this is so may be seen through further analysis of Garsiel's flagship analogy. True to his approach of "'foundations' first, 'super-structure' second," Garsiel identified all of the semantic elements common to the two narratives as the basis for the meaning that he subsequently established. Indeed, he presented them graphically as self-evident by virtue of the fact that they are shared terms. Yet, the identification of common lexical elements was executed as an exercise in identifying even common and unmarked words. Their contribution to the analogy was assumed on associative grounds alone, with no regard to their function in the advancement of the plot. Put differently, the criterion of rhetorical congruence that I proposed above was not adopted. When semantic or other "foundations" are laid in a process independent of meaning, it is no surprise that the phrase את הדבר הזה in 1 Kgs 2:23 is seen to parallel the same phrase in 2 Sam 12:12. Yet, as we demonstrated, the two phrases carry conflicting valences. Concerning Adonijah the phrase refers to his misdeed, while in 2 Sam 12 it refers to God's execution of justice. Within my proposed method of establishing analogical links, whereby identifying common elements and establishing meaning are concomitant and interdependent processes, the evolution of the analogy would have proceeded differently. Initial elements of the analogy would have been identified, such as the occurrence of uncommon word pairings in each narrative (e.g. אחת קטנה; ובחיקו תשכב). This would immediately invite the hypothesis of a set of possible correspondences: Adonijah = rich man = David; Abishag = the crown = the ewe. With these established, all elements subsequently proposed as the basis of the analogy would have needed to conform to these lines. The search for further analogical elements could have been conducted not only along semantic or formal lines but within the parameters of a consistent line of suggested meaning and interpretation. The inclusion of the shared phrase את הדבר הזה, which shares only associative but not functional similarity, serves only to obfuscate the attainment of a clear interpretation of the analogy. To summarize, interpretation is not a stage subsequent to the identification of the base elements of the analogy. Rather, proposed hypotheses of meaning can themselves be instrumental in the proper identification of the elements comprising the analogical base. The converse is true as well. As further analogical elements are identified and incorporated into the hypothesized web of meaning, they can help us refine, reject, or discover different shades of meaning within the initial hypothesis put forward.

In the case of the analogy between the parable of the ewe and the attempted appropriation of Abishag by Adonijah, the issue of how to handle the term את הדבר הזה in v. 12 is of minimal consequence. The meaning of the analogy as construed by Garsiel remains intact. Yet, in other instances where all shared terms are brought into the analogical base by the simple virtue that they are shared terms, the risk emerges within Garsiel's methodology that the analogy will be misinterpreted. If too many terms are posited as parts of the analogy and these terms lack rhetorical congruence as I defined it above, it will be, figuratively speaking, difficult to see the forest for the trees. Only by carefully admitting like terms that pass the test of rhetorical congruence and only by concomitantly executing the processes of identifying common base elements and offering them meaning, can we be sure to arrive at a proper definition of the analogy and a proper construal of its meaning.

Garsiel himself registers an awareness of the rigidity of his original formulation. Later in his introduction he writes: "Certainly on occasion we even continue during the second stage (that of the comparison itself) to uncover latent resemblances between the items in question

[and] the basic analogy widens and deepens."[45] Our contention, however, is that this happens not "on occasion" but is, rather, the rule. Moreover, we contend that as latent resemblances are identified they do not only "widen and deepen" the basic analogy. Rather, they have the capacity to alter its meaning. The discovery of additional elements when identified within the criterion of rhetorical congruence can lead us to re-construe the correspondences that we have established between the two narratives and hence the meaning of the analogy between them.

The ensuing case studies will be presented according to this approach. Initial elements of analogy will be identified and a hypothesis of meaning suggested. As further analogical elements are identified the initial hypothesis of meaning will be continually refined and the different shades of its meaning explored.

An additional issue that requires elucidation concerning the poetics of the narrative analogy as defined by Garsiel is that of the sequential structure of the base elements of the analogy. The theoretical underpinnings of this consideration are again derived from the writings of Propp. Central to his notion of the 31 functions of the Russian wonder-tale was the imperative that they should be uniformly ordered sequentially. Later critics took Propp to task on this account. If a hero receives a magic tool to overcome the villain, why, critics challenged Propp, did it matter substantively whether the hero received this power at birth in one tale, at the beginning of his quest in another, or immediately prior to accomplishing his feat in a third?[46]

The present writer is inclined to agree that Propp's insistence upon a single uniform sequence is too restrictive. Yet this does not mean that issues of sequence are altogether insignificant. I would like to propose a modified version of Propp's notion of sequentiality, and it is this modified version that will be adopted in our study. There are instances where it is evident not only that two analogical narratives share a common term, but that the appearance of these terms in each of their respective text continuums occupies the same position. The phrase ויקימו עליו גל אבנים גדול עד היום הזה (Josh 7:26; 8:29) links the trial of Achan with the execution of the king of Ha-Ai, not only because of the eight word chain, but because it appears in the final verse of

---

[45] Garsiel, *First Book*, 22.
[46] See discussion in Anatoly Liberman's introduction to Propp's *Theory and History and of Folklore*, xxxi.

each account. Similarly, both accounts bear a common phrase in the opening verse: ויאמר יהוה אל יהושע: קום (7:10; 8:1). Because no two plots are identical, it is inevitable that analogous lexical components will not align sequentially. To notice, however, that two analogous narratives share a number of common terms, and that the third terms on each list, say, are identical would be to require of the reader an unreasonable level of intimacy with each text. Yet openings and closings are more easily distinguished. The opening represents the tale's point of departure, and the closing its endpoint. Openings and closings therefore afford the narrative artist the opportunity to alert the reader to the presence of an analogical link between two narratives, by establishing a lexical link either precisely at the opening or close of each narrative.

A second example of sequential ordering of analogical elements is seen in the narrative analogy between the revelation to Moses at the burning bush (Exodus 3) and the theophany at Sinai (Exodus 19-20). Both contain many common motifs: these include revelation at Sinai from amid fire; oscillation between attraction to and cowering from the source of revelation; divine proscription from approaching the source of revelation. Yet, one way Scripture guides the reader toward an awareness of this analogy is by couching an even relatively prosaic element of each episode in similar language precisely at the opening of each account. The prelude to each account bears the motif of entry into the desert and arrival at the mount: וינהג את הצאן אחר המדבר ויבא אל הר האלהים חרבה ("he drove the flock into the wilderness, and came to Horeb, the mountain of God" - 3:1) is matched in the Sinai theophany: ויבאו מדבר סיני ויחנו במדבר ויחן שם ישראל נגד ההר ("they entered the wilderness of Sinai and encamped in the wilderness. Israel encamped there in front of the mountain" - 19:1).

The comments thus far relate to the metaphor plot generally. As we mentioned earlier, the case studies in this work focus upon the biblical battle report. Further methodological comments concerning our study of narrative analogy stem from some of the characteristics of this genre of biblical literature, and thus we turn at this point to set out some of the salient literary aspects of the biblical battle report in this regard.

Literary Aspects of The Biblical Battle Report

Within modern scholarship, the exposition of the literary form of the biblical battle report began with an inquiry into the theological ramifications of battle in ancient Israel. Building upon earlier work by Friedrich Schwally,[47] Gerhard von Rad contended that when Israel engaged in battle as God's troops, it constituted "holy war," a political and military activity based in the cultic institution of the amphictyony.[48] Von Rad attempted to uncover the evidence for a real-life institution of sacral warfare associated with the tribal amphyctyony. Later scholars, most notably Stoltz, rejected the notion of Holy War, asserting that the reports of battles in pre-monarchal Israel share no common ritual or ideological pattern nor a common cultic or political setting.[49]

From a literary standpoint, however, von Rad made a substantial contribution to our understanding of the typical features of biblical battle report. While he may have failed to establish a social institution of Holy War, von Rad was the first to identify many of the typical features of the biblical battle report: shofar blowing (Judg 3:27; 6:34-35; 1 Sam 13:3); sexual renunciation prior to battle (1 Sam 21: 5; 2 Sam 11:11-12); sacrifice on the eve of battle (1 Sam 7:9; 13:9-10, 12); consultation with the oracle or prophet prior to engagement (Judg 20:13,18; 1 Sam 7:9; 14:8; 14:37; 23:2,4,9-12, 28:6; 30:7-8; 2 Sam 5: 19, 23); God's declaration that Israel's enemies have been given into her hand (Josh 2:24; 6:2; 6:16; 8:1; 8:18; 10:8; 10:19; Judg 3:28; 4:7; 4:14; 7:9; 7:15; 18:10; 20:28; 1 Sam 14:12; 17:46; 23:4; 24:4; 26:8; 1 Kgs 20:28); divine exhortations not to fear (Exod 14:13-14; Deut 20: 3; Josh 8:1; Josh 10:8; 10:25; 11:6; 7:3; 1 Sam 23:16-17; 30:6; 2 Sam 10:12);[50] repentance and mourning in the camp in the wake of defeat (Judg 20:23, 26; 1 Sam 11:4; 30:4).

Whereas von Rad focused on motifs and plot elements commonly

---

[47] Friedrich Schwally, *Der Heilige Krieg im Alten Israel*, (Semitische Kreigsaltertumer 1; Leipzig: Deitrich, 1901).

[48] Gerhard von Rad, *Der Heilige Krieg im Alten Israel* (Zurich: Zwingli-Verlag, 1951).

[49] Fritz Stoltz, *Jahwes und Israels Kriege* (Zurich: Theologischer Verlag, 1972); Manfred Weippert, "'Heiliger Krieg' in Israel und Assyrien: Kritische Anmerkungen zu Gerhard von Rads Konzept des 'Heiligen Krieges im alten Israel,'" *ZAW* 84 (1972) 460-93, esp. 490; J.L. Licht, "War," *EB* 4.1061.

[50] See E.W. Conrad, *Fear Not Warrior: A Study of "al tira" Pericopes in the Hebrew Scriptures* (BJS 75; Chico: Scholars Press, 1985); P.E. Dion, "The 'Fear Not' Formula and Holy War," *CBQ* 32 (1970) 565-70.

found in the biblical battle story, Richter and Plöger looked for lexical elements common to the Bible's battle reports. They found that battle reports (*Kampfbericht, Schlachtbericht*) frequently contained verbs of movement (נ.ס.ע., ה.ל.ך., ב.ו.א.), verbs of military activity (א.ס.פ., ח.נ.י., ל.ח.ם.), and verbs indicating the outcome of the battle for the vanquished party (ל.כ.ד., ל.ק.ח., נ.כ.ה., נ.ג.פ., נ.ו.ס., ר.ד.פ.), and a description of the magnitude of the defeat (מגפה גדולה, מכה גדולה).[51]

Susan Niditch has found repeated themes in these stories, such as an act of valor to merit marriage (Josh 15:16; Judg 1:12; 1 Sam 18: 24-27); taunting as a prelude to armed engagement (Judg 5:18; 1 Sam 17; 2 Sam 21:21; 2 Sam 23:9; 2 Kgs 19:23; Is 37:23; Zeph 2:8-10); armed victory that ensues from an act of trickery by underdogs (Gen 34; Judg 3; Judg 4:17-24 [cf. 5:24-31]; Judg 14-15); and battles won via miraculous divine intervention (Exod 17:8-13; Josh 6:20; 8:18; 10: 12-13; 1 Sam 7:9-11; 2 Kgs 6:18; 7:5-7; 19:35-37; 3:20-25).[52]

For all of this, however, scholars have questioned whether we may properly speak of a common form of the biblical battle report. The lexical elements identified by Richter and Plöger, asserts Gunn, are indeed prevalent in most of these stories. Yet, they are features that lack specificity and could be expected in any account of battle. The lexical terms identified here would be expected in scribal or oral traditions anywhere in the ancient Near East.[53] The claim that these terms represent a "form" of the biblical battle story, concludes Gunn, is too general to be of help and lacks proper attention to the circumstances of particular passages, and offers only a loose indication of a possible biblical form.[54] The consensus within scholarship today is that a set form of the biblical battle report is unavailable.[55] Yet, when we look across the entire biblical corpus, what may be discerned are typical

---

[51] Wolfgang Richter, *Traditiongeschichtliche Untersuchungen zum Richterbuch* (BBB 18; 2nd ed; Bonn: Peter Hanstein, 1966) 262-66; J.G. Plöger, *Literarkritische Formgeschichtliche und Stilkritische Untersuchungen zum Deutoronomium* (BBB 26; Bonn: Peter Hanstein, 1967) 16-19.

[52] Susan Niditch, *War in the Hebrew Bible* (Oxford: New York, 1993).

[53] David M. Gunn, "The 'Battle Report': Oral or Scribal Convention?," *JBL* 93 (1974) 517.

[54] Ibid., 518.

[55] Ibid., 518; Timothy L. Fearer, "War in the Wilderness: Textual Cohesion and Concept Coherence in Pentateuchal Battle Tradition," Ph. D. dissertation, Claremont Graduate School, 1993) 48; Lori L. Rowlett, *Joshua and the Rhetoric of Violence: a New Historical Perspective* (JSOTS 226; Sheffield: Sheffield Academic Press, 1996) 60; Anton Van der Lingen, *Les Guerres de Yahvé: L'implication de YHWH dans les guerres d'Israël selon*

features of the battle report. "Typical" features here does not mean
elements that appear in most battle reports. Rather, they appear even
in a small handful of reports and may be said to be part of a large
corpus of conventional elements from which the biblical narrators
drew in their depiction of battle in ancient Israel.

Significant for our study of the battle report as metaphor plot is an
assertion made by Gunn in his study of several battle reports in the
Book of Samuel. Commenting upon the difficulty of identifying a set
form for the biblical battle report, Gunn writes:

> We are dealing with passages of narrative, each of which is a subsidiary
> segment or constituent part of a larger story. In fact, in the cases we
> have looked at, it is hard to detach any of them without doing violence
> to the larger story, for they are part and parcel of it.[56]

Gunn's comment may be widely applied. Unlike annalistic traditions
elsewhere in the ancient Near East, battle reports in the Bible never
stand in isolation. Rather they are embedded within larger narrative
units. This observation speaks directly to the heart of the present
study. The fact that so many scholars have concluded that a fixed
form of the battle report is unavailable is of no surprise. The formal
and rhetorical aspects of each battle report will ultimately emerge as a
function of the role of the pericope within the larger narrative within
which it is embedded. This study seeks to look above particular issues
of form and motif as already identified by the scholars mentioned
earlier and to make a statement about the fashion in which the battle
report interacts with its surrounding literary unit.

We may further expand upon Gunn's assertion that battle reports
are an integrated part of the larger story. Consider the following
observation. When seeking to depict a battle, a biblical author can
choose from a wide stock of conventional aspects of the battle to
mention in his report:

1) Spiritual preparations for battle (sacrifice, prayer, mass assembly).
2) Consultations prior to battle (the leader may confer with God,
   prophet, or with other leadership figures).

---

les livres historiques de l'Ancien Testament (LD 139; Paris: Cerf, 1990) 215; John A. Wood,
Perspectives of War in the Bible (Macon, GA: Mercer University Press, 1998) 33.

[56] David M. Gunn, "Narrative Patterns and Oral Tradition in Judges and Samuel,"
VT 24 (1974) 295.

3) Sending of spies and receipt of their report.
4) Physical preparation for battle (draft, enumeration of weapons and troops).
5) Pre-battle instructions from leader to his troops.
6) Enumeration of the various stages of the battle.
7) Summary reports of casualties, prisoners and booty, and geographic parameters of the battle.
8) Detail of victory celebrations or of collective responses to defeat.

These eight elements, in fact, constitute sixteen variable elements for the biblical author, for while his focus is upon Israel he may also choose to detail any of these elements with regard to the enemy camp as exhibited in detail, for example, in the battle at Eben-ezer (1 Samuel 4). If a particular element plays a dramatic role in the lessons of the battle, the author's choice of including it in his account is well-understood. That Scripture chose to tell us that Joshua sent out spies prior to the battle of Jericho is understandable in light of the misadventure that befalls them. That Goliath was armed to the hilt is significant in contrast to the lack of armaments brought to the dueling ground by David. Yet, by and large, the battle details of the type listed above enumerated by the biblical authors seem to contribute primarily to the effect of verisimilitude.

The question emerges: by what rules did a biblical author decide which of these elements to include and which to highlight? I would suggest that Gunn's comment about the integrated nature of the biblical battle story goes a long way in helping us understand which of the many conventional elements of a battle a biblical writer would seek to include in his creation. We may expect that the elements of the battle that are reported contribute to the literary tapestry of the larger unit alongside their contribution to the effect of verisimilitude.

Consider the first battle report in the Bible, the battle of the four kings against the five in Genesis 14. Throughout the account great detail is accorded to the issue of booty. In fact, one might even say that disproportionate attention is paid to the issue of booty. 14:11 states that the victorious kings made off with all of the belongings (רכש) of the people of Sodom. It is only in the next verse that Scripture tells us that they also made off with Lot as captive and, the text stresses, it was with his belongings (רכשו) as well. The same disproportionate attention to רכ(ו)ש over life is displayed in the depiction of Abram's heroic raid to free Lot. Verse 16 states first that he retrieved all of the

רכ(ו)ש. Only then does the text mention that Abram also saved Lot or, rather, "Lot and his belongings" and only after that does Scripture say that Abram retrieved the women and the people (14:16). The negotiation with Malki-Zedek sheds light on this disproportion. For some within the story רכ(ו)ש is a primary issue. The victorious kings sought to despoil the vanquished kings, among them the kingdom of Sodom. Malki-Zedek feels duty-bound to reward Abram with these belongings, rather than returning them to their original and rightful owners. Abram's refusal reflects his utter dependence on God, but also signifies his sense of respect for the property of others. The spoils should remain with their rightful owners.[57]

Yet the pericope and its lexical and thematic emphasis on רכ(ו)ש takes on even greater significance when the battle story of Genesis 14 is seen within the context of the Abram stories of chapters 12-15. Throughout, the stories attend to a theme of fairness and respect for property. Pharaoh's appropriation of Sarai constitutes a flagrant violation of respect for ownership. The separation between Lot and Abram serves to properly respect the property that belongs to each one. The word רכ(ו)ש, a *Leitwort* in the narrative of chapter 14 (vv. 1, 16, 21), is also a *Leitwort* in the larger narrative of the Abram stories of chapters 12-15. Abram comes to Canaan with the רכ(ו)ש that rightfully belongs to him (רכשם אשר רכשו) (12:5). The great רכ(ו)ש that he attained as a result of Pharaoh's indemnity and the רכ(ו)ש of Lot (13:6) are properly respected in the agreement to separate. Abram's exemplary treatment of רכ(ו)ש in chapter 14—retrieving all the רכ(ו)ש which had been violated, yet taking virtually none for himself—is the highpoint of this theme in chapter 14. Abram receives his reward through this *Leitwort* in chapter 15: His descendants will leave from enslavement ברכש גדול, with great possessions (15:14). Only by seeing the battle narrative and its particular attention to booty within the context of the larger narrative unit can the focus within the battle report be fully understood.

---

[57] Abram's exemplary behavior in this regard is discussed with respect to prevailing booty restoration agreements in the ancient Near East in Yochanan Muffs, "Abraham the Noble Warrior: Patriarchal Politics and Laws of War in Ancient Israel," in idem, *Love & Joy: Law, Language and Religion in Ancient Israel* (New York and Jerusalem: Jewish Theological Seminary of America, 1992) 67-96.

Battle Narrative and Parallel Narrative:
Their Respective Places Along the Plot Continuum

It is to broader discussions of critical theory that I turn once more to flesh out a particularly acute issue for this study, this time a question of structure: within our case studies of the biblical battle report, where does the battle report appear within the larger work relative to its parallel narrative? *A priori*, we could hypothesize three different models:

1)

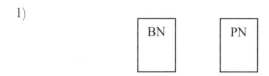

Here, the battle narrative (BN), in whole, precedes the parallel narrative (PN), also in whole, along the text continuum. It may appear immediately before or it may appear at quite a distance prior to its paralleled text. Conversely, we could find the parallel narrative, in whole, prior to the battle narrative:

2)

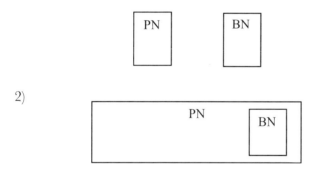

In this scenario, the battle narrative parallels not another narrative along the text continuum, but rather the entire narrative within which it is embedded. This is referred to as a *mise en abyme*.[58] A *mise*

---

[58] The definitive work on the *mise en abyme* is Lucien Dällenbach, *Le Récit Spéculaire: Essai sur la mise en abyme* (Paris: Seuil, 1977). See also Ann Jefferson, "*Mise en abyme* and the Prophetic in Narrative," *Style* 17 (1983) 196-208; Mieke Bal, *Lethal Love: Feminist Readings of Biblical Love Stories* (Bloomington: Indian University Press, 1987) 75-87; idem, "Mise en abyme," *On Meaning-Making: Essays in Semiotics* (Sonoma: CA: Polebridge Press, 1994) 45-58. On Mise en Abyme within biblical studies see Edward

en abyme is defined as "any aspect enclosed within a work that shows
a similarity with the work that contains it (*est mise en abyme toute enclave
entretenant une relation de similitude avec l'œvre qui la contient*)."[59] Within the
plays of Shakespeare its classic expression is in *Hamlet*, where the play
within the play, "The Murder of Gonzago," dramatizes the king's own
crime and the queen's disloyalty.[60] Here, again, variation is possible;
the battle narrative can appear later within the overall plot, as I have
graphically placed it here, or earlier. Conversely, in theory, the larger
box, i.e. the main narrative, could be the battle narrative, and within
it a smaller parallel narrative.

3)

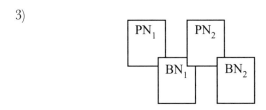

This scenario, whereby the battle narrative and parallel narrative
alternate along the text continuum, is the standard form of the Elizabethan drama. Each of the plots unfolds over the course of the play,
with some degree of overlap between the characters and events of the
two plots, from act to act, and from scene to scene.

How are narrative analogies arranged along the text continuum
within the Bible's poetics? In the Joseph narratives a degree of shifting occurs between stories that are Judah based and others that are
Joseph based while some points of analogical similarity exist between
the two characters.[61] Likewise, one sees repeated shifting between
scenes about David and scenes about Saul with some overlap between
them in 1 Samuel.[62] This is about as close as one comes to our third

L. Greenstein, "The Retelling of the Flood Story in the Gilgamesh Epic," in Jodi
Magness and Semour Gitin (eds.), *Hesed Ve-Emet: Studies in Honor of Ernest S. Frerichs*
(Atlanta: Scholars Press, 1998) 199-200; Yitzhak (Itzik) Peleg, "Going Up and Going
Down: A Key to Interpreting Jacob's Dream," Ph. D. dissertation, Schechter Institute
of Jewish Studies, 2000 (Hebrew).

[59] Dällenbach, *Le Recit*, 18. The English translation is taken from Lucien Dällenbach, *The Mirror in the Text* (trans. Jeremy Whiteley with Emma Hughes; Cambridge:
Polity Press, 1989) 8.

[60] Dällenbach, *Le Recit*, 22.

[61] See Ackerman, "Joseph, Judah, and Jacob," 85-113.

[62] See Garsiel, *First Book*, 135-37.

graphic figure, or what we called the classic Elizabethan plan of the multiple plot. No full length treatment of the *mise en abyme* has been conducted within biblical studies though literary theorist Mieke Bal has classified the Ruth story as a *mise en abyme* of the larger story of the history of Israel.[63]

Yet, overwhelmingly, it would seem that doubled narratives within the Bible follow the form delineated in our first graphic figure: along the text continuum, two distinctly bounded stories are found to be analogous to one another. It may be that their respective contents exist in relationship; cause and effect, or two stories about the same character at a different stage in the plot, but formally, the two narrative sections are seen to be distinct units, often in close proximity to each other, yet without direct overlap.[64]

The issue of the location of the two narratives along the text continuum is of cardinal importance for our study. The battle narrative, we would expect, should behave as other narrative analogies do. By the law of averages, then, we should find that sometimes the battle narrative precedes its parallel narrative, and sometimes follows it. In all six of the cases under study the battle narrative and parallel narrative are distinctly ordered along the text continuum, and, in fact, are immediately juxtaposed and contiguous. It is remarkable that in all of them the form that is revealed is:

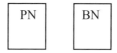

The battle narrative is a metaphor plot, time and again, of the story that precedes it. This observation is significant for several reasons. In describing his methodology, Garsiel classifies juxtaposed narratives in a separate category: "if [two stories] have been placed in contiguity, then whether they are linked by plot or theme… their very juxtaposi-

---

[63] Bal, *Lethal Love*, 87.

[64] Yair Zakovitch (*Through the Looking Glass*), however, has shown that what he calls mirror texts, whereby two figures are contrasted through analogy, often bear the property of intertextuality, accessing and referencing stories from other earlier works. On intertextuality and biblical studies see Danna Nolan Fewell (ed.), *Reading Between Texts: Intertextuality and the Hebrew Bible* (Louisville: Westminster, 1992). Several more recent perspectives on intertextuality and biblical studies are found in A. Lemaire and M. Sæbø, eds. *Congress Volume Oslo 1998* (Leiden: Brill, 2000).

tion urges the reader to look for hidden links."[65] All of the links that
we will establish, therefore, will be that much more credible because
universally we will be comparing juxtaposed texts.

Moreover, the fact that the battle narrative will always be shown to
appear immediately following its corresponding metaphor narrative
suggests that we may be able to conclude something distinct about
the relationship between form and function within these biblical battle
reports. If, time and again, the battle report mirrors the story that
precedes it, we may be able to deduce from this some type of statement about war in the Bible. But we will be able to do so only after
examining the cases under study and hence such findings perforce will
need to wait until the presentation of our conclusions.

Another point of significance stems from the relationship between
genre and rhetoric. Earlier we noted that while scholarship has been
unable to concretely define the characteristics of the battle report
in generic terms many typical features have been identified. These
included both semantic (.נ.כ.י, ל.ח.ם, נ.ג.ף.) and motival (trickster,
single combat warfare, taunting) elements. The present study aims
to extend that range of typical features to a third realm: that of the
structural. A typical feature that can be found in the composition of
battle reports is that they can form metaphor analogies with the narrative units that surround them.

A well-pointed question could be asked of the scope of this study:
narrative duplication is a common staple of biblical narrative. It stands
to reason, then, that across the entire corpus of biblical narrative we
will find instances where the battle, or elements of it, stand in analogical relationship to other elements along the text continuum. Is
there anything unique, therefore, in finding techniques of duplication
employed particularly in the composition of the battle report?

The answer, it will be clear by now, is yes, twice over. First, the
battle report can be seen to reflect a particular technique of narrative
doubling, that of the metaphor plot. Second, by examining the battle
story in relation to its parallel narratives, we have been able to see
already, in an initial way, that the battle report follows the narrative
that it doubles, rather than vice versa.

---

[65] Garsiel, *First Book*, 21.

The Functions of Narrative Duplication

As we analyze our case examples our aim will be not only to document the formal existence of analogical elements, but ultimately to question their meaning and implications: toward what end has Scripture created these analogies? A number of generic issues surround the function and meaning of these types of structures, and I wish now to review these in advance of delving into the study of the particular cases.

We open with a disclaimer made both by Levin with regard to the structures that he examined within English Renaissance drama, and by Sternberg with regard to structures of repetition generally in the Bible: when discussing the relationship between form and function overarching rules are hard to come by. In the words of Levin: "Throughout this study we have insisted that no multi-plot structure could be understood apart from its specific function within its concrete dramatic context."[66] Sternberg likewise speaks of the error of trying to link form and function in a regular and systematic way: "Given the appropriate contexts, the same means may serve different semantic and rhetorical ends, and different means, the same end."[67]

Having said that, there are two basic questions that need to be asked and whose parameters need to be defined before we turn to our case studies:

1) *What interpretive effect do the two analogous narratives have upon each other?* Empson, in one of the first treatments in contemporary criticism of the double plot, sees within the double plot a vehicle for mutual illumination.[68] It is in this vein that Levin finds the tragedy of Lear so pronounced and intense.[69] By observing Gloucester's parallel tragic fate we realize that it pales in comparison to that of Lear, and hence our heightened sense of the enormity of his tragedy.

Conversely, the parallel dramas of Lear and Gloucester have been interpreted by Thompson in a fashion that allows us a second way to look at the relationship between two analogous narratives. She sees in the double plot a *composite statement*, not about the characters, Lear and Gloucester per se, but about the potentially universal phenomenon

---

[66] Levin, *The Multiple Plot*, 222.
[67] Sternberg, *Poetics*, 437.
[68] Empson, *Some Versions of Pastoral*, 34.
[69] Levin, *The Multiple Plot*, 19.

of ungracious children.[70] Thompson's comments articulate a poetics
stemming from a psychological or sociological position on the part of
the artist. Within the poetics of the Bible, Sternberg has made a similar
comment about narrative analogies, but ascribing a theological agenda
for the phenomenon, instead:

> Such… coupling may recur often enough to signal a divine law or
> logic that governs the march of history…like the "unnatural" rise of the
> younger over the older, especially in Genesis…As the chain of analogy
> unfolds along the sequence… the cumulative lessons of induction solidify
> into a general rule or historical paradigm, which grows in predictive
> determinacy and ideological force with each new application.[71]

In her comments on the *mise en abyme*, Mieke Bal raises a structural
point that is particularly germane for the issue of illumination between
analogous narratives. The placement of the embedded, or mirror text
will play a great role in determining its function. A mirror text placed
at the beginning of the frame narrative can serve readers as a proleptic
tool and allow them to predict the outcome of the story.[72] Similarly,
when a mirror text is embedded toward the end of the primary text it
may serve as a retrospective, or analeptic device.[73] Its primary function, she claims, is significance enhancing. While our case examples
do not exhibit the *mise en abyme*, the issue of the relative placement
of one narrative vis-à-vis the other is a crucial issue. Since in all of
the examples that we will be examining the battle report appears
immediately following its parallel narrative we may expect to find the
battle narrative functioning as an oblique commentary on the story
that precedes it.

2) *Do the analogical linkages result in internal as well as external reception?*
One of the great divides between modern and classical literature is
the question of reception: Does the author allow the reader a higher
vantage point of understanding than the internal characters of the
story, or does the reader grope in unawareness for as long as do the
story's characters? The modern novel allows for no such superiority,

---

[70] Thompson, "Who Sees Double," 47, 75.

[71] Sternberg, *Poetics*, 269.

[72] Mieke Bal, *Narratology: Introduction to the Theory of Narrative* (Toronto: University
of Toronto Press, 1985) 146.

[73] Ibid., 147. See also Dällenbach, *Le Récit*, 82-83.

and blurs any distinction between internal and external reception.[74] This is supported, for example, by Jefferson's observation concerning the use of the *mise en abyme* in contrasting ways by Poe and in *Oedipus the King*. In Poe's tale, *The Fall of the House of Usher*, the reader shares the narrator's ignorance in spite of the presence of a *mise en abyme* ("The Mad Trist") that portends the events to come. In contrast, the oracles of Oedipus, which form *mises en abyme* of the entire play, contribute to the reader's observation of the characters' follies from a superior vantage point of knowledge.[75]

In his discussion of verbatim repetition in the Bible, Sternberg states the Bible's norm with respect to the issue: there are times when the repetition reflects the psychological motives of the characters while at times the device of repetition is solely a function of signals received only from the transmission of author and text to reader.[76]

The question is particularly germane to a study of metaphor plots and narratives. In standard cases of narrative analogy the resemblance of chains of events between two scenarios may more easily allow a character to notice the linkages formed for the reader by the artist; the common plot may be readily apparent to an internal character as well. But in a metaphor analogy the very basis for comparison is established through poetic and rhetorical devices alone; the events themselves display no similarity. As we proceed, then, through our case studies we will ask: are the associations being drawn by the reader also being realized by the internal characters? What evidence does the text give us to decide the point? When there is evidence of internal reception is it concurrent to ours as readers or only upon reflection late in the episode?

We turn now to our six case studies. In each we will identify initial common elements and propose a hypothesis of meaning. As our probe of the metaphor analogy continues, more base elements will be considered for inclusion as we adhere to the criterion of congruence and evolve our hypothesis as to the meaning of the analogy. In each case study we will consider the question of illumination between the two narratives and the question of reception of the analogy's meaning by the internal characters. In an appendix we will offer reflections

---

[74] Dällenbach, *Le Recit*, 111.
[75] Jefferson, "*Mise en abyme*," 203.
[76] Sternberg, *Poetics*, 410.

concerning narrative analogy and the biblical battle report through a comparative study with epigraphic inscriptions of battle reports from the ancient Near East.

Translations of biblical passages are my own in consultation with the major modern Bible translations, particularly that of the Jewish Publication Society of America.

CHAPTER TWO

THE SECOND BATTLE AT HA-AI (JOSH 8:1-29) AND
THE TRIAL OF ACHAN (7:10-26)

As we mentioned in our introduction, the juxtaposition of two passages is a *prima facie* basis for seeking possible analogy. This is all the more so when the two narratives are components of a larger literary unit as is the case with the account of the trial of Achan in Joshua 7 and the second battle at Ha-Ai in Joshua 8. In each, Joshua is the protagonist of the story. Moreover, the outcome of chapter 8, victory over the inhabitants of Ha-Ai, is explicitly made dependent by Scripture upon the full implementation of the trial procedures of chapter 7: "You will not be able to stand up to your enemies until you have purged the proscribed from among you" (Josh 7:13). It is against this backdrop that we proceed to identify common lexical terms and propose a hypothesis of meaning that emanates from the correspondences established.

"They raised a huge mound of stones over him, which is still there to this day"

Both the narrative of the second battle of Ha-Ai and of the trial of Achan conclude with the narrative description, "They raised a huge mound of stones over him, which is still there to this day" (ויקימו עליו גל אבנים גדול עד היום הזה) in reference to Achan (7:26) and to the king of Ha-Ai (8:29). The presence of a lengthy lexical string depicting a rarely attributed motif in two passages is a *prima facie* basis for finding an analogy, as is the presence of a common formula at the same point in each narrative respectively, in this case at its close. Before assessing the meaning that this link might bear I would like to further substantiate my claim that a linkage must be proposed, in light of an examination of how and when comparable commemorative cairns are depicted elsewhere in the Bible.

Indeed, cairns are not unique to the narrative unit of Joshua 7-8. Boling likens the cairn heaped upon Achan to that found concerning Absalom (2 Sam 18:17)[1] and many commentators have linked the

---

[1] Robert G. Boling, *Joshua* (AB 6; Garden City NY: Doubleday, 1982) 228.

cairn heaped upon the king of Ha-Ai to a similar action taken against
the kings of the southern confederacy in 10:27. Yet it is significant
that, Achan notwithstanding, only one other instance can be found
in which a villainous individual (i.e. Absalom) has a cairn built over
him. Moreover, aside from the king of Ha-Ai, there is only one other
instance in which enemy kings earn the same treatment.[2]

Moreover, the language employed in the two instances under study
is not only identical, but also distinctive. When a formula is distinct to
two juxtaposed passages, there is *prima facie* evidence to seek analogical
meaning. Concerning the kings of the southern confederation, Scripture
writes (10:27): "Large stones were placed over the mouth of the cave
that are there to this day" (וישמו אבנים גדלות על-פי המערה עד-עצם היום
הזה). Here the verb וישמו appears in place of the verb ויקימו found
in both Joshua 7 and 8, while the term גל is absent. The phrase עצם
היום הזה in the Ha-Ai accounts is expressed simply as, עד היום הזה. A
structural difference concerning the stones may be discerned as well.
The king of Ha-Ai himself was buried beneath a large cairn while the
southern kings were deposited in a cave and it is the cave that is sealed
with large stones. The Absalom account reads, "and they piled up a
very great heap of stones over it" (ויצבו עליו גל-אבנים גדול מאד), again
employing a different verb while omitting the phrase עד היום הזה.

To summarize then, while the cairn is not unique to Joshua 7-8, it
is not commonly found elsewhere. The language employed in the two
juxtaposed accounts is not only identical across an eight-word string,
but is distinctive at several points in comparison with the formulations
utilized in the other occurrences of the cairn. If we consider the narrative structure of each account, a further likeness is seen. The erection

---

[2] The function of these stone structures has been variously explained. Nelson (R.
D. Nelson, *Joshua* [OTL; Louisville: Westminster, 1997] 106), in his comment concerning the cairn over Achan, says that the mound of stone was presumably thought
of as disempowering the dead and entombing any further potential damage from
them. Similar expressions are found in the medieval commentaries of Abarbanel
and R. Joseph Kara to 8:29. Gray (John Gray, *Joshua, Judges, Ruth* [NCBC; London:
Nelson, 1967] 89) suggests that such structures may have been associated with an
accursed person on whose grave passers-by would cast stones as, he claims, was until
recently the custom at the Tomb of Absalom in the Kidron Valley. Alternatively,
he offers, the cairn in chapter 7 may have been a boundary cairn between Judah
and Benjamin. Gersonides (8:29) sees the cairn of chapter 8 as serving the function
of perpetuating the victory there and thereby forewarning other kings waiting to
engage Israel in battle.

of the cairn constitutes the final note of the battle report of the second battle of Ha-Ai and in similar fashion is the final action taken in the account of the trial of Achan, with the remainder of 7:26 representing an etiological note.[3] The connection begs for an explanation.

There have been various accounts of the relationship between the two passages. Coming at the issue from a diachronic perspective, Nelson maintains that the unit of Joshua 7-8 is the redaction of two independent tales, one about Achan and one concerning Ha-Ai that have been joined in a single plot movement.[4] The cairn in each is reflective of a final redactive effort in which the two tales are joined together.

This study, however, seeks the possible meanings that stem from a synchronic reading of the text. Galil and Zakovitch state on the etiological note in 7:26 that "the extirpation of the sinner Achan paved the way for the successful conclusion of the capture of Ha-Ai in precisely the same fashion."[5] The underlying message, within their interpretation, seems to be an idea of cause and effect. The victory over Ha-Ai, Scripture intimates, emerges only because Achan had been properly dispatched. The event commemorated by the second cairn is only made possible by the event marked by the first. Woudstra suggests a different account of the link between the two cairn passages: "God's past acts of deliverance for Israel and of judgment on those who disobey him, be they Israelite (Achan) or non-Israelite, could thus be recalled by generations to come."[6] Both narratives end with cairns because both episodes are worthy of commemoration. What is unclear from Woudstra's commentary is the reason for this particular villain (i.e. Achan) and for this particular act of deliverance. Further,

---

[3] This stands in particular contrast to the positioning of the detail of the cairn within the Absalom narrative, which continues for several more verses .

[4] Nelson, *Joshua*, 98. This view is shared by Butler (T.C. Butler, *Joshua* [WBC 7; Waco, TX: Word Books, 1983] 81), Gray (*Joshua Judges*, 81), Miller and Tucker (J.M. Miller and G.M. Tucker, *The Book of Joshua* [CBC; Cambridge: Cambridge University Press, 1974] 67), Soggin (J.A. Soggin, *Joshua: A Commentary* (OTL; trans. R.A. Wilson; London: SCM Press, 1972] 96), and Woudstra (M.H. Woudstra, *The Book of Joshua* [NICOT; Grand Rapids: Eerdmans, 1981]120). Kaufmann (Y. Kaufmann, *The Biblical Account of the Conquest of Canaan* [2nd ed; Jerusalem: Magnes, 1985] 117-18 [Hebrew], and Y. Kaufmann, *Joshua* [Jerusalem: The Israel Society for the Study of the Bible, 1963] 116 [Hebrew]), however, argues that the unit is an integral whole.

[5] Gershon Galil and Yair Zakovitch, (eds.), *Joshua* (Olam HaTanakh; Tel Aviv: Davidson-Eti, 1994) 82 (Hebrew).

[6] Woudstra, *Joshua*, 142.

it is unclear from his words toward what end Scripture brought the
two into conversation through the shared phraseology.

Particularly helpful here, and the conception upon which we will
expand, is the accounting proposed by Hamlin:

> The pile of stones in the Valley of Achor (Trouble Valley), which marks
> the conclusion of ch. 7, is a reminder of the inner struggle in the heart
> of Israel against temptation and corruption. The pile of stones at the
> ruin mound of Ha-Ai, referred to in 8:29, tells of a victory over outside
> forces.[7]

The key here is Hamlin's resolution of the matched cairns through the
prism of a duality: the two cairns signify that Israel has two enemies,
one internal and one external. The external enemy is the Canaanite
nations. The internal enemy, the potentially wayward Israelite, is an
enemy "internally" in two senses of the word. He is a member of the
people of Israel and hence internal to the nation. Second, the threat
that he poses is not to the physical state of the people, but to their
spirit, and hence represents an "internal" threat. It would seem that
Hamlin meant "internal" in this second, perhaps more homiletic,
sense. Modifying Hamlin's hypothesis slightly, we suggest that the two
cairns equate processes of struggle against two enemies—the "enemy
without," namely the Canaanite nations, and the "enemy within," in
the first sense defined here, within the people of Israel.

To grasp why the message of this duality is so appropriate at this
juncture in the Book of Joshua we need to see the unit of Joshua
7-8 within its wider narrative context. The theft of *ḥerem*, banned
and consecrated property, by Achan constitutes the first crisis encountered by Joshua and Israel upon crossing into the land of Israel. It
is significant that God delays his response to the theft until after the
debacle of the first battle of Ha-Ai. In so doing, He creates a linkage
between the theft and the rout that is explicit within the conceptual
and semantic fields of His words to Joshua in 7:12. In that verse, the
term חרם refers both to the fate of Israel before her neighbors and
to Achan and the stolen booty.[8] The lesson to Joshua in the wake of

---

[7] Hamlin, *Joshua*, 56.

[8] This understanding of the phrase אם לא תשמידו החרם follows Kaufmann (*Joshua*,
119), and Woudstra (*Joshua*, 126). Nelson (*Joshua*, 101) and Butler (*Joshua*, 86) however,
identify the term *ḥerem* here as referring exclusively to the stolen booty and not to Achan.
For more on *ḥerem* see Philip D. Stern, *The Biblical Ḥerem: A Window on Israel's Religious
Experience* (BJS 22; Atlanta: Scholars Press, 1991); M. Greenberg "Ḥerem," *EJ* 8.344-
49; Y Kaufmann, *The Religion of Israel* (trans. Moshe Greenberg; New York: Shocken

the debacle of the first battle of Ha-Ai is that he and Israel must be cognizant that they face two enemies as they wage their campaign of conquest. On the one hand they face the nations of Canaan, what may be termed not only the external enemy but the more apparent enemy, the enemy they had knowledge of even before their redemption from Egypt (Exod 6:8). Within the words of God's admonition in vv. 11-12 they learn through their own experience that they face a second enemy, the enemy within their own ranks; an enemy so numerically insignificant that it can number even a sole deviant who violates the word of God. The tenacity with which the external enemy is pursued must be matched by a concomitant and commensurate effort against the enemy within. The two cairns erected at the close of the trial narrative of chapter 7 and the battle narrative of chapter 8 represent the two corresponding endpoints of equivalent processes: the pursuit of the two enemies of Israel, internal and external. With a working theory established that provides meaning to the initial analogous elements identified between the two narratives, we proceed to identify the other elements of the common pursuit against Israel's two enemies as recorded in the narrative of Joshua 7-8.

Equivalent Processes of Six Activities:
לקום, להשכים, להקריב, ללכוד, לרוץ, לשרוף

Sternberg notes that the lexical plays within a story that guide us as to the story's meaning are often done through the agency of the story's verbs. Thus, the verb "to take" in the account of the rape of Dinah refers to the rape at the beginning of the story, but also to the proposed marriage later on. Likewise, asserts Sternberg, the verb "to see" is often variously used in multivalent fashions in anointment scenes.[9] Recall, that in like fashion, we saw that Propp defined his functions around the actions taken in a plot.[10] Concerning the establishment of narra-

---

Books, 1972) 247-54; N. Lohfink, "חרם" in *TDOT* 5.180-99; *NIDOTTE* 2.276-77; H. Horbury, "Extirpation and Excommunication," *VT* 35 (1985) 13-38; C. Sherlock, "The Meaning of *hrm* in the Old Testament," *Colloquium* 14 (1982) 13-24; André Lemaire, "Le Hérem Dans Le Monde Nord-Ouest Sémitique," in L. Nehmé (ed.), *Guerre et Conquête Dans Le Proche-Orient Ancien* (Antiquités Sémitiques 4; Paris: Maisonneuve, 1999) 79-92.

[9] Sternberg, *Poetics*, 480.

[10] Propp, *Morphology*, 21. The notion of looking toward the verb patterns of a

tive analogy, we may posit that while lexical allusions between two narratives may be established around any word, the verbs of a story play an especially important role in establishing the analogical base.

This section delineates six activities common to each of the narratives. Our aim here is not merely to continually underscore the aggregate of mounting evidence that the two stories indeed stand in analogous relationship, but to explore the unique contribution of each element of the analogy. As was the case when we probed the significance of the cairns, we will need again to establish that the parallels are indeed significant, and not solely plot exigencies of each account. As we asserted earlier, the analogous elements need not appear in the same order so long as the criterion of rhetorical congruence is maintained.

We begin with the word קום, "arise." As was the case with the formulation of the cairn erection, the parallel here is not only linguistic, but also structural. The identical formula appears at the same critical juncture of both passages. If cairns conclude each of the processes, the divine call to Joshua to "rise up" commences them (7:10, 8:1. see also 7:13). The call to Joshua to arise, of course, is not unique to these passages, and is found also in 1:2. The appearance at the beginning of the book is instructive for its meaning in the Achan-Ha-Ai narratives of chapters 7-8. Within the Book of Joshua, the call to Joshua to arise is not merely a call to action, as commonly found elsewhere (cf. e.g. Gen 13:1, Deut 9:12, Jonah 3:2, Ezek 3:22, Ezra 10:4). Rather it is a call to action (to cross the Jordan River) out of an understanding of and in response to Joshua's sullen state. This is evident at the opening of the book: "After the death of Moses the servant of the Lord, the Lord said to Joshua the son of Nun, Moses' attendant: My servant Moses is dead. Rise up and cross the Jordan," etc. (1:1-2). The identification of Joshua as Moses' attendant in the same statement that records the aftermath of his passing, represents a focalization of the narrative through Joshua's perspective, reflective of the loss and spiritual orphaning suffered with the death of his personal mentor. The call to rise up, then, is a call to rise out of the paralysis engendered by Moses' loss (cf. Gen 23:3, 2 Sam 12:21).

The calls to Joshua to rise up in 7:10 and in 8:1 stem from a similar circumstance, namely the debacle of the first battle of Ha-Ai. Hav-

---

text as a form of analysis is evident in Roland Barthes' notion of the proairetic code demonstrated in his *S/Z* (Paris: Seuil, 1970).

ing prostrated himself in grief and bewilderment (7:6-9), Joshua is now led upon a dual path of revival and rehabilitation. The amends concerning the enemy within begin with a call to Joshua to rise up and to extirpate the cause of the defeat. The call to rise up and attack the city of Ha-Ai is likewise a response to the hesitancy and paralysis engendered by the setback on the battlefield.[11]

A second phrase common to the two accounts, one that likewise comments on the mental state through which the activity is executed is the term, "and Joshua arose in the morning" (וישכם יהושע בבקר) (7:16, 8:10), understood by Boling[12] following Speiser as not merely "to rise," but "to act persistently or diligently."[13] In all, the phrase appears four times in Joshua (3:1, 6:12, 7:16, 8:10), and so it cannot be said to be a unique feature to these two accounts. Nonetheless, it allows us to perceive within both occurrences a sense of diligence and perhaps even eagerness on the part of Joshua, not merely to act, but to implement the divine instructions given him and to overcome the earlier battlefield defeat. In each instance, the phrase וישכם יהושע בבקר serves as an adverbial complement to an action which constitutes the fulfillment of an earlier divine command. In His rebuke, God tells Joshua, "Tomorrow morning you shall present yourselves by tribe, and whichever tribe that the Lord shall snare" (ונקרבתם בבקר לשבטיכם והיה השבט אשר-ילכדנו יהוה) (7:14). When Joshua arises diligently the next morning, his actions are cast in language taken from that divine imperative: "Joshua arose the next morning and had Israel come forward by tribes, and the tribe of Judah was snared" (וישכם יהושע בבקר ויקרב את-ישראל לשבטיו וילכד שבט יהודה) (7:16). The same phenomenon is exhibited within the narrative fabric of chapter 8. God commands Joshua, "Take with you the fighting troops and arise against Ha-Ai" (קח עמך את כל-העם המלחמה וקום עלה העי) (8:1). Joshua's diligence in 8:10 is in precise execution of this command: "Joshua arose in the morning, and mustered the troops, and arose against Ha-Ai, together with the elders of Israel at the head of the troops" (וישכם יהושע בבקר ויפקד את-העם ויעל הוא וזקני ישראל לפני העם העי). The formulation of Joshua arising in the morning is not unique to these two passages.

---

[11] There is, of course, a slight syntactic distinction between the two occurrences, as the phrase וקום עלה in 8:1 is a verbal hendiadys (cf. 7:13), while that of 7:10 is not. This does not detract, however, from the parallel import of the call to rise in each instance.

[12] Boling, *Joshua*, 159.

[13] E.A. Speiser, *Genesis* (AB 1; Garden City, NY: Doubleday, 1964) 138.

Nonetheless, the author creates a tight correspondence between them by endowing the phrase with identical functions in each: to act diligently in precise accordance with God's word in the wake of the episode in which His word went unheeded (7:11).

The activities of 'rising up' and of 'performing diligently' in terms of the content of the two narratives, are subordinate to the central theme of each story, embodied in each through the semantic field of לכד. Within the framework of a battle report such as Joshua 8, the term וילכדוה (8:10) is unremarkable, as the root ל.כ.ד. often appears in reference to military conquest (cf. e.g. Num 21:32; Judg 7:24; 1 Kgs 16:18; Jer 6:11). The use of the term in reference to the identification of Achan (7:14 [3x], 15, 16, 17 [2x], 18), however, is an uncommon usage. Lindblom identifies 35 biblical passages that refer to lot-casting generally and other processes of divinely determined selection.[14] Of these, the language of לכד is found elsewhere only in 1 Sam 10:20-21, and 1 Sam 14:41-42.[15]

---

[14] J. Lindblom, "Lot-Casting in the Old Testament," *VT* 12 (1962) 164-66. Division of the land - Num 26:52ff., 33:54, 34:13, 36:2; Josh 13:6, 14-17, 18-19; Levite cities—Josh 21; 1 Chr 6:39ff.; Achan—Josh 7; Canaanites allotted to Israel—Josh 23:4; Ps. 78:55; Selection of soldiers—Judg 20:9ff.; Selection of Saul—1 Sam 10:19ff.; Detection of Jonathan—1 Sam 14:38ff.; Temple officiants—1 Chr 24-26; Temple firewood duty—Neh 10:35; Repopulation of Jerusalem—Neh 11:1; Haman's lots—Esth 3:7, 9:24; Abuse of orphans—Job 6:27; despoiling raiment—Ps 22:19; Sign of friendship—Prov 1:14; God divides Edom—Isa 34:17; Choosing between two highways—Ezek 26:25ff; Division of food—Ezek 21:25ff; Division of land after Messiah—Ezek 45:1, 47:22; Pagan lot-casting—Hos 4:12; Enemies cast lots about Israel—Joel 4:3; Foreigners cast lots for Jerusalem—Obad 1:11; Trial of Jonah—Jon. 1:7; Lots for territory after the destruction—Mic 2:5; Lots cast over men of Thebes—Nah 3:10; Scapegoat on Day of Atonement—Lev 16; In everyday life—Prov 16:33, 18:18.

[15] It is difficult to identify the process by which Achan was selected, and this for two reasons. First, the general relationship between the institution of lots (גורלות) and that of the Urim and Thummim is unclear. Lindblom ("Lot Casting," 170), for example, states that all cultic lot-casting was carried out in the presence of the Urim and Thummim, while NIDDOTE 1.841 identifies lot-casting and the Urim and Thummim as two distinct processes. The most recent discussion of this issue is found in Cornelis Van Dam, *The Urim and Thummim* (Winona Lake: Eisenbrauns, 1997), ch. 10: "The Procedure for Using the Urim and Thummim," pp. 194- 214, particularly p. 202 n. 38. See also Wayne Horowitz and Victor (Avigdor) Hurowitz, "Urim and Thummim in Light of a Psephomancy Ritual from Assur (LKA 137)," *JANES* 21 (1992) 95-114. Second, the narrative of Joshua 7 neither utilizes the term גורלות nor that of אורים ותומים. It is not surprising therefore, that a panoply of opinion concerning the mechanism here can be found in both critical and rabbinic sources. On the basis of the appearance of the term לכד in 1 Sam 14:41-42 in conjunction with the Urim and Thummim, some scholars have determined that the same mechanism was employed with respect to Achan. See Kaufmann (*Joshua*, 120), McCarter (P. Kyle McCarter, *I Samuel* [AB 8; Garden City, NY: Doubleday,

Intricately connected with the term לכד in chapter 7 is the verb קרב (7:14 [4x], 16, 17, 18), meaning, "brought forth for judgment."[16] In like fashion, we find the same process reported with regard to the king of Ha-Ai in 8:23.[17] This is the only instance in the Bible where a defeated king is brought before his captors for judgment or sentencing through the agency of the verb קרב.[18]

The verbal analogy, however, poses a difficulty with regard to the criterion of rhetorical congruence. The term לכד refers to Achan in chapter 7, and to the *city* of Ha-Ai in chapter 8. While the term נקרב likewise refers to Achan in chapter 7, it refers to the *king* of Ha-Ai in chapter 8. This discrepancy challenges our working thesis, namely that the narrative of Joshua 7-8 establishes a narrative analogy to underscore the dual redress of the enemy within and the enemy without. The enemy within clearly is Achan. But who is the enemy without—the city of Ha-Ai, or its king? Strictly speaking, we should insist that all the terms found in reference to Achan in chapter 7 should find their parallels in unified reference to either the city of Ha-Ai, or, alternatively, to its king, but not to both. We will return to this issue later, noting

---

1980] 192, 249-250), Woudstra (*Joshua*, 127 n. 36 after J. Bright, *IB* 2.587); Robert G. Gordon *I & II Samuel* (Grand Rapids: Zondervan, 1988) 120; J. Lindblom, "Lot-Casting," *VT* 164-78. This possibility is likewise raised in medieval sources by Qimḥi, Ibn Caspi and Abarbanel to 7:14, and by Rashi to 7:16. Conversely, see H. P. Smith *The Books of Samuel* (ICC; Edinburgh: T & T Clark, 1961) 73 who sees the present instance as related only to 1 Sam 10:21-22 where no mention is made of the Urim and Thummim, and unrelated to 1 Sam 14:41-42 (ibid., 122). The conception that Achan was identified by lots without invoking the Urim and Thummim, is raised as a possibility by Qimḥi, Ibn Caspi and Abarbanel to 7:14 (cf. *b. Sanhedrin* 43b, and *Pirke De-Rabbi Eliezer* 38, which speak of lots, though it is unclear whether this is in conjunction with the Urim and Thummim or distinct from it).

A rabbinic tradition, quoted by Qimḥi to 7:14, maintains that the tribes were passed before the Ark and that the implicated tribe would be unable to move from its place, presumably on the basis of a more literal understanding of the term לכד, lit. "snared" or "caught."

Whatever the mechanism, the important point for our study is that the narrative employs an uncommon term to refer to the process by which Achan was identified. This enables us to hypothesize that this term was chosen in order to erect a semantic field around the root לכד in equivalence with the use of the root in chapter 8.

[16] Kaufmann, *Joshua*, 120; Yehuda Kiel, *The Book of Joshua* (Daat Miqra; Jerusalem: Mossad Harav Kook, 1985) 58 (Hebrew); Galil and Zakovitch, *Joshua*, 81. Cf. Exod 22:7; Num 27:5; 1 Sam 14:36; Is. 41:1. In conjunction with לכד, cf. 1 Sam 10:20-21. On this root as a legal term, see Y. Hoffman, "The Root QRB as a Legal Term," *JNSL* 10 (1983) 67-73.

[17] Kiel, *Joshua*, 58 n. 83.

[18] In contrast with the root י.צ.א. in Josh 10:24 and נ.ג.ש. in 1 Sam 15:32.

for the meantime, that our working theory of "the enemy without" suffers from a modicum of imprecision.

The shared lexical terms identified thus far bore as referents Joshua (וישכם יהושע בבקר and קום), on the one hand, and the enemy (לכד and קרב), on the other. With the root ר.ו.ץ. the Israelites are brought into the picture in equivalent capacities (7:22, 8:19). While the activity of running is perhaps implicit in a battlefield encounter, no other explicit occurrences of the term וירוצו or any other declension of the root are found within the entire corpus of biblical battle reports (though cf. in a similar sense, Joel 2:7, 9). In 7:22, the impetus of the running is debated amongst rabbinic exegetes. Qimḥi claims that the messengers ran out of joy and eagerness to retrieve the *ḥerem* and thereby assuage God's wrath.[19] The preponderance of opinion (Rashi, Gersonides, Abarbanel), however, maintains that the messengers ran to reach the *ḥerem* in advance of conniving members of the tribe of Judah, perhaps looking to save the good name of their tribe by contravening the lots. This interpretation allows for an equivalence to be established between the acts of running in the two accounts. In each account, members of the Children of Israel run on behalf of, and in the service of the entire nation; in chapter 8 it is in an endeavor to defeat the enemy from without; in chapter 7 it is in an effort to overcome the enemy from within. Here, too, we should note the lines of congruence between the analogies are blurred. Is the "enemy within" Achan, as we have maintained until now, or is it some extended group, such as the tribe of Judah? We shall return to this point later.

The final verb that unites the two narratives is the verb שרף, "burn." In chapter 7 God commands that the perpetrator and all that he owns should be burnt (7:15), implying not only execution via a particular method, but rather utter obliteration. A similar import can be seen in the burning of the city in 8:28: "Joshua burned down Ha-Ai and turned it into a mound of ruin for all time, until this very day" (וישרף יהושע את-העי וישימה תל-עולם שממה עד היום הזה).[20]

To round out the list of common lexical terms between the two analogous narratives we may add the root נ.ב.ל. (7:15, 8:29), though

---

[19] Shmuel Ahituv, *Joshua* (Miqra LeYisrael; Tel Aviv: Am Oved, 1995) 128 (Hebrew).

[20] It is worthy of note that the burning of a conquered city was the exception, not the rule in the course of Joshua's conquests. Other than Jericho (6:24), only Hazor is burnt, a point that Scripture underscores (11:13). See discussion in Ahituv, *Joshua*, 138.

explication of each of the verses is first required. The appearance in 7:15 is one of many similar occurrences in which the noun נְבָלָה "represents actions bearing serious guilt and consequences for the community."[21] The use of the root in 8:29, however, represents somewhat of an anomaly. At first glance the use of the root here seems unremarkable, clearly reflecting the influence of Deut 21:22-23. Yet, a broader look at episodes of hangings and the treatment of corpses throughout the Bible reveals the singularity of this passage. The Bible records seven other episodes of death through the root ת.ל.י. (Gen 40: 22; Josh 10:26; 2 Sam 18:10 (by accident); 2 Sam 21:12; Esth 2:23; 7:10). Of these, only two address the treatment of the corpse. 2 Sam 18:17 reads: "They took Absalom and threw him into a large pit in the forest" (ויקחו את אבשלום וישלכו אתו ביער אל-הפחת הגדול), without recourse to the word נְבֵלָה. Even more striking is Josh. 10:27, where we encounter within the Book of Joshua a second episode in which vanquished Canaanite kings are hanged and stone structures erected over them. Yet, here as well, Scripture expresses itself without recourse to the use of the term נְבֵלָה: "At sunset, Joshua commanded that they should be lowered from the poles and cast into the cave where they had hidden" (ויהי לעת בוא השמש צוה יהושע ויורידום מעל העצים וישלכם אל המערה אשר נחבאו שם). Moreover, while the noun נְבֵלָה is often found in the latter prophets in reference to a corpse (Isa 5:25; Jer 7:33, 9: 21, 16:4, 19:7, 26:23, 34:20, 36:30. Cf. also Ps 79:2), this is never the case in the narrative histories except in reference to a corpse that has been mauled (1 Kgs 13:22, 24, 25, 28, 30, 37; 2 Kgs 9:37).

To date there is debate as to whether the terms נְבֵלָה and נְבָלָה are drawn from the same root or whether they are drawn from two distinct roots.[22] Even if we assume the minimalist position and that they are drawn from two distinct roots, the strong consonance between the two words coupled with the somewhat exceptional usage in 8:

---

[21] R.A. Bennett, "Wisdom Motifs in Psalm 14 = 53—*nābāl* and '*ēṣāh*," *BASOR* 220 (1975) 16. Cf. Gen 34:7; Deut 22:21; Josh 7:15; Judg 19:23, 24; 20:6, 10; 1 Sam 25: 25; 2 Sam 13:12; Isa 9:16; 32:6; Jer 29:23; Job 42:8.

[22] W.M.W. Roth, "NBL," *VT* 10 (1960) 394-409 sees all forms of נבל as carrying some connotation of "outcast" and that its origin reflects the Akkadian *nabālu(m)*, "to tear out." *BDB* distinguishes between *nābāl* and *nevālāh* for "foolish," "senseless" and *nābēl*, and *nevālāh*, in verb form to mean "to wither, fall, fade," and as a noun to mean "carcass," "corpse." *KBL*, however, derives them from one root, as does Caspari ("Über den biblischen Begriff der Torheit," *Neue Kirchliche Zeitschrift* 39.668-95). A middle position, that one source evolved along two separate paths, is adopted by Bennett, "Wisdom Motifs," 15-20. See discussions in *TWAT* 5.171-73; *THAT* 2.26-31, and most recently in *NIDOTTE* 2.11.

29, allows us to assert the two as equivalent elements of the narrative analogy between Joshua 7 and Joshua 8. The root נבל (even if
it reflects two etymologically unrelated words) describes in pejorative
terms the activity of Achan, the enemy within, and the king of Ha-Ai,
the enemy without.

To summarize, we have seen analogous terms that referred to Joshua
וישכם יהושע בבקר and קום reflecting the mood and mentality of the
leader of Israel in each account. We saw the term וירוצו as indicative
of the common mood of the children of Israel in the two narratives to
seize the moment and overcome the enemy. Nonetheless, terms that
refer to the "enemy within" of chapter 7 were seen to be imprecise;
לכד, קרב and נבלה refer strictly to Achan. The "enemy" overcome
by the messengers that ran, however, was not Achan, per se, but his
fellow tribesmen, i.e. a group related by extension to Achan himself.
The term שרף, at various junctures in the narrative, reveals different
referents. In 7:15 it refers both to Achan and "all that is his,"[23] while
in 7:25 it would appear that burning was the fate of some grouping
other than Achan, who is stoned. Thus it is unclear whether the internal
enemy is Achan, or some more inclusive group.

The picture is no clearer with regard to the "external enemy" of
chapter 8. The terms וירוצו, לכד and שרף refer exclusively to the city
of Ha-Ai, while the terms קרב and נבלה pertain to the king of Ha-
Ai. The eight-word string, "they raised a huge mound of stones over
him, which is still there to this day" (ויקימו עליו גל אבנים גדול עד היום
הזה) refers exclusively to Achan and to the king of Ha-Ai.[24] While the

---

[23] Both critical and rabbinic sources allow for the possibility that Achan's family
members were killed with him. Mitchell (G. Mitchell, *Together in the Land: A Reading
of the Book of Joshua* [JSOTSup 134; Sheffield: Sheffield Academic Press, 1993] 74)
suggests that there is evidence here of a form of corporate personality, or that family
members were considered subordinate and indeed subsumed within the identity of
the head of the household. This latter opinion is found within the commentary of
Qimḥi to 7:15: בניו ובנותיו הקטנים בכלל ממונו אצל העונש. Adult children, he goes on
to say, would also be liable to death since they presumably knew of the offense and
were therefore complicit offenders. Soggin, *Joshua*, 105 and Rashi (vv. 24-25) take
the position that the only human life taken was that of Achan while וישרפו אתם
refers to some of his belongings. For more on the notion of corporate personality
and collective responsibility in the Bible, see J. Porter, "The Legal Aspects of the
Concept of 'Corporate Personality' in the Old Testament," *VT* 15 (1965) 361-80; J.
Kaminsky, *Corporate Responsibility in the Hebrew Bible* (JSOTSup 196; Sheffield: Sheffield Academic Press, 1995) 67-95; J. Scharbert, *Solidarität in Segen und Fluch im Alten
Testament und in seiner Umwelt* (vol. 1 of *Väterfluch und Vätersegen* [BBB 14; Bonn: Peter
Hanstein, 1958]).

[24] Having concluded my accounting of the common terms that form the basis

semantic cues afforded us by the analogy leave a somewhat blurred picture, clarity of the issue is attained through an examination of other rhetorical strategies employed in the construction of the analogy.

The first is a question of imagery. In his treatment of the burning of Achan's family and his possessions, Mitchell observes that:

> If the account is related to the wider context of the conquest of the nations, then Achan's family receives exactly the same treatment as the doomed cities of the land. The battle reports contain a catalogue of the destruction of women and children. Even though accounts of destroying the nations can be very brutal, they cannot match those describing the treatment of fellow Israelites. The closest comparison to the Achan story is to be found in the regulations concerning the destruction of an apostate city in Deut 13... Achan is punished for disobedience. The extent of the destruction is an expression of abhorrence for apostasy and thereby places Israel in the same category as the nations.[25]

We began our analysis of chapters 7-8 in Joshua by positing a message of duality, based on a string of semantic parallels, of an enemy without—the Canaanites—and an enemy within—the disobedient or apostate Israelite, embodied by Achan. What we have demonstrated through common lexical terms, Mitchell highlights through imagery. Achan is "cast" in the terms of a Canaanite city, for he is, like the cities of Canaan, an enemy that must be vigorously fought and extirpated. He is, one might say, the "Canaanite city" dwelling within the very camp of Israel. Mitchell's observation explains why the lines are blurred between Achan and those around him. To highlight and underscore the proportions of Achan's infamy the narrative refuses to address him alone; to do so would be to minimize the proportions of his offense and their implications for Israel. By implicating his family members, his tribe, indeed the entirety of Israel (7:11), Achan is seen to be a wide-ranging phenomenon.[26]

---

of the analogy between the two narratives, I wish to list all the other roots that are common to the two narratives: ל.ק.ח. (7:1, 11, 21; 8:1), נ.פ.ל. (7:10; 8:25), צ.ו.ה. (7:11; 8:4, 8), ע.ש.ה. (7:15, 20; 8:2), ש.ל.ב. (7:21; 8:2), ש.ל.ה. (7:22; 8:3,9), ש.ו.ב. (7:26; 8:21). I have omitted them from consideration, for I believe that only those terms that fulfill the criterion of rhetorical congruence contribute to the substantiation of the analogy. Frank Polak has alerted me that the word שלל may function in contrastive fashion. In chapter 7 it is the source of woe for Israel; upon its extirpation Israel is invited in chapter 8 to partake of it. To broadly claim that the presence of these roots in both narratives indicates parallelism between them serves only to blur the function of the equivalence as a whole and to weaken the base of the analogy.

[25] Mitchell, *Together in the Land*, 74-75.

[26] The mechanism by which others are implicated for Achan's wrongdoing has been

The notion of a central figure whose implication condemns concentric circles of kin and clan is paralleled nicely in the rhetoric of the first verse of chapter 8, as seen in Scripture's treatment of the relationship between the king of Ha-Ai and his subjects. God's call to Joshua to take Ha-Ai in 8:1, is, on the one hand, formulaic, incorporating stock terms such as, אל-תירא[27] and ראה נתתי בידך את, while going on to specify the impending target kingdom and its king. The concluding phrase of the verse, however, is anomalous in two respects. Throughout the Book of Joshua, the target city and its king are listed in a single, uniform convention, whereby the city is listed first, with subordinate mention of the king in the possessive, as in את יריחו ואת מלכה (6:2) and את חצור ואת מלכה (11:10). The Book of Joshua employs ten such phrases in all (6:2, 8:2 [2x], 10:1 [2x], 10:30, 39 [3x], 11:10). Only here does the mention of the king precede that of his city. Had the king of Ha-Ai played a distinct role in the earlier battle of 7:4-5 the justification to vary from the convention would be abundantly clear. No mention at all is made, however, of the king of Ha-Ai in that earlier episode. Kiel posits that the author simply chose to vary his style here,[28] but such an approach seems unsatisfying inasmuch as later in the book Scripture repeats the formulaic structure two and even three times within the same verse.

A second anomaly emerges in the formulation of the conquest target. The conventional formula employs the name of the city alone. Here, by contrast, Joshua is told that he will take "the king of Ha-Ai, his

---

variously explained. Some view the *ḥerem* as possessing the properties of a contagion (cf., for example, Butler, *Joshua*, 86; Nelson, *Joshua*, 101; Ahituv, *Joshua*, 126) while others understand the dynamic as reflective of a theology of corporate personality (cf., for example, Mitchell, *Together in the Land*, 74). My own opinion is that a behavioral explanation is in order: Scripture views Achan as merely symptomatic of a larger phenomenon in Israel, namely haughtiness following the battle of Jericho and inappropriate attribution of victory to their own battle prowess. This may be seen in the report of the spies prior to the first battle for Ha-Ai (7:3). Note that God responds to the sin of Achan only following the debacle of Ha-Ai and not immediately in the wake of Achan's act. To develop this fully, however, would require to me to grapple with the extensive literature surrounding the concept of corporate personality and to engage in a close reading of chapter 6 and the beginning of chapter 7. To do so would be to go beyond the scope of this chapter.

[27] For a form-critical examination of the phrase, see E.W. Conrad, *Fear Not Warrior: A study of 'al tîrā' Pericopes in the Hebrew Scriptures* (BJS 75; Chico, CA: Scholars Press, 1985). Particular attention is paid to the present narrative, ibid., 6-12. See also P.E. Dion, "The 'Fear Not' Formula and Holy War," *CBQ* 32 (1970) 565-70.

[28] Kiel, *Joshua*, 53.

people, his city, and his land." This tripartite reference to a kingdom is nowhere else found in the Bible. Boling maintains that "his people" refers to the king's family and attendants, to civil servants, troops and mercenaries, as well as to officials, members of the aristocracy and their families.[29] Kiel suggests that within the biblical lexicon Canaan is split into various "lands," each one constituting its own kingdom.[30] The king would sit in the capital city and rule from there over the city and its environs.

I would like to suggest that Scripture abandons convention here on both these accounts to establish greater congruence between Achan in chapter 7, and the king of Ha-Ai in chapter 8. Achan in chapter 7 is portrayed as the epicenter of a problem that incriminates his possessions, his family, clan, tribe, indeed, all of Israel. Nowhere is this more graphically seen than in the process of identification (7:14-18) which arrives at Achan only by first implicating successive levels of kinship, starting with the whole nation, and moving inward from tribe, to clan, to ancestral house to man. Just as the narrative of chapter 7 casts Achan in images reminiscent of a doomed Canaanite city, the narrative of chapter 8 casts the city of Ha-Ai in structural terms that allow the reader to more clearly identify the twinning of Achan and the king of Ha-Ai, by erecting concentric circles around him—"*his* people, *his* city, and *his* land."[31]

Point of View and the Narrative of Joshua 8

Another striking similarity exists between the casting of Achan and the king of Ha-Ai that is not readily apparent through semantic parallels alone. The issue here concerns point of view. A perusal of battle reports across the Bible demonstrates, unremarkably, that most of the interaction between Israel and her neighbors is described from the perspective of Israel, her leaders, her prophets, and her protagonists on and off the battlefield. Nonetheless, it is not unusual to find in these battle reports some element of the story depicted from the vantage point of the enemy (e.g. Judg 1:7, 7:13-14, 1 Sam 4:6-7,

---

[29] Boling, *Joshua*, 237.
[30] Kiel, *Joshua*, 53.
[31] The LXX omits "his people" and "his city" retaining only "his land." See Woudstra, *Joshua*, 135 n. 7.

14:11-12, 1 Kgs 22:31-32, 2 Kgs 3:21-23). In most cases we can fathom the rhetorical ends of the author and how the enemy point of view contributes in a way that would be lost were the tale told solely through the prism of the Israelite perspective. One example will serve to illustrate the point. Gideon descends to the edge of the Midianite camp, and overhears the dream of the Midianite soldier and the interpretation offered (Judg 7:13-14):

> Listen, I had this dream: There was a commotion—a loaf of barley bread was whirling through the Midianite camp. It came to a tent and struck it, and it fell... The other responded, "This can only mean the sword of Gideon..."

Scripture could easily have cast the entire scene from Gideon's perspective: "And Gideon overheard one soldier telling another about his dream in which a loaf of bread... after which the second soldier interpreted it as a sign of Gideon's impending victory." By switching point of view and taking us directly into the Midianite tent, Scripture accomplishes several objectives. First, we share in the sense of dread experienced by the Midianites. Moreover we discover that the Midianites are more confident of Israel's victory than is Gideon himself. Through portrayal of the Midianite perspective the narrative succeeds in leveling a subtle criticism against Gideon for his repeated hesitance to engage Midian in battle.

With regard to point of view within the battle report, the Book of Joshua adopts a highly distinct strategy. As a rule, the battle reports of the Book of Joshua steadfastly avoid relating anything from the perspective of the enemy cities, kings, or inhabitants. Indeed, the narrator does open the final three conquest accounts in a formulaic fashion whereby a Canaanite king hears of Israel's success and initiates the establishment of a coalition (9:1-2, 10:1-5, 11:1-5).[32] Yet, in the ensuing battles (10:8-28, 28-43, 11:6-15), even where the action is depicted at length, Scripture adopts a rhetorical strategy of entirely avoiding depiction from the Canaanite point of view. This is also the case in the earlier battle accounts (6:12-26, 7:2-5).

Were the battle accounts of Joshua to demonstrate a preference for the Israelite perspective, with occasional recourse to that of the Canaanites, we would conclude that the narrative policy adopted by the Book of Joshua on this score was essentially in line with that found in the other narrative histories. We would then attempt to account

---

[32] Kaufmann, *Joshua*, 133; Kiel, *Joshua*, 63.

for the shift to Canaanite perspective on a case-by-case basis, as illustrated through the Gideon narrative above. The fact that such perspective is absent from any of the battles of the Book of Joshua begs explanation.

I believe that an approach to this observation may be found in the work of literary theorist Susan Lanser. Todorov[33] addresses the issue of point of view via a distinction between subjective and objective knowledge of a character. Subject information is conveyed through a character's temperament, personality and responses as recounted through a narrative voice. Object knowledge of a character is presented from the vantage point of a narrator or another character, and effectively renders the person into a state of object-hood. Lanser observes that this distinction plays a crucial role in developing reader affinity for the characters portrayed:

> Affinity with a character thus depends to some extent on the degree to which that character is "subjectified"—made into a subject, given an active human consciousness. The more subjective information we have about a character as a rule, the greater our access to that persona and the more powerful the affinity.[34]

If affinity with a character is bolstered by conveying the story from his or her perspective and a character is rendered an object by denying the reader access to that perspective, we may hypothesize as to why the Book of Joshua chooses to steer clear of the Canaanite perspective as these battles are waged. The battles recounted in the other narrative histories are either battles of expansion or battles of defense. The battles of Joshua, however, are battles of obliteration. This is the charge laid down in Deuteronomy (20:17), is seen through the centrality of the word ḥerem in nearly every battle (6:21, 8:26, 10:1, 28, 35, 37, 39, 40; 11:11, 12, 20, 21), and is epitomized by the summary statement (10:40): "Thus Joshua conquered the whole country: the hill country, the Negeb, the Shephelah, and the slopes, with all their kings: he let none escape, but proscribed everything that breathed—as the Lord, the God of Israel, had commanded." In entirely foregoing the perspective of the Canaanites, the narrative adopts a rhetorical strategy that is in consonance with the ideology of the Book: the Canaanites are to be

---

[33] Tzvetan Todorov, *Poetique* (Paris: Seuil, 1973) 58ff.

[34] Susan Lanser, *The Narrative Act: Point of View in Prose Fiction* (Princeton: Princeton University Press, 1981) 206.

obliterated. What is depicted in the plot action of the Book, is achieved rhetorically. The "objectification" of our perception of the Canaanites denies them humanity, and contributes to our perception of the process of annihilation across the narrative of the Book of Joshua.

The one exception to this strategy is in the narrative fabric of chapter 8. Here we perceive the unfolding of events from within the camp of Ha-Ai, and this on two occasions. First, when the King of Ha-Ai takes notice of the Israelite encampment (8:14) and rushes headlong with his troops to meet them;[35] second, when the men of Ha-Ai look behind them and see smoke rising above their city and realize that they themselves are entrapped (8:20).

Galil and Zakovitch have correctly noted that the use of the verb "to see" in each, functions in contrastive fashion.[36] In v. 14 the king of Ha-Ai sees but is completely fooled,[37] blind to the true reality: "he was unaware that a force was lying in ambush behind the city." This contrasts with the corrected vision of v. 20, where they realize the enormity of their earlier misperception.

We may speculate as to why the author of Joshua deviated from his general policy of "objectifying" the condemned Canaanites. Ha-Ai, as a foe, stands in a unique position here in chapter 8. Ha-Ai constitutes the only enemy to have scored a victory over Israel since the Exodus. The author wishes, therefore, to draw attention to the blind hubris of the king of Ha-Ai and to receive the "confession" of error, as it were, by subjectifying them, precisely at the moment of full realization in v. 20. This rhetorical end apparently warranted the sacrifice of the impression of "objectification" employed uniformly by the Book's author in every other battle narrative.

A second level of interpretation may be offered, however, in light of the equivalence we have drawn between the battle report of chapter 8 and the trial account of chapter 7. The contrast between the two actions of "seeing" in 8:14 and 8:20 may be seen through the prism of the paradigm of the "'before' and 'after'" form of commercial advertise-

---

[35] The subject of the second clause of the verse has been debated. Kaufmann (*Joshua*, 124) proposes emending the text to read "and the men of the city," while Soggin (*Joshua*, 95) prefers the reading here of the LXX and Vulgate which preserves the second clause in the singular, in continued reference to the king of Ha-Ai. The foregoing argument however, is valid regardless of the position adopted on this issue.

[36] Galil and Zakovitch, *Joshua*, 81.

[37] Cf. Nelson, *Joshua*, 114.

ment. 8:14 represents the state of "before"—a state in which the king of Ha-Ai, in his haste to conquer Israel and consequently despoil her, sees only the object of his desire. In the state of "after," the vision is corrected. Whereas Galil and Zakovitch's interpretation contrasts the two scenarios of seeing, the "before" and "after' form of advertising focuses attention on the two scenarios as revolving around a pivotal event. In a commercial advertisement the stages of "before" and "after" may revolve around a hair restoration treatment, or a dieting scheme. In Joshua chapter 8, the pivotal event, of course, is the battle, or, in a word, the semantic field of לכד (8:19) that we referred to above. This sequence exemplifies a rhetorical strategy described by Aristotle in chapter 11 of the *Poetics* as the *anagnorisis* immediately following *peripeteia*. The anagnorisis (Greek for "recognition") is that moment in a drama when a character recognizes the true state of affairs, having previously been in error or ignorance. According to Aristotle, the ideal moment of anagnorisis coincides with peripeteia (Greek for "sudden change"), or the reversal of a character's fortune, giving rise to the opposite of what events had seemed to portend.[38] In Joshua 8, the peripeteia of the men of Ha-Ai as they watch their city burn with nowhere to turn engenders the moment of anagnorisis, as they realize that they will not again emerge victorious over Israel.

All of this dovetails with the narrative treatment of Achan and his point of view in Joshua 7. Achan is subjectified only in vv. 20-21. Yet, within Achan's extended confession, we have references to two essentially separate moments of narrative time. Verse 20 is a statement made in the present and a confession of "I have sinned" at the conclusion of a lengthy process. This is not so of verse 21. Verse 21 takes us back in narrative time to an earlier time frame, the moment of the crime. The JPS translation captures this sense in highly effective fashion:

> It is true, I have sinned against the Lord, the God of Israel. This is what I did: I saw among the spoil a fine Shinnar mantle, etc.

The colon following the phrase "This is what I did" indicates to the reader that the narrative wishes to convey not only a sense of remorse

---

[38] In chapter 6 of the *Poetics* Aristotle refers to these two tactics as "tragedy's greatest means of emotional power." See further Stephen Halliwell, *The Poetics of Aristotle: Translation and Commentary* (Chapel Hill: University of North Carolina Press, 1987) 116-18; D.W. Lucas, *Aristotle—Poetics: Introduction, Commentary and Appendixes* (Oxford: Clarendon Press, 1972) 291-98.

at the present, but to return to the narrative scene of the crime, and allow the reader to go through the steps of the crime together with Achan as it actually happened. Just as the king of Ha-Ai was led to a skewed vision, blinded by his desire to conquer and despoil Israel, so too Achan was blinded by his desire for the spoils, and led by a skewed vision: "I *saw* (ראיתי) among the spoil a fine Shinnar mantle," etc. Hence, here in chapter 7 we have a contrast of "before" and "after," much like that exhibited in chapter 8. Verse 21 represents the stage of the crime itself, born of vision skewed by greed. Verse 20, a later moment in terms of narrative time, constitutes the stage of "after," of proper recognition. In chapter 8, the pivotal event between the stage of "before" and the stage of "after" was the event of לכד, and so it is as well in chapter 7. The recognition of "I have sinned" is separated from the folly of "I saw among the spoil" by a single process: the change of fortune embodied in the semantic field of לכד in vv. 14-18.[39]

We may summarize our findings thus far in schematic fashion:

	The Enemy Within (Josh 7:10-26)	**The Enemy Without** (Josh 8:1-29)
Divine Call to Joshua to Act	ויאמר יהוה אל-יהושע קם לך (7:10)	ויאמר יהוה אל-יהושע... וקום עלה העי (8:1)
Alacrity in Fulfillment of Divine Command	+ (7:16) וישכם יהושע בבקר language of 7:14	+ (8:10) וישכם יהושע בבקר language of 8:1

---

[39] The extended metaphor I have proposed in this chapter is given an alternative explanation by Qimḥi. Whereas I have proposed a reading of Joshua 7-8 that established the equivalence of Achan = Ha-Ai, Qimḥi suggests two independent equations: Achan = Jericho, and Ha-Ai = Jericho. Concerning the sentence of burning imposed upon the perpetrator in 7:15, Qimḥi (7:16) writes: "Just as the city that was *ḥerem* was burned, so too he who transgresses concerning the *ḥerem* is burned, together with all of his possessions (כמו שנשרפה העיר שהיתה חרם, כן ישרף העובר בחרם וכל אשר לו שהוא חרם) (See also Abarbanel to 7:15). Qimḥi later sees the command to burn the city of Ha-Ai (8:8) as an extension of the command in 8:2 to do unto Ha-Ai as had been done unto Jericho (also R.S. Hess, *Joshua: An Introduction & Commentary* [Tyndale Old Testament Commentaries; Leicester: InterVarsity Press, 1996] 169). While this position adequately accounts for the call for burning in each story, the thesis of this chapter encompasses the broad range of analogous elements that have been identified herein, most of which cannot be understood as derivatives of a Jericho paradigm for both Achan and Ha-Ai independently.

	The Enemy Within (Josh 7:10-26)	The Enemy Without (Josh 8:1-29)
Israelites Run to Overcome Enemy	וישלח...מלאכים וירצו האהלה (7:22)	והאורב קם ... וירוצו (8:19)
Entrapment of Enemy	ל.כ.ד. (7x in 7:14-18)	וילכדוה (8:19)
Enemy Brought for Judgment	ק.ר.ב. (8x in 7:14-18)	ואת-מלך העי תפשו חי ויקרבו אתו אל-יהושע (8:23)
Enemy Depicted Through Root נ.ב.ל.	וכי עשה נבלה בישראל (7:15)	ויורידו את-נבלתו מן-העץ (8:29)
Enemy Sentenced to Burning	ישרף באש אתו ואת-כל-אשר-לו (7:15) ישרפו אתם באש (7:28)	תציתו את-העיר באש (8:8) ויציתו את העיר באש (8:19) וישרף יהושע את העי (8:28)
Conclusion: Cairn atop the Enemy	ויקימו עליו גל-אבנים גדול עד היום הזה (7:26)	ויקימו עליו גל-אבנים גדול עד היום הזה (8:29)
Central Personality and Hierarchy of Accomplices	עכן, בניו ובנתיו וכל אשר לו (7:24), שבט יהודה, בני ישראל	את מלך העי ואת-עמו ואת-עירו ואת-ארצו (8:1)
Skewed Vision Prior to Entrapment (ל.כ.ד.)	ואראה בשלל אדרת שנער אחת טובה... (7:21)	ויהי כראות מלך-העי וימהרו.. ויצאו...לקראת ישראל (8:14)
Anagnorisis Following Peripeteia (ל.כ.ד.)	אמנה חטאתי ליהוה אלהי ישראל (7:20)	ויראו והנה עלה עשן העיר השמימה ולא היה לנוס..והעם ... נהפך אל הרודף (8:20)

The arrangement of the data in this schematic presentation reflects a cardinal methodological point. In our introduction, we examined Garsiel's presentation of the metaphor plot between the parable of the ewe and Adonijah's attempt to appropriate Abishag. Recall that the texts were cast in parallel columns, with the common terms highlighted in bold. In our graphic presentation here, we add a third, critical, column at the left: the column that defines the functional role of the base elements of the analogy. When the parallel terms alone are presented graphically, in the fashion that Garsiel presented them, they may be seen to be related only by association. The left-hand column provides the additional, and to our mind essential, criterion of rhetorical congruence.

Equivalent or Identical?

As mentioned, our purpose in identifying the various elements that form the base of the analogy is also to classify them and highlight their varying functions. Toward this end I would like to draw attention to a distinction that will help us classify the various parallel elements that have been identified between Joshua 7 and 8. In our introduction we cited Levin's distinction between the standard double-plot Elizabethan drama, and what he termed the equivalence plot (and we, the metaphor plot), whereby two different spheres of human action are drawn into conversation and comparison. The present study reveals such a metaphor, for chapter 7 details a trial, while chapter 8, a battle. The trial and battle stand in symbolic, or metaphoric relationship to one another. But does this likewise characterize the relationship between each pairing of the constituent elements of the analogy? Here we may distinguish between two poles of classification. At one end, we can identify analogies between the constituent elements of the equivalence that are themselves highly symbolic or metaphoric in nature. The two appearances of the root נ.ב.ל. represent the outstanding example of this. Even if we maintain that the two words derive from a common root they remain fundamentally different terms, for a despicable deed is not a corpse. Just as the overall relationship between the two narratives is one of equivalence, so too is the relationship between these two common elements. They are "equi-valent" terms in the most literal sense—they share an equal valence, for they are both pejorative references. At the other end of the spectrum, we saw parallel elements that stood not only in metaphoric similarity, but constituted the very same action taken in both narratives. The elements of erecting a cairn over Achan and over the king of Ha-Ai, are *identical* elements, for the same action is taken in both accounts.

The other analogous elements identified exist along a continuum between pure equivalence (such as the consonance exhibited through the root נ.ב.ל.) and pure identity (as seen through the two cairns). The act of presenting for judgment before God through the root ק.ר.ב. is fairly identical within the two narratives. The semantic field around the root ל.כ.ד., conversely, which we saw as the central element of comparison, is of a fundamentally equivalent nature. In each account, a process of seizure is executed, but in very different realms. To summarize, while the relationship between two analogous narratives may be metaphoric, the relationships between the constituent parts of the analogy will be varied. Some elements will themselves exist in an equivalent relationship, particularly in cases of analogy via assonance. Other elements, however, may be of a highly identical nature, even as the nature of the overall analogy is metaphoric.

Vector of Rhetorical Influence

In our introduction we touched upon the issue of proleptic vs. analeptic strategies within biblical narrative. Concretely, the question arises for the first time in this study with regard to the vector of rhetorical influence between the two narratives under discussion here: is Joshua 7 a commentary on Joshua 8, or vice versa? In investigating this issue, I would like to do so from a limited perspective. I would like to assume an implied reader who has no foreknowledge of the story past the point that one has read—a reader who reads the story of Achan with no knowledge of the battle that is to follow in chapter 8.

Conceptually speaking, the notion that chapter 8 elucidates chapter 7 seems the more thematically compelling. Chapter 8 is a battle account essentially undifferentiated from any of the other battle accounts of the Book of Joshua. Ha-Ai, its king, and its inhabitants are subsets of the familiar class of Canaanites. The reasons for the battle waged against them are well understood and require no elucidation. Yet, whereas chapter 8 is conceptually typical, chapter 7 is not. The challenge here before the author of Joshua was how to convey the full implications of an individual violation of the *ḥerem*. Israel had no prior experience with this set of circumstances and thus the situation required elucidation. In turning to narrative analogy the author could have drawn from other instances of lone transgressors as models such as the blasphemer (Lev 24:10-23) or the wood-gatherer (Num 15:32-36). To cast Achan in his proper light, however, means to cast him as the enemy within on a par with the enemy without, and therefore reject all earlier models of lone transgressor, and create a new typology: Achan as Canaanite city. The vector of rhetorical influence, then, seems to be retrospective; the details of the story of the battle for Ha-Ai elucidate facets of the struggle against the enemy within reported in chapter 7. As we mentioned at the outset, the import of the analogy is not that Israel has an external foe, the Canaanites. The import of the analogy stems from the realization that there is an internal foe of equally threatening proportions.

Finally, this leads us to the question raised in our introduction of external vs. internal reception. To what extent may we say that the internal characters of the story are aware of the metaphor that the author has created for the reader? The question here focuses exclusively on the character of Joshua. Achan and the King of Ha-Ai, while set in analogous relationship, are unaware of each other within the story. In each account, men from Israel are depicted as running to defeat the enemy. Yet, it seems more probable that this link is for the reader's sake and not born out of a conscious understanding on Israel's part that in running to take the city they are mirroring their earlier actions with regard to the recovery of the stolen goods.

For Joshua, however, the equivalence is not only something of which he is conscious, but indeed something that he takes action to further. The divine call to action in each (indeed, in identical language), coupled with his own response with alacrity could not have been lost on him. His initiative at the end of chapter 8 to erect a cairn demonstrates that, certainly by that point, he is aware of an equivalence between Achan and the King of Ha-Ai. By erecting a cairn so similar to the one erected at the close of chapter 7, Joshua may be clearly seen as demonstrating to the people of Israel the equivalence between the enemy within and the enemy without.

CHAPTER THREE

THE BATTLE AGAINST BENJAMIN (JUDG 20:40-48) AND THE RAPE OF THE CONCUBINE (JUDG 19:22-27)

While the previous chapter examined the narrative analogy formed by the account of an entire battle, the conquest of Ha-Ai in Joshua 8, the present chapter explores the way in which the narrator employs the vehicle of the metaphor analogy with regard to a single significant segment of his battle report. Judges 20 tells of three battles against the tribe of Benjamin conducted over three days and constitutes one of the longest battle reports in the biblical record. In contradistinction to the first two days of battle in which the tribe of Benjamin scored victories over the allied tribes of Israel, the account of the third day witnesses a turn of fortune and tells of the decimation of the tribe of Benjamin. In this chapter the account of the decimation of the tribe of Benjamin as related in Judg 20:40-48[1] will be explored as a metaphor analogy to the story of the rape of the concubine as reported in Judg 19:22-27.

---

[1] The account of the earlier events of the third day of battle between Israel and the tribes of Benjamin, those prior to the rout of Benjamin (20:29-39), has presented exegetical difficulties. These result from its numerous repetitions, lacunae and inconsistent use of pronouns to refer to the various forces in action in the theatre of battle. Of those who have attempted a synchronic reading of the account, some have proposed a strategy of resumptive reading (E.J. Revell, "The Battle with Benjamin [Judges xx 29-48] and Hebrew Narrative Techniques," *VT* 35 [1985] 417-33; P. E. Satterthwaite, "Narrative Artistry in the Composition of Judges xx 29ff," *VT* 42 [1992] 80-89), while others have attempted to see cohesiveness in the text by positing the employment of summary headings followed by detailed elaboration (Yehuda Elitzur, *The Book of Judges* [Daat Miqra; Jerusalem, Mossad Harav Kook, 1976] 177-79 [Hebrew]; Martin Noth, *Das System der Zwölf Stämme Israels* [Beiträge zur Wissenschaft vom Alten und Neuen Testament; Stuttgart: W. Kohlhammer, 1930] 166-68; Gershon Galil [ed.], *Judges* [Olam HaTanakh: Tel Aviv: Davidson-Eti, 1994] 162-65 [Hebrew]; Rachel Reich, "The Concubine at Gibeah: Judges 19-21—A Literary Analysis," M.A. thesis, Bar-Ilan University, 1985 108 [Hebrew]). Still others, undaunted by the repetition (twice Israel prepares to fight Benjamin; two accounts of a retreat [32, 39]; two times Benjamin fells thirty soldiers [31, 39], twice Benjamin believes that victory is theirs [31-32, 39]), have maintained that the account here tells of two primary stages of

Judges 20:41 and the Semantic Field of הרעה

Our investigation of the action begins with 20:40, where we are told that having charged out of Gibeah to pursue the feigned retreat of the Israelite force, the Benjaminites turned around to behold the entire city going up in smoke. This had been the appointed sign for the Israelite troops executing the feigned retreat to reverse direction and go on the attack (41a). The men of Benjamin are taken by surprise, "for they realized that disaster (הרעה) had overtaken them" (v. 41b). Reich has drawn attention to the semantic field created around the term רעה in light of its earlier appearances in the story.[2] It recalls the old man's censure to the inhabitants of Gibeah in 19:23, "Do not commit such a wrong" (אל-תרעו נא), which is further echoed by the subsequent charge of the tribes, "What is this evil thing (הרעה הזאת) that has happened among you?" (20:12) and the demand that they be handed over, "hand over those scoundrels... so that we may... stamp out the evil from Israel" (20:13) (ונבערה רעה מישראל).

While Reich's evidence is perhaps suggestive of a connection between the two episodes, we need first to subject the appearance of the phrase "for they realized that disaster (הרעה) had overtaken them" to a test of significance. If the phrase is found to be commonplace in battle narratives as a description of a force's mood concerning impending defeat then the argument for meaningful paralleling to the story of Judges 19 becomes less compelling. A priori, this phrase could give expression to the collective feeling of any troop facing defeat on the battlefield. Upon inspection, however, the phrase is, in fact, found to be a singular one within the corpus of biblical battle reports. In no other battle report do we find the mental state of a vanquished

---

battle, which both happened to contain several common elements (Yehezkel Kaufmann, *The Book of Judges* [Jerusalem: Kiryath Sefer, 1968] 294 [Hebrew]). It is this author's position that none of these three approaches has been proven conclusively. It may well be that an expanded, or even different analogy could be adduced were one of these positions to be adopted regarding these verses. But then our conclusions would be that more tenuous as well, for we would be basing our findings upon only one of several options for accounting for verses 29-39.

The narrative that records the latter events of the third day (vv. 40-48), the decimation of the tribe of Benjamin, however, presents far fewer difficulties. All synchronic opinions have read these verses chronologically. We may focus upon this stage of the battle and draw conclusions that in theory would be commensurate with all three positions mentioned above concerning vv. 29-39.

[2] Reich, "The Concubine," 113.

force depicted through a phrase in any way similar to "they saw" or "then they realized that disaster (רעה) had fallen upon them." Moreover, within 20:41, the phrase may even be regarded as superfluous; the astonishment of the Benjaminites, ostensibly, already implies the dawned awareness of impending danger. The semantic parallel, then, is significant, and its meaning is worthy of exploring.

Reich rightly points to the double meaning of the word רעה in these passages. With reference to the episode of chapter 19 it means wickedness; it is a moral valuation. In the battle narrative of chapter 20, however, it is morally neutral; רעה here implies disaster, misfortune (cf. Job 2:11), but does not bear the implication of wickedness. It implies the theme of measure for measure; through the establishment of the semantic field, the "evil" of chapter 19 is punished through the "disaster" of chapter 20.[3] Taken a step further, we may posit that the semantic field established around the word רעה, allows for an intertextual extrapolation. On the primary level of reading, what has befallen Benjamin is the רעה—the sudden turn of fortune, in the form of the now advancing Israelite force. On a secondary level of reading, however, they become aware that what has befallen, or literally "touched" them is "the רעה"—their own evil deeds and their attenuating consequences.

20:43—The Phrases and Phases of an Attack

The body of the analogy is continued in verse 43, but for the sake of demonstrating how the unit may be read as a cohesive whole, a few words are in order concerning the role of verse 42 as a summary heading of details elaborated in verse 43. The men of Benjamin turn toward the desert. Note that, in contradistinction to verse 45 and verse 47 where the flight is described through the hendiadys ויפנו וינסו, here we find only ויפנו אל המדבר immediately followed by והמלחמה הדביקתהו. The formulation in vv. 45 and 47 implies that they fled and that a distance was opened between the fleeing force and the pursuer. The implication in verse 42, however, is that as soon as they began to turn toward the desert they were already overcome. I read the

---

[3] Ibid.. On the theme of measure for measure and word play see Yael Shemesh, "Measure for Measure in Biblical Literature," *Beit Miqra* 44 (1999) 261-70, and the response by Yitzchak Peleg in that same volume, pp. 357-60.

highly ambiguous 42b, as does Amit,[4] to the effect that Benjaminites
from other cities who came to assist were annihilated together with
their brethren from Gibeah.[5] In short, verse 42 reports in general
terms the annihilation of the main force of Benjamin together with
supporting forces from other cities.

This takes us to verse 43, which describes the unfolding of this
development in greater detail. It is our contention that the stages of
the battle are analogous to stages and aspects of the assault of the
concubine in ch. 19.

V. 43a tells of the encircling of the Benjaminite camp. The detail
is exceptional, as—with the exception of 1 Sam 23:26—no other biblical battle story reports the encircling of a force, though this could
hardly have been a singular development within the history of biblical
warfare. The act is reminiscent of the behavior of the inhabitants of
Gibeah who surrounded the house of the old man in 19:22. While
the word employed here is כתרו and in 19:22 נסבו, the two evidently
bear highly similar connotations as they stand as equivalent verbs in
the parallelism established in Ps 22:13.[6]

The third phrase, 43c, reports that the Benjaminites were pursued until Gibeah, though several commentators have called for an
emendation of the MT. The identity of the terminus of the chase is
significant for the meaning of the story, thus warranting a review of

---

[4] Yairah Amit, *The Book of Judges* (Miqra LeYisrael; Tel Aviv: Am Oved, 1999) 306
(Hebrew). This interpretation is also found within the commentary to the verse of the
eighteenth century rabbinic commentary *Metsudat David* by R. David Altshuller.

[5] The phrase ואשר מהערים משחיתים אותו בתוכו has proven enigmatic as it bears
three pronouns whose referents are unclear. The Targum, Rashi, Qimḥi, and Abarbanel, all take the phrase "those of the cities" (ואשר מן הערים) to refer to the Israelite
ambush force, as do the JPS and RSV translations. The understanding of *Metsudat
David* (and of Amit, *Book of Judges*), however, more closely concurs with the plural
(הערים) and the meaning of its usage in 20:41. The word אותו in the singular simply
continues the grammar initiated by the phrase ואשר מהערים "that from the cities"
which may also be seen as singular. The phrase אותו בתוכו is taken by R. Isaiah of
Trani and Elitzur (*Book of Judges*, 178) to mean that the Benjaminites from the other
cities were massacred in their respective cities. The initial reference to those cities,
however, was in plural, which should have yielded בתוכן—"within them" at the
end of the verse. The reading of בתוכו—"within it/him" to mean within the main
Benjaminite force, however, encounters no such difficulty. Amit (*Book of Judges*, 306)
proposes an emendation of בתוכו to read בתוך, "in the middle." No textual witness,
however, sustains this reading.

[6] The LXX here apparently read either כתתו, "crushed," or כרתו, "cut down."
See Robert G. Boling, *Judges* (AB 6A; Garden City NY: Doubleday, 1975) 287 and
Gray, *Joshua, Judges*, 388. The verb כתר in the sense of "surrounding" also appears
in Ps 142:8.

the positions on this issue. Moore[7], Kaufmann,[8] Boling,[9] and Amit[10] all propose an emendation of the text to read Geba instead of Gibeah. The reasoning for this may be understood from Boling's translation of the verse: "They surrounded the Benjaminites. They pursued them vigorously from Nohah and completely subjugated them, *as far as* a position opposite Geba to the east" (italics mine). Boling has understood the phrase "they were chased until... (עד.הרדיפהו)" to imply distance from the point of origin, and hence Boling's addition "as far as." Since the point of origin was Gibeah, the verse is rendered unintelligible if the point of terminus is likewise Gibeah, and hence the proposed emendation of Geba.

The MT (as well as the LXX and V, which also read Gibeah) however, is perfectly intelligible without the emendation to Geba, and without the supplementary phrase "as far as" preceding it. The Benjaminites set out from Gibeah in pursuit of the feigned retreat (v. 39). Upon being caught between the complementary Israelite forces, they began to flee toward the desert (v. 42). They were surrounded and hounded to the point of exhaustion until... "a point just opposite Gibeah to the east." The Benjaminites meet their demise on the outskirts of their own city. This creates an equivalence with the concubine, who, likewise, was assaulted to the point of exhaustion and collapsed at the threshold of her one-time shelter, the old man's house: "She collapsed at the entrance of the man's house... and there was a woman, his concubine, lying at the entrance of the house" (19:26-27).

There may be a further line of analogy here, though it must be stated with a degree of caution. The motives of the concubine to return to the old man's house, it would seem, are clear: having been ravaged and with no place to go, she tried pathetically to return to the place which she already knew could not offer her protection: the erstwhile shelter that was the old man's house. Can the same pathetic motive be discerned in the battle report of 20:43? Here, the picture is less clear. We are told that the corporate "Benjamin" was hounded to exhaustion and we are told that it was cut down opposite Gibeah to the east. But how, and why did the Benjaminites wind up precisely there? Here the text is silent, and three possibilities exist. The first is

---

[7] George F. Moore, *A Critical and Exegetical Commentary on Judges* (ICC: Edinburgh: T & T Clark, 1895) 441.

[8] Kaufmann, *Book of Judges*, 297.

[9] Boling, *Judges*, 283.

[10] Amit, *Book of Judges*, 306.

that the battle proceeded randomly, with Benjamin surrounded on all sides, running in confusion, cut down, finally, at the point at which the Israelite forces closed in on them, which turned out to be opposite Gibeah to the east. Alternatively, it may be that the Israelite force that executed the about face, deliberately chased the Benjaminites back toward Gibeah and into the hands of the ambush force that had torched the city. Within either of these scenarios the analogy to the concubine, then, is exclusively in formal terms: each is seen to reach demise at the outskirts of the former place of protection.

A third possibility of explanation, however, exists in understanding the unfolding of the battle in v. 43c. Finding themselves engulfed, the Benjaminites attempted to retreat toward their garrison in an attempt to reach more secure positions. The garrison, Gibeah, of course, was not what it once was, having now been torched, rendering their attempted retreat pathetic, for their own torched city is the only place of respite available to them. If this reading is accepted, then the analogy to the concubine goes beyond formal terms and attains psychological equivalence as well: the shared experience of pathetically attempting to reach the former shelter, even with the knowledge that the sanctuary now available there is of a very limited nature. As mentioned, though, the text is silent on this issue, and either of the first two scenarios drawn are equally valid readings.

Before leaving our examination of v. 43c, I would like to attend to the choice of terms used to denote the location to which the Benjaminites were chased, "to a point opposite Gibeah on the east." The use of the term here for "east," (מ)מזרח-שמש‎, is unusual. The term מזרח השמש‎ (inclusive of all its grammatical prefixes and suffixes) appears 19 times in the Bible. Six of these bear the connotation of "farthest east" in apposition with farthest west, and imply "east" within a context of great expanse (Isa 45:6; 59:19; Mal 1:11; Ps 50:1; 113:3; cf Isa 41:5). Six more are used as a descriptor of the entire region of the Transjordan (Deut 4:41, 47; Josh 1:15, 12:1, 19:34; 2 Kgs 10:33). Two imply heading in an eastward direction (Josh 19:12, 27). One implies "from the east" (Judg 11:18), and one, "the eastern side of" (Num 21:11). The usage here is different, and refers to a specific point that lies to the east of another specific point. This usage is found in only two other passages (Josh 13:5; Judg 21:19).

The more conventional way in which Scripture denotes one specific point that lies to the east of another is through the agency of מקדם‎, found nine times throughout the Bible in this capacity (Gen 3:24, 12:

8 (2x); Num 34:11; Josh 7:2; Judg 8:11; Ezek 11:23; Jonah 4:5; Zach 14:4). Admittedly, the usage here of ממזרח-שמש is not unique, and is found again even within the narrative unit of the rape of the concubine and its aftermath (21:19—מזרחה השמש), suggesting that this may have simply been the preferred term by the author of this unit (although within the wider context of the Book of Judges we do find מקדם used for this purpose in 8:11).

Nonetheless, I would like to suggest the possibility that the choice of ממזרח-שמש over מקדם here was deliberate and was intended to buttress the analogy between the fate of the concubine and the fate of the Benjaminites in formal terms, through the invocation of a common image. Verse 43c may be translated in a highly literal fashion as "to a point opposite Gibeah toward the *place the sun rises*." The invocation of the literal term "toward the place the sun rises" (ממזרח-שמש) and not "to the east" (מקדם), may be seen, in formal terms, as matching the sun imagery repeatedly invoked at the close of the account of the attack on the concubine: "They raped her and abused her all night long until *morning*; and they let her go *when dawn broke*. *Toward the morning* the woman came back; and *as it was growing light*, she collapsed... When her husband arose in the *morning*, he opened the doors...(19: 25-27)."[11]

To summarize: the Benjaminites are punished in like measure for their offense against the concubine. They, like she, are surrounded, hounded, and ultimately (limiting ourselves to an analogy in form alone) meet their demise on the threshold of what once had been a sanctuary of security.

Our analysis of the battle in verse 43 reveals an exercise in a methodological mode that we have not previously employed in this study. None of these parallels employs semantic markers, as there are no

---

[11] Invoked five times, the sun imagery in the rape account contributes to the story in a fashion beyond the level of simply supplying information. It is reflective, perhaps, of a reality of life in biblical times expressed by the Psalmist (104:20-23): "You bring on darkness and it is night, when all the beasts of the forest stir. The lions roar for prey, seeking their food from God. When the sun rises, they come home and couch in their dens. Man goes out to his work, to his labor until the evening." Man may venture out of his house in safety only by day, when the wild animals have retired to their dens. By night however, to remain outside is to subject oneself to hungry animals stalking their prey. For the husband, the morning ushers in safety. He opens the doors (pl.!) that shielded him from the pounding throng outside. But all of this is reversed with regard to the concubine; the dawn ushers in her demise. She too approaches the door, only to collapse there into unconsciousness, or even death.

shared lexical terms between 20:43 and the rape account of chapter
19. What is common here is imagery ((1) surrounding and hounding,
(2) demise near former shelter, (3) demise coupled with sun-imagery).
Yet, imagery is a considerably more vague entity than a quantifiable
semantic marker. When speaking of common imagery, the strength of
the analogical link is only as strong as the distinctiveness of the image,
and this writer is the first to acknowledge that not all three shared
images highlighted here are equally compelling. The shared image of a
surrounding, encircling, superior force seems to us the most compelling, as it is a highly uncommon one across the whole of the Bible.
Equally strong is the image of the demise of the victim near a former
source of shelter, again, a highly distinctive feature. The invocation of
sun-imagery is the weakest of the shared images, for theoretically any
mention of daylight, or of the sun, could be claimed to bear semiotic
meaning. It is redeemed here, however, by the somewhat unusual use
of the term ממזרח שמש in 20:43, coupled with the five occurrences of
the term daybreak, or morning, in the rape narrative of chapter 19.

Two Stories of ע.ל.ל.

Moving forward now in the narrative of Judges 20 to v. 45, we come
to an uncommon use of the verb ע.ל.ל.: "They turned and fled to
the wilderness, to the Rock of Rimmon; but [the Israelites] picked
off (ויעללהו) another 5,000 on the roads." The use here of the verb
parallels the use of the same verb ע.ל.ל. in 19:25, "They raped her
and abused her (ויתעללו-בה) all night long." While there is a strong
resemblance between the words, the common root does not perforce
indicate that we have here two occurrences of the same word, and thus
we must first define each carefully and discern its shades of meaning
in order to appreciate the full significance of this parallel.

The use of the term in the non-*hitpael* form, as exhibited in 20:
45, is figurative and may best be translated as "gleaned." Within the
context of battle reports, it is found elsewhere only in Judg 8:2, as
Gideon extols the "gleanings" of Ephraim. Its occurrence within the
battle report of Judges 20, then, may be deemed an exceptional, if
not singular phenomenon.[12] The precise import of this "gleaning"

---

[12] Beyond battle reports, divine punishment of a people resulting in its decimation
is also depicted through this term (Isa 3:12; Jer 49:9).

imagery, however, is the subject of debate, and has bearing on the establishment of the narrative analogy with the rape scene beyond the level of assonance. As it is used in 8:2, the image is clear. Gideon states that his troops performed the "harvest," i.e. the main action of the battle, certainly from a quantitative standpoint of casualties inflicted and lands captured. But following this "harvest," he maintains, Ephraim performed an act of gleaning—of attending to that which had not yet been attained, namely, the subduing of the princes of Midian, which was of decisive significance. "Gleaning," in military terms, implies a "mop-up" action. This interpretation is adopted by Qimḥi and by Amit[13] with regard to 20:45. Following the main action of the battle in which 18,000 Benjaminite troops are felled, as reported in vv. 42-44, verse 45 reports an act of "gleaning" whereby Israelite forces further subdue an additional 5000 of the remaining soldiers of the Benjaminite force.

Others[14] argue for an alternative interpretation of the gleaning image. The gleaning image of 20:45 does not imply a primary action followed by a "mop-up" operation performed on the remainder. Rather the gleaning image refers to the successive waves of "gleaners" who act upon the field in serial fashion. In Rashi's words, "killing after killing, like gleaning after the harvest" הריגה אחר הריגה כעוללות שאחרי הבציר). The emphasis then, is not upon a secondary, smaller action in the wake of a primary one, but rather on the same action being executed repeatedly.

This second interpretation of the gleaning imagery has bearing for the narrative analogy at hand. The assault on the concubine of ch. 19 and the decimation of the tribe of Benjamin of ch. 20 are cast in lexical congruence as the victims of processes of the phonetic field of ע.ל.ל. Yet, the congruence runs much deeper than the level of assonance. For in each instance, the act executed via the verb ע.ל.ל. is an act executed upon the victim over and over again; even as the verb ויתעללו בה of 19:25 is, as we shall see, etymologically unrelated to the word לעולל, "to glean," the act perpetrated through this act of התעללות is that of gang rape, an act perforce carried out in serial fashion; Scripture itself alludes to the fact that this victimization was not a momentary assault but one executed over many hours: "They

---

[13] Amit, *Book of Judges*, 307.
[14] Rashi and R. Joseph Kara to 20:45; Elitzur, *Book of Judges*, 179; Galil, *Judges*, 165.

raped her and abused her all night long until morning" (19:25). To summarize, the concubine is victimized through the semantic field of ע.ל.ל. in a serial attack of rape after rape. The tribe of Benjamin in ch. 20 suffers measure for measure through the same lexical field, in a serial victimization, as Rashi stated of killing after killing.

The term ויתעללו־בה in 19:25, like ויעללהו in 20:45, also bears multiple valences. The *hitpael* form in reference to people, as exhibited here, occurs seven times across the Bible to mean "to mock," or "dally with." The present instance is the only one that bears a sexual connotation of any kind. Five of the occurrences are within the context of military foes making sport of one another. Three depict earthly foes behaving thus (1 Sam 31:4 = 1 Chr 10:4; Jer 38:19) and two depict God making sport of his enemies in war (Exod 10:2; 1 Sam 6:6). Even the sixth instance—Balaam's remonstration of the donkey—may be seen to be a borrowed image from the battlefield. Furious at his donkey for having mocked him (Num 22:27), Balaam exclaims two verses later (22:29), "If only I had a sword in my hand, I would kill you." The image of the sword in hand prepared to kill, which would be fully appropriate in a battle setting, may be invoked to convey Balaam's stance vis-à-vis the obstinacy of his mount. Beyond merely disobeying him, she has become in his eyes a foe, who mocks him as a victor mocks a vanquished opponent. In response, he desires only to draw a sword, and smite his four-legged foe.

These data, whereby all other occurrences of the term appear within a military context, can lead, from a methodological standpoint, to one of two conclusions about the meaning here. The more conservative approach is to view the term as meaning "to make sport of" or "to mock" in a generic sense, without a specific context beyond the parameters of each individual occurrence. The fact that all six of the other occurrences are within a battlefield context or borrowed from that context means only that in those stories the author chose to employ the generic term for mockery. Alternatively, however, we may conclude that the preponderance of attestations within a battle context suggests that the term's most basic meaning is within the context of battle, and that the use of the term in any other context is a borrowed usage, as exhibited by the example from the Balaam story. The image here is, unarguably, unique in its context of sexual abuse and exploitation. At the same time, however, it may be seen to be borrowed from a battle-narrative context. The Levite and his concubine, as strangers, were unwelcome in Gibeah as a matter of norm.[15] The rapacious behavior of the Gibeanites is not only an expression of licentiousness but through the designation of the act as התעללות it emerges as an expression of mocking by the victor over his vanquished foe, in this case the unwanted strangers, through the physical agency of the concubine.

An intertextual use of the root ע.ל.ל. emerges between the two narratives as the use of the verb in each narrative invokes the meaning, or context, of the other. As we saw earlier, the term ויעללהו in 20:45 may imply a serial act of victimization, reminiscent of the serial act of aggression against the concubine. Now the reverse is seen to be true as well. The term ויתעללו-בה of ch. 19, implying abuse within a sexual context, is a term whose most basic milieu is that of the battlefield. Through the crossing of lines of the semantic field of ע.ל.ל., the battle against Benjamin takes on overtones of a gang rape, and the gang rape of the concubine those of a battle. This conclusion, of course, rests on several assumptions that are debatable, such as the correct implication of the gleaning imagery in 20:45, or the assertion that the verb להתעלל bears a primary battlefield context. Yet what seems unassailable from our discussion of the verb ע.ל.ל. in Judges 19-20, is the minimalist conclusion. The two words may, in fact, be unrelated. Yet the high degree of assonance between two uncommon words that satisfy the criterion of rhetorical congruence (each refers to an act of aggression against the victim) suggests that the author of the unit has employed these terms to further the equivalence between the crime committed against the concubine and the punishment suffered by the tribe of Benjamin.

The Semantic Fields of ש.ל.ח. and of נ.פ.ל.

The final act taken by the tribes of Israel against Benjamin is the act of burning the cities of Benjamin (20:48). While torching a conquered city is commonly found in biblical battle reports, the particular term שלחו באש is found elsewhere in a battle context only in Judg 1:8 and in Ps 74:7. By contrast, the more conventional שרפו באש (in both singular and plural) is found 19 times (Num 31:10; Deut 13:17; Josh 6:24, 11:9, 11:11; Judg 9:52, 18:27; 1 Sam 30:14; 2 Kgs 25:9; Jer 21: 10, 32:29, 34:2, 34:22, 37:8, 10, 38:18, 39:8, 51:32, 52:13), and hence

---

[15] Elitzur, *Book of Judges*, 169.

the term here is exceptional, if not unique. The term שלחו באש is
matched by use of the same verb in the rape account: "They raped
her and abused her all night long until morning; *and they cast her off*
(וישלחוה) when dawn broke (19:25)." Before discussing the possible
meanings of this parallel, however, I must justify my rendering here
of the term וישלחוה as "they cast her off."

The JPS translation, and indeed, most modern commentators,
translate וישלחוה as "they let her go," or "they released her." I have
opted for stronger language for several reasons. Mieke Bal[16] has written
of rape as an act of hatred, and the context of the rape scene—as an
expression of Gibeah's hatred for strangers—bears out Bal's assessment. The apex of this hatred, of course, is related in the verse that
details the night-long gang rape, verse 25. To end the account of the
night of torture by stating, "They raped her and abused her all night
long until morning; *and they released her* when dawn broke," creates an
anti-climax, and belies the violence of their actions, by making their
final act not only passive, but one of compassion. The phrase "and
they released her" is, moreover, redundant. Once the reader has been
told that they raped and abused the concubine all night long *until
morning*, the reader implicitly understands that the torture ended then,
and that she was released.

My rendering of the word וישלחוה as "cast off" is based on the use
of the verb elsewhere in a highly similar context: Amnon's rape of
Tamar. Following the rape, Scripture says (2 Sam 13:15-17):

> And Amnon said to her, "Get out!" She pleaded with him, "Please don't
> commit this wrong; to send me away (לשלחני) would be even worse"...
> He summoned his young attendant and said, "Get that woman out
> (שלחו-נא) of my presence and bar the door behind her."

Amnon's final act of brutality is hardly one of "release," but rather
an expulsion that expresses his disgust and repulsion. Note further,
the similar language of sexual violence there and here: "he grasped"
(ויחזק) v. 11 (compare to Judg 19:25); "vile thing" (נבלה) v. 12 (compare to 19:24); "he would not listen to her" (ולא אבה לשמע בקולה) v.
14 (compare to 19:25). The same may be said of the term וישלחוה
in 19:25. Even the act of releasing her is an act of violence. Hardly
passive, "they cast her off."

Although the two actions are highly differentiated (casting off

---

[16] Mieke Bal, *Lethal Love: Feminist Literary Readings of Biblical Love Stories* (Bloomington: Indiana University Press, 1987) 20.

and torching, respectively), they uphold the criterion of rhetorical congruence. In each episode, the aggressor performs an act of .ש.ל.ח upon the victim, respectively, the concubine, and the cities of the Benjaminites.

Once again, we can see how *structure* plays a role in the establishment of an analogy between two stories. Recall that in our discussion of the equivalence between the trial of Achan in Joshua 7 and the conquest of Ha-Ai in Joshua 8, we noted the identical phrase "they raised a great heap of stones over him, which is there to this day." Yet, we further noted that the basis for viewing these two phrases as parallel elements stemmed from the fact that they each appear respectively as the final phrase of each account. The same, we saw, was true of the words, "And God said to Joshua... 'Rise...'" (ויאמר ה' אל יהושע... קום) which constituted the opening phrases of each account. The same structural consideration is evident here. The parallelism between the elements of .ש.ל.ח is structural as well as lexical. Through the verb .ש.ל.ח the tribes torch the Benjaminite cities as their final act of battlefield aggression. Through the agency of the verb .ש.ל.ח, the inhabitants of Gibeah ignominiously cast off the concubine as a final act of violence capping a night of rape and molestation.

The final semantic parallel between the two passages that we will consider surrounds the root .נ.פ.ל. As we saw in the introduction, this root was identified by Plöger and Richter as one of the conventional terms used in biblical battle reports; hence, there is nothing distinct about the use of this verb in depicting the Benjaminite casualties in vv. 44 and 46. Nor is there anything exceptional about the use of the verb .נ.פ.ל to depict the collapse of the concubine at the doorstep of the old man's home in 19:26-27. Thus, on the one hand, the criterion of rhetorical congruence is met, as the victim in each is seen "to fall." Yet, the usage of .נ.פ.ל in each passage may be justified on its own terms. Here we encounter an example of a semantic parallel between two passages, where the significance test leaves us with inconclusive results. When the use of a particular word or phrase can be demonstrated to be distinct we have the right to posit that its placement in parallel to a similar word or phrase elsewhere contributes to the formation of the narrative analogy. The converse, however, is not true. Failure to find distinctiveness in either of the words under inspection (as in the present instance) does not mean, perforce, that these do not contribute to the establishment of the parallel. There is no reason to insist that narrative analogies be constructed entirely out of unusual words and

usages. The result here, therefore, is not negative, but simply, inconclusive. It may be that the author used the root .נ.פ.ל in each passage
because it was the word that most aptly suited his purposes in each
instance. Alternatively, we may see within the use of the word .נ.פ.ל
in each the fulfillment of two objectives: the term expresses the action
being described in the most apt and natural terms and at the same
time adds another paired element that contributed to the establishment
of his narrative analogy. Were the narrative analogy built entirely on
elements such as this the very proposition that the passages stand in
analogy would need to be questioned. When an analogy has been
documented, as we feel the case is here, inconclusive parallels that
satisfy the criterion of rhetorical congruence may be included, with
the appropriate disclaimer as to the strength of the parallel.[17]

Group as Corporate Entity

The contention that the battle account of ch. 20 and the rape account
of chapter 19 are equivalent stories is further buttressed by what I
perceive to be a highly distinctive rhetorical strategy that permeates
nearly the entire literary fabric of the battle account of the demise
of the tribe of Benjamin.

The rhetorical device I refer to here is the consistent reference to a
group, in this case the men, or, tribe of Benjamin, through use of *collective pronouns* and their *coreferents*. By collective pronouns, I mean terms
that are morphologically singular, yet refer to a group of individuals.
Coreferents are terms in a sentence which have the same referent as
does the collective pronoun. These may be pronouns, adjectives or
participles. When the coreferent of the collective pronoun is in the
singular it expresses "grammatical" concord. When the coreferent is
expressed in the plural, it demonstrates "notional" concord.[18] Through-

---

[17] In both passages the root .נ.פ.ל appears twice (19:26, 27; 20:44, 46). Were
the declension identical or even the form identical in both instances, we would be
able to claim that significance has been demonstrated. But that is not the case here.
While in both 19:26 and 20:44 we encounter a verb form (*piʿel*), the latter two in
each narrative (i.e. 19:27 and 20: 46) do not match. הנפלים in 20:46 is a noun, lit.
"the fallen," while נפלת in 19:27 is the participle form of the verb, and refers to her
position, lit. "was lying."

[18] These are the terms used by E.J. Revell in his unpublished essay on the topic,
"The Logic of Concord with Collectives in Biblical Narrative" (section 1.1). I am
grateful to Prof. Revell for sharing the article with me and granting me the privilege
to cite his work here.

out verses 1-39, we see that while the narrative usually refers to the rogue tribe as the *sons of* Benjamin (i.e., grammatically plural) it does not hesitate to vary in style and opt for the collective pronoun "Benjamin" (20:17, 20, 25, 35 [2x], 36, 39) in reference to the entire force, or the entire tribe. In sentences that refer to "the sons of Benjamin," all subsequent coreferents to the group are in the plural. Yet even in clauses that invoke the collective pronoun, "Benjamin," subsequent coreferents are typically expressed in the plural, employing notional concord, as in 20:20, "The men of Israel took the field against *Benjamin* (עם בנימן); the men of Israel drew up in battle order against *them* (אתם) at Gibeah," or as in 20:25, "*Benjamin* came out from Gibeah against them... and *struck (pl.)* down (וישחיתו), with exceptions found only in 32b (ונתקנהו) and 39a (ובנימן החל).

The section that has been the focus of our close reading, 20: 40-48, stands apart in this regard. Here, the rogue tribe is referred to through the collective "Benjamin" and its singular coreferents in unusual proportions. To appreciate the phenomenon fully, we would do well to divide the section of 20:40-48 along lines of content. We have here three distinct foci: vv. 40-46 describe the decimation of the main Benjaminite force, that left nearly all of its members dead (25,000 out of an original force of 26,700). Verse 47 chronicles the flight of 600 survivors to shelter for four months. Verse 48 reports of the ethnic cleansing and genocide committed by the tribes across all the cities of Benjamin. The concentrated use of collective pronouns and singular coreferents is limited to the first section, vv. 40-46, the account of the decimation of the Benjaminite army. Here we find 16 collective pronouns and coreferents in the singular, and only three in the plural: v. 41—"they retreated (ויפנו)"; v. 44—"they fell (ויפלו)"; v. 45—"they turned and fled (ויפנו וינסו)" (this is a verbal hendiadys, and hence the two verbs are essentially one act).[19] Such a phenomenon

---

[19] I am unable to explain adequately what functional advantage is achieved by employing the plural coreferents in these instances, especially in light of the fact that in each of these verses all of the other coreferents are in the singular.

It is perhaps of significance that all three of these plural coreferents appear as the opening word of their respective verses. It may be that a convention dictated that where the subject of the verse is not explicit, clarity mandated that the opening verb employ a plural coreferent when referring to a group. De Regt (L.J. De Regt, *Participant Pronouns in Old Testament Texts and the Translator* [Assen: Van Gorcum, 1999] 14) notes that an explicit reference with a proper name often marks the start of a new paragraph, referring to a major participant. Hence, in like fashion, we see in Judg 1: 20 a plural verb that opens the verse, even though the previous verse refers to Judah

in the Former Prophets is found elsewhere only in Judges 1 and in
Judges 11:12-20 (Revell section 9.4). Revell offers the following suggestion concerning the rhetorical function of this device:

> The[se] actions are viewed abstractly, as undertaken by population
> groups seen as "states." In more vivid narrative passages, such political
> actions are typically depicted by the leader of the group treated as an
> individual...In the three passages of historical synopsis (i.e. Judg 1, 11:
> 13-21, and 20) the narrator presents the political struggles as background
> to the narrative of those aspects of the history of Israel which are his
> major interest. The predominant designation of population groups as
> singular is one of the marks of this intention.

Revell's generalization may be challenged. It is unclear, for instance,
why the narratives of Judges 11:13-21 and Judges 20 are mere "background," and even less clear why they are to be considered "abstract"
rather than vivid; the battle account of Judges 20, if anything, is one
of the most vivid battle accounts found in the biblical record. Rather, I
would like to suggest, as Sternberg does, that there is no unique linkage between form and function, and that the same rhetorical device
may serve various functions.[20] Two examples from within the Pentateuch in which groups are referred to through collective pronouns
and singular coreferents will serve to underscore the point.

In Exod 1:9-12a, the narrative exclusively refers to the emerging
nation of Israel through collective terms and singular coreferents. This
stands in sharp contrast to 1:7, where the depiction of the prolific
nature of the Israelite birthrate employs five plural coreferents. The
subsequent account of vv. 9-12a underscores their unity and hence their
threat in Pharaoh's eyes; the "whole," in Pharaoh's estimation, is far
more threatening than the sum of its parts. Unity likewise seems to be
the underlying theme inherent in Israel's vow concerning the conquest
of the King of Arad in Num 21:1-2. The conquest and expression of

---

in the singular throughout all its coreferents. This theory corresponds with Revell's
finding (section 2.2) that collective pronouns such as "Benjamin" rarely appear as the
subject of a verse, less than 10% of their occurrences by his calculation. Likewise, we
find that in contrast to ויפלו at the beginning of v. 44 here, where the subject is not
stated explicitly, the word ויפל elsewhere refers to a group only mid-verse (Exod 32:
28; Judg 12:6; 1 Sam 4:10; 2 Sam. 11:17). Cf. Num 21:2 and 2 Sam 10:18 where a
singular verb refers to a collective entity as the first word of the verse. In both these
instances, the collective that serves as the subject of the verse is explicitly stated.
Admittedly, the opening verb of Judg 11:18 challenges this theory. On the entire
subject of pronouns in the Hebrew Bible see De Regt, *Participant Pronouns*, and with
particular reference to coreferents, pp. 85-88.

[20] Sternberg, *Poetics*, 437.

trust in God were carried out in a unanimity of belief.

Toward what end has the author of Judges 20 cast the tribe of Benjamin—or more pointedly, the routed army of Benjamin in vv. 40-46—in corporate, or personified terms? The unity thesis, exhibited in the Pentateuchal examples just cited, seems insufficient here: why would the narrator strive to stress unity in vv. 40-46, and not in all of the action earlier depicted in vv. 1-39?

I would like to interpret that at this critical junction in the plot of Judges 19-20, the army of Benjamin is cast as an individual human being. Some of the phrases within vv. 40-46 are almost awkward as references to a group, and read far more naturally as descriptions of an individual. This is the case with the final clause of v. 41, literally, "for *he* realized that disaster had overtaken *him* (כי ראה כי נגעה עליו הרעה), or v. 43—literally, "They encircled *Benjamin*, hounded *him* and drove rest from *him*" (כתרו את בנימן הרדיפהו מנוחה הדריכהו). All of these seem to underscore our sense of Benjamin here as a personified individual rather than as a mass corps. Yet, it can hardly be said that the didactic aim here is to elicit pity, or identification with the sufferings of the tribe of Benjamin by making their travails more individual and hence more "human." Judges 20, if anything, seems to be highly critical of the tribe of Benjamin for not disciplining the residents of Gibeah, and some have even seen the chapter as an anti-Benjaminite polemic.[21]

I would suggest that the decimation of the Benjaminite army in individual, more "human" terms serves to strengthen the analogy between the victimization of the tribe of Benjamin and the victimization of the concubine. "Benjamin," and not the *tribe* of Benjamin, nor the *sons* of Benjamin, nor the *men* of Benjamin is the subject of the decimation account. This explains the absence of this literary device earlier in the chapter, during the account of the first two days of fighting, 20:1-39. Only once the tide of fortune turns, does the fierce fighting force of the *sons* of Benjamin, and the *tribe* of Benjamin, evolve into a victimized individual. "Benjamin," the corporate person, like the concubine, is harassed and ravaged to the point of exhaustion; "Benjamin," like the concubine, collapses just short of reaching the enclave that would have provided shelter.

---

[21] Cf. Ben-Zion Luria, *Saul and Benjamin* (Jerusalem: Israel Society for the Study of the Bible, 1970) 180 (Hebrew); Galil, *Judges*, 76. See most recently, Yairah Amit, *Hidden Polemics in Biblical Narrative* (Leiden: Brill, 2000) 178-88.

To summarize to this point: we began by noting that even before engaging in a close reading of the accounts, it was evident, from the standpoint of biblical theology, that the annihilation of the tribe of Benjamin was an extreme punishment exacted in retribution for an extreme and heinous crime, the gang rape of the concubine and subsequent refusal by the entire tribe to bring the offenders to justice. Through the semantic field surrounding the word רעה the notion of measure for measure was proposed as underlying the lexical fabric of the text and laying the conceptual groundwork for the subsequent analogy to be established. Through this analogy we are to view the רעה suffered by the tribe of Benjamin, that is, the entire unfolding of their demise as recorded in vv. 40-48, as equivalent to the רעה suffered by the concubine in the attack, as recorded in 19:22-27. The search for equivalent terms and images followed suit. Each, we saw, was outnumbered and surrounded. Each was pursued to the point of exhaustion in an effort to return to the only shelter at hand, though that shelter was effectively no longer available. The city of Gibeah had since gone up in smoke, and the old man's house was the very point from which the concubine had been thrust out to the frenzied mob. We saw further that the analogy was perhaps strengthened in formal terms. The ubiquitous prevalence of sun imagery used to portray the close of the concubine's suffering in chapter 19 is matched by the final stage of the Benjaminite army's demise which occurred opposite Gibeah, not, toward *qedem* (as convention would dictate), but toward *the rising sun*. In a matching of uncommon terms, we saw that each suffered a fate through the root ע.ל.ל., bringing a battlefield term into the account of the rape, and underscoring the common victimization through a serial act of cruelty. The semantic fields of נ.פ.ל. and ש.ח.ל. rounded out the terms employed to portray the onslaught against both the concubine and the tribe of Benjamin. Amid these parallels we further saw that the section of the account which focuses on the collapse of the Benjaminite army, vv. 40-46, casts them in individual terms, in a fashion that allows the depiction of victimization to parallel more closely that of the concubine.

The Meaning of the Equivalence: A Second Layer

In our introduction we noted the interrelationship of twin processes of assimilation when reading analogous stories: the process of identifying common analogical elements and the process of establishing meaning were intertwined and reciprocal. Thus far we have examined the analogy as a vivid illustration of the principle of measure for measure. This was posited when we examined the first common element, the semantic field of רעה, and it was further borne out as subsequent elements were identified. The foregoing element of comparison, however, will shed light on another dimension of the meaning of the analogy.

In the wake of each account, respectively, we see that all of Israel gathers together to confront the travesty that has just occurred. The Israelites interrogate the Benjaminites in 20:3, in response to the mutilated limbs they had received: "Tell us, how did this evil thing happen? (דברו, איכה נהיתה הרעה הזאת). A similar question is expressed following the decimation of the Benjaminites, this time to God (21:3): "O Lord God of Israel, why has this happened in Israel? (למה יהוה אלהי ישראל היתה-זאת בישראל). The spirit in which each question is raised, is, of course, markedly different; in chapter 20 the question of how "this came to be" is asked in indignation and in self-righteousness. The question is a challenge to which the Benjaminites are called upon to respond. In chapter 21, however, it is said in sorrow and perhaps even self-reflection and remorse. Formally, the question is posed to God. But the ensuing offer of sacrifices (21:4) and resolve to find wives through which to rebuild the decimated tribe suggest that the question is asked as much of themselves as it is of God. Having judgmentally pondered the travesties committed at the hands of the Gibeans, they are now forced to ponder the travesty wrought by their own hands.

Scholars have noted several aspects of the campaign against the tribe of Benjamin that support the contention that the text is highly critical of Israel's conduct here. Nowhere in the Book of Judges is unity displayed amongst the tribes of Israel as it is in the campaign to exterminate the tribe of Benjamin.[22] Amit has noted that of the nine times that the Bible states that an entity acted as "one man" (איש אחד), three appear here in Judges 20.[23] While the confederation's original war aims were to retaliate against the residents of Gibeah alone (20:11) in an act of moral cleansing, the result is an unbridled act of ethnic cleansing, in which women (21:16), children and chattel (20:48) were annihilated.[24]

---

[22] Moore, *A Critical*, 404; Hamlin, *Joshua*, 168.
[23] Amit, *Book of Judges*, 299.
[24] Cf. Hamlin, *Joshua*, 168; Boling, *Joshua*, 277. Reich has noticed a further parallel

All of the findings thus far may be arranged schematically, in a fashion that categorizes and differentiates between the various elements that we have seen:

	Measure For Measure – Punishment of Benjaminites Analogous to Victimization of Concubine	
	Decimation of Benjaminites	**Rape of Concubine**
Victim of רעה	כי ראה כי נגעה עליו **הרעה** (20:41)	אל-אחי אל-**תרעו** נא (19:23) מה **הרעה** הזאת אשר נהיתה בכם (20:12)
Victim Encircled	כתרו את-בנימן (20:43)	בני-בליעל נסבו את הבית (19:22)
Hunted to Exhaustion	הרדיפהו מנוחה הדריכהו (20:43)	וישלחוה..ותבא..ותפל פתח בית-האיש אשר-אדניה שם עד-האור (19:24-25)
Demise at Threshold of Shelter	הדריכהו עד נכח הגבעה..ויפלו מבנימן שמנה-עשר אלף איש (20:43-44)	ותפל פתח בית-האיש אשר-אדניה שם (19:25)
Sun Imagery at Point of Demise	הדריכהו עד נכח הגבעה ממזרח-שמש (20:43)	ויתעללו-בה..עד-הבקר..וישלחוה בעלות השחר (19:25) ותבא האשה לפנות בקר..עד האור (19:26) ויקם אדניה בבקר (19:27)
Victimization through ע.ל.ל.	**ויעללהו** במסלות חמשת אלפים איש (20:45)	**ויתעללו**-בה (19:25)
Victim falls – נ.פ.ל.	ויפלו מבנימן (20:44) ויהי כל **הנפלים** מבנימן (20:46)	**ותפל** פתח בית-האיש (19:26) והנה האשה פילגשו **נפלת** (19:27)
Vicitim is cast – ש.ל.ח.	כל-הערים הנמצאות **שלחו** באש (20:48)	**וישלחוה** בעלות השחר (19:25)
Israel Reflects on the Tragedy	למה יהוה אלהי ישראל **היתה-זאת** בישראל (21:3)	איכה **נהיתה** הרעה הזאת (20:3) מה הרעה **הזאת** אשר **נהיתה** בכם (20:12)
	Decimation of Benjaminites	**Rape of the Concubine**
	Atrocity of the Tribes Equivalent to the Atrocity of the Gibeans	

---

that casts the act of the tribes in terms equivalent to that of the residents of Gibeah. The language used by the tribes to demand the handing over of the residents of Gibeah in 20:13 is highly reminiscent of the language used by the residents of Gibeah themselves in demanding the handing over of the guest by the old man in 19:22, in a sense that foreshadows the atrocity that will later follow:

תנו **את האנשים** בני בליעל.....הוצא **את האיש**

אשר בגבעה....**אשר** בא אל ביתך

ונמיתם...ונדענו

The chart graphically illustrates that the narrative analogy between the rape of the concubine and the decimation of the tribe of Benjamin is, in fact, two analogies: one, which features the punishment of the tribe of Benjamin in terms analogous to the sufferings they inflicted upon the concubine (light shaded area). The second narrative analogy focuses on the identity of the tribes of Israel as offenders, even as were the inhabitants of Gibeah (dark shaded area). While the quantitative proportions are obviously much greater in Israel's offense, the purpose of this analogy is to highlight the viciousness common to each offending party.[25] In terms of their constituent elements these two analogies display a high degree of overlap, yet they are not identical. The elements common to both analogies are the elements in the medium shaded area. These contribute to the respective lessons of each analogy. The "gleaning" reported in v. 45, for example, demonstrates on the one hand, from the perspective of the victim, that the Benjaminites suffered a fate similar to that of the concubine. Yet, the same phonetic field of ע.ל.ל. demonstrates equally well—this time from the perspective of the viciousness of the perpetrator—that the tribes were as ruthless on the battlefield as were the Gibeans during their assault.[26] The analogies overlap, but they are not identical. The first analogical element, the use of the word רעה, and the final element, the reflection by Israel on each tragedy pertain, respectively, to only one of these analogies.

The word רעה in 20:41 comments neither upon the guilt of the tribes, nor upon the analogy between their behavior and that of the Gibeans. Their savagery only began to exhibit itself in subsequent verses, through "gleaning" the scattered and confused strays from a vanquished army; through wiping out women and children across all the cities of Benjamin. Recall that the outset of the campaign on the third day was waged with God's explicit blessings (20:28), and to this point (v. 41) all that they have done is to successfully execute a winning strategy. The word רעה, therefore, is a member only of the analogy that brings the punishment of the Benjaminites into equivalence with the rape of the concubine.

---

[25] This is in sharp contrast with Amit's reading of Judges 19-21 as a depiction of " a period more illustrious than any other in the history of Israel and Judah prior to the exile" (*Book of Judges*, 281).

[26] Cf. Reich, "The Concubine," 117.

The element of the word רעה may also be seen as the exclusive member of the analogy of measure for measure from another perspective. Above we raised the possibility of reading a second layer of meaning into the word רעה here. On a primary level, it reflects "Benjamin's" consciousness that misfortune was falling upon himself. Secondarily, however, we suggested that the realization here was that it was "his" (i.e. the corporate entity that I have called "Benjamin") own misdeeds that were catching up with him in the form of the closing Israelite ranks. If this reading is accepted, then the word רעה is again seen to be a member only of the analogy of measure for measure. Indeed, the message of the entire analogy becomes encapsulated within the form of this single word.

The final shared feature, the reflection of Israel upon each of the atrocities, is likewise a member of only one of the analogies, this one a member of the analogy equating the ruthlessness of the Israelites with the ruthlessness of the Benjaminites. This is so, because by this point in the narrative, the action that had been the focus of the analogy of measure for measure, has since ended. When the Israelites ask God, "Why has this happened?" they are the only ones on the narrative stage; there are almost literally no more Benjaminites left to victimize. In fact, the conciliatory tones here give way to ad hoc remedies for the rebuilding of the tribe. With the torching of the cities described several verses earlier in 20:48, the suffering of the Benjaminites comes to an end and with it the analogy between their punishment and the suffering they inflicted upon the concubine. The question of the tribes before God, however, does have an eerie ring to it, reminiscent of the undignified charges that the tribes themselves raised in 20:3. This element, therefore, is a member, exclusively, of the analogy between the ruthlessness displayed by the Israelites and the ruthlessness displayed by the tribe of Benjamin. The lesson of this analogy, then, is to contribute to the impression of the overall wayward slide of the whole of Israel at this time.[27]

I would like to conclude our study of this metaphor analogy by placing our findings here within the context of the methodological

---

[27] Cf. Elitzur, *Book of Judges*, 12. Reich ("The Concubine," 110) has noted similarities between the account here and the injunction concerning the wayward city (Deut. 13:13-19). The tribes, she claims, acted toward the cities of Benjamin as if they were wayward cities, with the important distinction that whereas the Torah mandates a procedure of due process, the tribes heard only the account of the concubine's husband (cf. Satterthwaite, "Narrative Artistry," 86; Amit, *Book of Judges*, 306).

innovations that I delineated in the introduction. The criterion of rhetorical congruence has emerged as crucial to our interpretation of the analogy. We saw that the lexical marker רעה was a distinct member of the analogy that cast the punishment of the Benjaminites in terms similar to that of the rape of the concubine, in punishment measure for measure. We also saw that Israel's reflection upon each tragedy through the shared words היתה זאת was only a member of the analogy that equated the atrocity of the tribes with that of the Gibeans. By carefully assessing the role and function of each shared term we were able to delineate two distinct analogies here. Not merely two explanations of the same analogy, but two distinct analogies, each with its own meaning.

Moreover, recall that we extrapolated from the work of Propp the working principle that when a shared lexical term is a highly common one, it may be considered as part of the analogical base if we find it positioned in both narratives at key positions—either at the opening or at the closing of the analogy. The principle is vividly at play in the present instance. The final element of the analogy is Israel's reflection upon the tragedy through the (rather common) words, היתה זאת. Yet, we may confidently include them in the analogical base, for in each narrative they constitute the concluding shared element of the analogy.

Joshua 8 and Judges 20: A Reassessment

The structure of this study has thus far probed the second battle of Ha-Ai (Joshua 8) and the battle of Israel against the tribe of Benjamin as independent illustrations of battle stories in the Bible cast as narrative analogies to the stories that respectively precede them. The two accounts, however, have been viewed by many as interdependent, though the nature of this interdependence has been widely debated. Were we interested in the textual history of the Book of Judges, the question of the influence of Joshua 8 on Judges 20 (or vice versa) would be of apparent importance. Our interest in the question, however, stems from a different consideration. Our attempt to document the existence of a convention of narrative analogy in the crafting of biblical battle stories is predicated, in primary fashion, on a strategy of demonstrating a significant number of examples of the phenomenon across the Bible.

There is a second strategy, however, that supports the contention that such a topos exists: the documentation of broad influence of one text upon another that might point to the transmission of the topos—as one of many shared elements—from one text to another. The nature of our study is for the most part synchronic. Yet, to determine whether the rhetoric of the metaphor plot in one book may have been inspired by its presence in another, requires that we engage this diachronic issue.

The question of the interrelationship between Joshua 8 and Judges 20, as mentioned, is widely debated; some, such as Galil and Zakovitch, see the many parallels between the two texts as indicative of an ideological agenda.[28] Others, also citing the many shared features, see a process of textual borrowing but with no ideological agenda. Finally, one scholar, Leah Mazor, has asserted that there is no textual relationship whatsoever between the two accounts.[29] To make the discussion intelligible, we need first to present the basic data that have spawned the debate. In graphic form, we may see that the two accounts share many terms in common:

Judges 20	Joshua 8
עלו כי מחר **אתננו בידך** (28)	ראה **נתתי בידך** את מלך העי (1)
וישם ישראל **ארבים** אל הגבעה סביב (29)	**שים** לך **ארב** לעיר מאחריה (2) **וישם** אותם **אורב** (12)
ויעלו בני ישראל אל בני בנימן (30)	ויקם יהושע וכל העם המלחמה **לעלות** העי (3)
ויצאו בני בנימן **לקראת** העם (30)	והיה כי **יצאו לקראתנו** (5)
כבראשונה (32)	**כאשר בראשונה** (5)
ובני ישראל אמרו **ננוסה** (32)	**ונסנו** לפניהם (5,6)
נתקנהו מן העיר (32)	עד **התיקנו אותם מן העיר** (6)
וכל ישראל **קמו** ממקומו (33)	ואתם **תקמו** מן הארב (7)
ויבאו מנגד לגבעה (34)	**ויבאו נגד** העיר (11)

---

[28] Galil and Zakovitch, *Joshua*, 76.

[29] Leah Mazor, "The Account of the Victory over Ha-Ai (Joshua 8): A Textual and Literary Analysis," in Sara Japhet (ed.), HaMiqra BeRei Mefarshav (Jerusalem: Magnes Press, 1994) 99-100 (Hebrew).

Judges 20	Joshua 8
והם לא ידעו כי נגעה עליהם הרעה (34)	**והוא לא ידע כי** אורב לו מאחורי העיר (14)
ויפנו... אל **דרך המדבר** (42)	וינסו **דרך המדבר** (15)
והאורב החישו... ויך את כל **העיר**	**והאורב** קם מהרה ממקומו וירוצו... ויבאו **העיר** וילכדוה (19)
והמשאת החלה לעלות מן העיר עמוד **עשן** ויפן בנימן אחריו והנה **עלה** כליל העיר **השמימה** (40)	**והנה עלה עשן העיר השמימה** (20)
ואיש ישראל **שבו** אל בני בנימן (48) **ויכום לפי חרב.**.. (48)	**וישבו ויכו** את אנשי העי (21) ויפלו כלם **לפי חרב** עד תמם וישבו כל ישראל העי (24)
עד כל הנמצא (48)	**עד** אשר החרים את כל ישבי העי (26)
גם כל הערים הנמצאות שלחו באש (48)	וישרף יהושע את העי (28)

Beyond the lexical similarities there is similarity found with regard to the basic structure of the two accounts. In each, a force suffers a loss (Israel in Joshua 7; the tribes during the first two days of fighting in Judges 20), and returns to turn that setback into the successful opening of a feigned retreat leading to ambush of the foe. No other biblical battle story so neatly follows the common pattern exhibited in these two accounts.

For Galil and Zakovitch the meaning of all this is clear: the author of Judges 20 has cast the tribe of Benjamin in terms used to describe the decimation of a Canaanite city, in an example of an anti-Saul, anti-Benjamin polemic, *par excellence*.[30] Yet, in spite of all the parallels, this theory, first advanced by Güdeman,[31] has been challenged on several fronts. As Rudin has pointed out we would expect a polemic to draw a sharp distinction between the proverbial "good guys" (presumably the

---

[30] Galil and Zakovitch, *Joshua*, 76. Cf. Amit, *Hidden Polemics*, 178-88.

[31] M. Güdeman, "Tendenz und Abfassungszeit der letzten Kapitel des Buches der Richter," *MGWJ* 18 (1869) 357-68.

tribes of Israel) and "bad guys" (presumably the Benjaminites) of the story.[32] Yet Judges 20 fails to do so. While the tribe of Benjamin is deeply implicated, the tribes of Israel hardly emerge scot-free. Much of the evidence garnered in the earlier part of this chapter demonstrated Israel's guilt in the near-genocide of an entire tribe and this without touching upon the problematic behavior of the tribes toward Jabesh Gilead in chapter 21. Moreover, were Judges 20 an anti-Benjaminite polemic, then its author would presumably be someone with pro-Davidic leanings. And yet, we find that the author of Judges 20 has placed at the helm of this troubling campaign of the tribes none other than the tribe of Judah (20:18).[33]

Many scholars therefore, have preferred to describe the influence here as textual, with no unambiguous ideological or didactic intention.[34] Looking to document the feigned retreat successfully executed by the Israelites, the author of Judges 20 looked to the only precedent he had on how to craft such a battle report, namely the text of Joshua 8.

Yet these scholars have failed to comprehensively address the challenges raised by Mazor. She not only rejects the notion of a polemic in Judges 20 based on its similarity to Joshua 8, but indeed rejects the notion of any connection whatsoever—ideological or textual—between the two stories. The textual similarities, she claims, all fail on what we have called the significance test; either the terms are highly common or they are the terms necessary for the depiction of a feigned retreat. On lexical grounds therefore, there is no reason to presuppose an intentional relationship between the two accounts. Nor does she see any reason to assert a relationship between the two stories on account of the common tactic of feigned retreat leading to ambush. Like Moore,[35] she sees it as quite plausible that the same successful

---

[32] Talya Rudin-Ubarsky, "The Appendix to the Book of Judges (Judges 17-21)," *Be'er Sheva* 2 (1985) 158 (Hebrew).

[33] Boling (*Joshua*, 236) has proposed an alternative ideological link between the two passages: the shared notion of a change in fortune on the battlefield demonstrates that no defeat is final, if Yahweh is allowed to take command. Yet his claim likewise suffers from the incongruences between the two passages.

[34] See on this: W. Roth, "Hinterhalt und Scheinflucht: der stammespolemische Hintergrund von Jos 8," *ZAW* 75 (1963) 296-304; R. de Vaux, "La prise de 'Ay," *Histoire Ancienne d'Israel* (2 vols; Etudes Bibliques; Paris: J. Gabalda, 1971-73) 1.563-70; H. Rösel, "Studien zur Topographie der Kriege in den Büchern Josua und Richter," *ZDVP* 91 (1975) 159-90; 92 (1976) 31-46; Rudin, "The Appendix," 155-58; Amit, *Book of Judges*, 283. Unlike most scholars, Ahituv, *Joshua*, 140 and Malamat (Abraham Malamat, *Israel in Biblical Times* [Jerusalem: Bialik Institute, 1983] 72) see the Ha-Ai narrative as patterned after the Gibeah account, and not vice versa.

tactic would be employed at different times in different places. In fact, citing Malamat, she demonstrates that the tactic of feigned retreat is documented in several ancient Near Eastern battle accounts.[36]

The present writer finds most of Mazor's argument compelling. With the studies of Richter and Plöger in front of us, we can see that, indeed, most of the parallel language, is not only "commonly found," as Mazor claimed,[37] but commonly found as the stock of biblical battle reports. Other terms, she claimed, were particular for the circumstances of a feigned retreat and ambush and thus likewise were not indicative of textual borrowing. A verb such as נ.ת.ק., while not commonly found in other battle stories, is the most appropriate word to indicate that an unwitting foe was lured out of his stronghold. Each author could have independently decided to use it. Her challenge, in effect, is this: To claim an intended textual relation between the two passages we must find parallels that are significant. They must be significant in that they do not appear routinely in other battle stories and they must be significant in that they do not stem perforce from the narrator's need to describe a feigned retreat ambush.

Upon inspection, we find that, in fact, we have four phrases that are neither common stock of the biblical battle report, nor elements absolutely necessitated by the tactic of feigned retreat that are uniquely shared by the two passages:

1) Both accounts refer to smoke that rose above the city toward the sky (Josh 8:20, Judg 20:40). Elsewhere in the Bible, the words "smoke" (עשן) and the verb "to rise" (ע.ל.י.) appear in conjunction in four other places (Exod 19:18; 2 Sam 22:9 (=Ps 18:9); Isa 34:10; Song 3:6). Yet only in these two passages do we find the image of smoke rising *to the sky* (השמימה).

2) In reference to the movements of a military force, the phrase "to advance near" (ויבאו מ[נ]גד) appears only in these two battle accounts (Josh 8:11; Judg 20:34). In fact, nowhere else in the Bible is the root ב.ו.א. juxtaposed with the word נגד.

---

[35] Moore, Joshua, 435.

[36] Malamat, *Israel*, 51. Polybius (5.70.6) attests to an action like this by Antiochus III against a Ptolemaic garrison atop Mount Tabor in 218 B.C.E.. Josephus attests that in 68 C.E. the tactic was employed by Placidus, one of Vespasian's generals against Jewish defenders (*Jewish Wars*, 4.6.8). See further E. Galili, "The Conquest of Palestine by the Seleucian Army," *Maarachoth* 82 (1954) 64-66, and additional examples cited more recently by Malamat, *Israel*, 74-77.

[37] Mazor, "The Account," 100.

3) In our introduction we noted that casualty summaries are a typical feature of the biblical battle report. Yet the precise phrase "the total of those who fell" (ויהי כל הנפלים) appears in these two stories alone (Josh 8:25; Judg 20:46).

4) The use of a verb to describe the "setting" or "planting" of an ambush occurs 28 times across the Bible. To set an ambush through the verb שם is found in only four of these instances. Three of the occurrences are found in these two accounts (Josh 8:2,12; Judg 20:29). There is only one other instance in which the phrase שם ארב occurs (Judg 9:25).[38]

5) The expression that a foe was unwitting of the imminent danger through the agency of "he/they were unaware that... (והוא/הם לא ידעו כי...)," is found only in these two battle reports (Josh 8: 14, Judg 20:34). Only a single other phrase even approximates it (Neh 4:5).

As mentioned earlier, there is great debate even among those who do posit textual influence, as to the evolution of textual history here: is the text of Judges 20 patterned after that of Joshua 8, or vice-versa?[39]

It is not my purpose to take sides in the debate, for I wish to state something about the relationship between the texts that holds true according to both sets of opinion. I wish to contend that based upon these five uniquely distinct phrases we may state that the textual influence here—one way or the other—is clear, contra Mazor. On the basis of these findings it seems fair to say that many of the other terms common to the two narratives were employed not only because they were stock terms in the crafting of a battle story, but because the author of one of the narratives was working closely with the other open in front of him. What may we conclude from this evidence of borrowing?

One possibility is to adopt the position taken by Reich who assumes that the account of Joshua 8 served as a paradigm for Judges 20.[40]

---

[38] The most prevalent verb used to connote setting an ambush is the verbal form of the root א.ר.ב. itself (Deut 19:11; Josh 8:4, 14; Judg 9:32, 34, 43, 16:2, 21:20; Mic 7:2; Ps 10:9, 59:4; Prov 1:11, 18, 7:12, 12:6, 23:28, 24:15; Job 31:9; Lam 3:10, 4:19). Other verbs are found as well: to establish an ambush (ק.ו.ם.—1 Sam 22:8, 13), to prepare (ה.כ.ן. - Jer 51:12), to provide (נ.ת.ן.—2 Chr 20:22).

[39] See above, nt. 34 for references. For a study of rabbinic positions that entertain the possibility that parts of Joshua may have been redacted after the Book of Judges see Eric Lawee, "Don Isaac Abarbanel: Who Wrote the Books of the Bible," *Tradition* 30:2 (1996) 65-73.

[40] Reich, "The Concubine," 96-97.

The borrowing is a deliberate part of the rhetoric of Judges 20 and the reader is meant to think of Ha-Ai as he or she reads this battle story. The third day of battle against Benjamin resembles the battle of Ha-Ai, because in the minds of the warring tribes of Israel the two episodes are identical. At Ha-Ai, a heathen foe that had registered a victory was defeated through the tactic of feigned retreat and obliterated. And on the third day of fighting Benjamin, Israel—having lost on the first two days—decided to adopt a similar strategy. The tribe of Benjamin, in the tribes' eyes, is an enemy on a par with the Canaanite tribes of old. With a sense of righteousness and mission, they successfully execute the strategy that God had given Joshua, and thereafter continue to relate to Benjamin as a heathen city, nearly until the point of obliteration.

At the very least, we may say that the author of one of these passages looked to the other, simply as a textual precedent, without wishing to make an ideological statement. Here he saw a battle that unfolded in a fashion similar to the battle he wished to document, and took the natural step of patterning his work stylistically after the precedent of the tradition within which he worked.

But could this later author, perhaps, see in that earlier text a model, not only for language, but for rhetorical strategies and vehicles as well? The focus of this chapter has been to demonstrate the metaphor analogy that may be seen in the relationship between the rape account of Judges 19 and the battle account of Judges 20. In our first chapter we delineated the way in which the conquest of Ha-Ai (Joshua 8) could be seen as a metaphor analogy to the trial of Achan (Joshua 7). Could it be that the later author/redactor was inspired in this regard as well by what he found in the earlier text?

It is impossible to reply definitively. Yet there is evidence that the two narratives share more than a common lexicon; they share at least two distinctive rhetorical strategies. In each, scholars looking to read these passages synchronically have had difficulties with the seeming repetitions found throughout each narrative. And in each instance, scholars have attempted to see in these repetitions a vehicle of rhetoric. For some, the repetitions are a sign of resumptive reading, whereby the narrator returns to further depict an earlier episode.[41] Others

---

[41] With regard to Josh 8:4-13 this approach is adopted by Boling (*Joshua* 239) and Goslinga (C.J. Goslinga, *Joshua, Judges, Ruth* [Grand Rapids: Eerdmans, 1986] 186-87). With regard to Judges 20 see Revell, "The Battle," 417-30, and Galil, *Judges*, 165 to 20:45.

prefer to see the repetitions as examples of a rhetorical strategy of
"general headers followed by detail," whereby a verse may proclaim
broadly what is enumerated in greater detail in subsequent verses.[42]
That each narrative bears these rhetorical strategies, of course, is not
an implicit sign that the author of Judges 20 borrowed them from the
text of Joshua 8. Examples of both resumptive reading and "general
headers followed by detail" are found in narrative passages across the
Bible. Yet, few are the battle reports that employ these strategies to
the extent that they are employed here.

In summation, we see evidence that both Joshua 8 and Judges 20
share at least two rhetorical strategies of repetition in the presentation
of the material. The entirety of this chapter has demonstrated a third
shared poetic: the crafting of the battle report as narrative analogy to
the events that form the prelude to the battle itself. We have established
that lexical borrowing is highly evident here. We are left, then, with
an open question: Did the later author borrow lexical terms alone, or
did he perhaps see within the earlier passage paradigms of rhetoric
as well? Did he come to craft his narrative analogy independently or
was this part of what he mined from the source he saw in the earlier
pericope?

The suggestion that the rhetoric of the metaphor analogy is to be
included as an aspect of the influence between these two passages is
of paramount importance for our study. The claim that the metaphor
plot is a typical feature of the biblical battle report may be substantiated by documenting repeated examples of the phenomenon. Alternatively, however, the claim that it represents a typical feature may
also be substantiated by documenting, as we have tried to do here,
broad textual influence in which this rhetoric appears as one of many
borrowed literary elements.

---

[42] This approach is taken by Woudstra, *The Book of Joshua*, 137 and Young (E.
J. Young, *An Introduction to the Old Testament* [London: Tyndale House, 1964] 165-66
concerning Josh 8:4-13, and by Galil and Zakovitch (*Joshua*, 81) and Ahituv (*Joshua*,
137) concerning Josh 8:20-21. With regard to Judges 20 see Galil (*Judges*, 162) in the
introduction to vv. 29-48, Noth (*Das Buch Josua*, 166-68), Satterthwaite ("Narrative
Artistry," 84), Elitzur (*Book of Judges*, 177-79). A different approach to reading these
repetitions from a synchronic perspective has recently been put forward by Eliyahu
Asis, "The Literary Structure of the Conquest Narrative in the Book of Joshua and its
Meaning," Ph.D. dissertation, Bar-Ilan University, 1999.

CHAPTER FOUR

THE APPOINTMENT OF JEPHTHAH AS COMMANDER IN CHIEF (JUDG 10:17—11:11) AND THE REPROACH OF THE PEOPLE BY GOD (JUDG 10:6-16)

In the preceding two chapters we examined two battle narratives as metaphor analogies of the stories that precede them. However, as we noted in our introduction, the biblical battle report often encompasses more than the battlefield action itself. It may also include descriptions of the preparation for battle both within the camp of Israel and of the enemy. It may detail the immediate aftermath of the battle with accounts of booty taken, etiological comments by one side or the other, and the like. While the two previous chapters drew a metaphor analogy between the battle and the prior, equivalent narratives (i.e. the capture of Ha-Ai as metaphorically equivalent to the capture of Achan; the decimation of the tribe of Benjamin as equivalent to the rape of the concubine), the present chapter draws a metaphoric equivalence between the *pre-battle* preparations of a battle report and the narrative that immediately precedes it. This chapter explores the analogy between the account of the appointment of Jephthah as commander over the people of Gilead in Judges 10:17-11:11 and the narrative of the reproach of the people by God in 10:6-16.

While the negotiation between Jephthah and the elders of Gilead occurs prior to the actual fighting (which is related in all of two verses, 11:32-33), the account of it may be categorically considered, from the perspective of form, to be a part of the battle report. The most pertinent argument for viewing these negotiations as an integral part of the battle report is the context; the elders of Gilead approach him only because war with Ammon looms in the air (10:17; 11:5). Moreover, the pericope of Jephthah's rise to power exhibits some of the linguistic conventions identified by Richter and Plöger and motival conventions as identified by von Rad as typical features of the biblical battle report. The mustering of the two armies is expressed through the verbs צ.ע.ק. and א.ס.ף. (10:17); the waging of war by Ammon is expressed in the conventional manner, "And [side 1] waged war (וילחם) with (עם) [side 2]" (11:4). Expressions of faith in God are expressed (11:9), and a religious convocation is convened on the eve of the battle (11:

11). A comparison, therefore, of the narrative of 10:17-11:11, which details the appointment of Jephthah as commander with the narrative that precedes it, falls well within the purview of our topic: the battle report as narrative analogy.

In the previous two chapters the process of comparison was undertaken with little introduction. Like terms and images were identified, verified to be significant, and the overall analogy interpreted. The foregoing comparison, however, mandates introductory remarks to clarify the import and even simple meaning of various passages within each of the two accounts under study. The reproach of the people by God in 10:6-16 needs to be understood in the contrastive light of similar reproaches at 2:1-5 and at 6:8-10, and in light of the positioning of this reproach within the context of the overall composition of the Book of Judges.

The narrative of Jephthah's rise to power also requires prefatory elucidation. Commentators in both the medieval and modern periods utilizing highly similar methods of close reading of the synchronic text have arrived at sharply differing accounts of Jephthah's character in this episode. The merits of the positive and pejorative readings, respectively, will be weighed in an attempt to attain a comprehensive reading of the section. With initial considerations concerning each of the sections clarified, the two passages will then be brought into intertextual treatment through the methodology of comparison utilized in the previous two case studies.

Divine Reproach Episodes in the Book of Judges: Convention and Variation

The narrative of 10:6-16 shares much in common with two other earlier narratives within the Book of Judges, namely 2:1-5 and 6: 7-10. In all three, Israel is censured by an anonymous prophet. In all three, the prophet cites episodes of divine salvation and in all three the prophet censures Israel for unfaithfulness to the covenant as exhibited through acts of idolatry. This recurring form contributes to the narrative strategy of cyclical narration adopted by the author of Judges, even if the form is not adopted with regard to every one of the salvation narratives in the earlier chapters of the book. At the same time, however, a proper reading of the reproach narrative of 10:6-16 is equally dependent on seeing the evolution of the form: how variation from episode to episode sets it apart from the two earlier instances of the form, and how its language borrows, yet deviates, from earlier expressions of reproach in the Book of Judges.

Yaakov and Ruti Medan have performed a close comparative reading of the phrases that recur throughout Judges 3-10 in an attempt to demonstrate that the reproach narrative of 10:6-16 reflects the nadir of a progression that evolves through these chapters, namely, Israel's slow yet steady decline. A graphic comparison of the language of transgression in each reproach passage reveals the following:

3:7   "The Israelites did what was offensive to the Lord; they ignored the Lord their God and worshipped the Baalim and the Asheroth."

3:12   "The Israelites again did what was offensive to the Lord."

4:1   "The Israelites again did what was offensive to the Lord."

6:1   "Then the Israelites did what was offensive to the Lord."

10:6   "Then the Israelites again did what was offensive to the Lord. They served the Baalim and the Ashtaroth, and the gods of Aram, the gods of Sidon, the gods of Moab, the gods of the Ammonites, and the gods of the Philistines; they forsook the Lord and did not serve him."

Verse 10:6 implies a more severe transgression than in the previous narratives. As the Medans point out, following the medieval rabbinic exegetes, the phrase (10:6) *they forsook the Lord and did not serve him* implies that in earlier periods of waywardness Israel had worshipped foreign idols while still worshipping Yahweh. Now, however, they served only foreign idols.[1] For the sake of comparison, contrast this state of affairs with Elijah's assessment of his own generation. He charges that the people are unfaithful, as they worship both Yahweh and foreign gods at the same time (1 Kgs 18:21).[2] The language of transgression of 10:6-16, then, may be seen as the most severe employed in the Book of Judges to that point.[3]

The Medans also trace the divine response to Israel's cries and see a pattern of increasing divine reticence to respond immediately:

---

[1] Yaakov Medan and Ruti Medan, "Jephthah in His Time," *Megadim* 6 (1988) 28; Amit, *Book of Judges*, 189.
[2] Medan and Medan, "Jephthah," 28.
[3] Ibid., 28; cf. Amit, *Book of Judges*, 188.

3:9   The Israelites cried out to the Lord, and the Lord raised
           a champion for the Israelites to deliver them: Othniel the
           Kenizzite.

3:15   Then the Israelites cried out to the Lord, and the Lord raised
           up a champion for them: the Benjaminite Ehud son of Gera.

4:3-4   The Israelites cried out to the Lord; for [King Jabin] had
           nine-hundred iron chariots, and he had oppressed Israel
           ruthlessly for twenty years... Deborah, woman of Lappidoth,
           was a prophetess...

6:7-10   When the Israelites cried to the Lord on account of Midian,
           the Lord sent a prophet to the Israelites who said to them...
           you did not obey me.

10:10-13   Then the Israelites cried out to the Lord, "We stand guilty
           before You, for we have forsaken our God. But the Lord said
           to the Israelites... No, I will not deliver you again."

The progression here is clear. In the first two episodes God's response
to the cries of Israel is immediate: a champion is raised up to deliver
them. By the third episode, that of chapter 4, a change is seen. Israel
cries out, yet the narrative no longer employs the phrase, "and the
Lord raised up a champion for them." Indeed, salvation does eventually
come, yet the absence of this phrase, suggest the Medans, indicates
that God was no longer willing to respond to the cry immediately;
the delivery would come, but it would be delayed. By chapter 6, even
delayed salvation is no longer the divine response. Here the cry is met
with prophetic censure. Only following the prophetic censure does
the angel appear to Gideon with his mandate to save the people.
The nadir of the process whereby the divine response to Israel's cry
is seen to diminish is found in the present narrative of chapter 10.
Israel's cry is met not only with rebuke, but with God's express refusal
to deliver them.[4]

To summarize, then, the pericope of censure in 10:6-16 should
not be seen in isolation but in its role within the composition of the
first half of the book of Judges. Once again Israel has sinned but the

_____

[4] Medan and Medan, "Jephthah," 27. The full import of God's refusal to deliver
Israel here is highly dependent on one's reading of 10:17 ותקצר נפשו בעמל ישראל,
a phrase to which we will attend later in the chapter. Suffice it to say at this point,
however, that God's expression of refusal to deliver Israel is a note unheard in the
earlier narratives and demonstrates the growing strain God feels in His relationship
with Israel.

language of transgression shows us that this time the nature of the breach is even more severe. Once again Israel calls upon God to deliver them, but this time the language of deliverance indicates that His response is equivocal at best.

10:6-16—The Use of a Unique Rhetorical Technique

While 10:6-16 bears elements common to earlier censure narratives (2: 1-5; 6:7-10), it stands apart from these, not only in detail and intensity, but through the employment of a distinct rhetorical technique: the censure is reported as *direct dialogue between God and Israel*. Thus, in 10: 11, the censure is portrayed as direct speech by God to Israel without the use of intermediaries: "But the Lord said to the Israelites, 'I have rescued you…'." Of course, Qimḥi, Kaufmann, and Elitzur are all correct when they comment that this message was actually conveyed to the people by an anonymous prophet.[5] But it is significant that while the role of the anonymous prophet is explicitly delineated in 2:1, 4 and in 6:8, here in chapter 10 it is not spelled out, leaving the unusual impression that God spoke directly to the people.[6]

The converse in this passage is true as well: Israel speaks directly to God. In 10:10, Scripture not only records the *fact* that Israel cried out to God (as in earlier episodes) but also records the content in the form of direct speech: "Then the Israelites cried out to the Lord, 'We stand guilty before You, for we have forsaken our God and served the Baalim.'" The same effect of direct speech is exhibited in Israel's response to God's refusal to save them (10:15): "The Israelites said to God[7]: 'We stand guilty . Do to us as You see fit; only save us this day!'"

Kaufmann and Elitzur, we saw above, proposed that the direct speech from God to Israel was actually conveyed through the conduit of an anonymous prophet. Yet, by what agency did Israel, in turn, speak to God in 10:10 and in 10:15? Boling has surmised that these statements were uttered in a public assembly.[8] Yet, here again, the

---

[5] Kaufmann, *Book of Judges*, 215; Elitzur, *Book of Judges*, 115.

[6] Amit, *Book of Judges*, 189.

[7] I have taken the liberty of deviating from the JPS translation, which reads "But the Israelites implored the Lord…," so as to harmonize the two identical statements of speech introduction in 10:10 and in 10:15.

[8] Boling, *Judges*, 192.

narrative of 10:6-16 stands in contradistinction to its earlier counter-
part in chapter 2. Verse 2:1 states explicitly that the messenger went
to Bochim and from 2:5 it seems that in fact some kind of collective
convocation took place there. Of course, the fact that the narrative
in chapter 10 fails to indicate that an assembly was held does not *ipso
facto* prove that Boling's proposition is incorrect. It is possible that a
public assembly was held, as Boling suggests, yet one which Scripture
chose not to highlight, but rather to leave as implicit.

Alternatively, however, we may suggest that, in fact, no public
assembly took place, and that Israel's declaration was never audibly
spoken. Rather, these statements reflect a verbal concretization of the
general spirit and sentiment of the entire people at the time. Scripture
casts this as stylized speech, in much the way that today a politician
may declare: "The people have spoken, and they say today: 'No
new taxes!'" The words purportedly uttered by the people, in fact,
represent a crystallized expression of consensus within the public at
large.[9] Whether Israel's proclamations in 10:10 and 10:15-16 were
uttered in an assembly, or whether they are the concretized sentiments of the time, the dialogue form of this narrative is affirmed: In
verse 10 Israel speaks to God. In verses 11-14, God speaks to Israel.
In verse 15 Israel again speaks to God, and in verse 16 God decides
on a course of action, to which we will attend shortly. While Richter
categorizes this pericope as a *Gattung* that he labels "the theological
dialogue story",[10] Boling is more to the point when he states that this
passage should not be classified as a form at all, but rather a "piece
without parallel."[11] Boling is correct here not only when this passage
is compared to the earlier censure narratives of 2:1-5 and 6:7-10, but
his contention is also confirmed when the text is examined in the
broader context of the entire Hebrew Bible. Nowhere else does one
find the unmediated phrase, "God said to Israel ויאמר יהוה אל בני
ישראל)," and nowhere else does one find the reverse phrase, "Israel
said to God (ויאמר[ו] בני ישראל אל יהוה)."

Toward what end has Scripture portrayed this censure in the form
of a dialogue? Alter writes that the Bible has a tendency "to transpose

---

[9] Similarly, see Alter's handling of the dialogue between God and David in 2 Sam
2:1. Alter (*Art of Biblical Narrative*, 69) maintains that the dialogue represents the gist of
a message conveyed through non-audible conventions.

[10] Wolfgang Richter, *Die Bearbeitungen des "Retterbuches" in der deuteronomischen Epoche*
(BBB 210; Bonn: Peter Hanstein, 1964) 88.

[11] Boling, *Judges*, 192.

what is preverbal or nonverbal into speech [as] a technique for getting at the essence of things, for obtruding their substratum."[12] This approach is well illustrated here. Dialogue, by its very nature, depicts a bilateral interaction. The framing of Israel's trespass and God's response in terms of interpersonal communication helps illuminate the dynamic between the two sides in evocative fashion.

The dialogue, on the one hand, lends insight into the full nature of Israel's crime. Her backsliding here could have been interpreted in dispassionate, juridical terms: an injustice; a crime; a serious breach of divine law—all of which are here true. Yet these terms do not convey the implications of the transgression from the perspective of God. When a criminal act in contemporary society is expressed in juridical terms such as "injustice," "crime" and "breach," the authority that adjudicates the crime is essentially dispassionate. The judiciary tries a criminal, sentences him, and metes out punishment—all in a dispassionate, if grave, disposition. The meter maid, if you pardon the anachronism, is a disinterested party when she writes out the parking ticket. Not so, however, the authority that adjudicates Israel's infractions, namely God. God is not merely heavenly judge and officer of the court; God is a covenantal partner. God experiences pain and hurt. Israel has not merely committed an infraction; Israel has betrayed. The notion of divine pain is difficult for the people of Israel in the Book of Judges to fathom, for they lack direct contact with God, and He remains, for most of the nation, an abstraction.[13] Scripture therefore casts God in human, emotive terms to lay bare the true nature of Israel's betrayal. The same attempt to reveal the nature of Israel's trespass in human terms explains the fact that in the first two censure narratives, Israel is chided not only for idol worship, but for ungratefulness (2:1-2; 6: 8-10). Idolatry, perhaps, is the legal, or narrow classification of the infraction. Casting Israel's behavior as ingratitude, however, gives expression to the psychic dimension of the infraction for its victim, namely God, in wholly human terms. The zenith of this rhetoric in chapter 10 is not in v. 13, where God refuses to save Israel, but in v. 14, where his tone is sarcastic, almost vindictive: "Go cry to the gods

---

[12] Alter, *Art of Biblical Narrative*, 70.

[13] Yairah Amit (*The Book of Judges: The Art of Editing* [Biblical Encyclopedia Library 6; Jerusalem: Bialik Institute, 1992] 350 [in Hebrew]) is correct, however, that the Book of Judges allows more direct contact divine contact with individual human agents (e.g. 6:12, 14, 16, 23) than is found in other books of the Deuteronomistic history.

you have chosen; let them deliver you in your time of distress!" As
Webb has correctly noted, the story "portrays [God's] involvement
as deeply personal and emotional rather than as merely formal and
legal; as not, in the final analysis, governed by abstract principles of
reward and punishment, justice and retribution."[14]

Beyond the concretization of the divine pain, there is a second aspect
of the nature of Israel's crime that is laid bare through the rhetoric
of stylized speech: the insincerity of Israel's plea. Note the content of
Israel's initial cry (10:10): "We stand guilty before You, for we have
forsaken our God and served the Baalim." As the Medans point out,
the language of transgression suggests that Israel had reached a new
low here, as "they forsook the Lord and did not serve Him" (10:6).
In earlier periods of waywardness Israel had served other gods while
still worshipping Yahweh; now they had abandoned Him altogether.
Their contrition (10:10) indicates at least a professed desire to renew
their relationship with Yahweh. Yet it is not fully clear that they are
prepared to sever all ties with the Baalim. Witness that only later, in
10:16, after they have received a tongue lashing from God, did they
actually "remove the alien gods from among them." The discrepancies,
therefore, between their first appeal and their final appeal, coupled with
decisive action, reveals self-preservation as their primary motivation.
To be sure, they desire a renewed relationship with God. Yet, this
is only because they see in Him the only way out of the Ammonite
oppression. From their perspective, they would just as well achieve
this assistance by merely "apologizing," as they do in v. 10. Only
once this is rejected in vv. 11-14 do they pledge to remove the alien
gods from their midst. Just as the rhetoric of stylized speech allowed
Scripture to bring God's pain to the fore, so too it brings to the fore,
especially in 10:10, the self-interest and insincerity that belie Israel's
protestations that they are in fact turning a new leaf.

The final phrase of 10:16 (16c) is the climax of the encounter for
it registers God's final response to Israel's plea. Yet this climax is cast
in ambiguous terms that have been widely interpreted. The crux of
the entire passage hinges upon an understanding of this clause, to
which we now turn.

---

[14] B.G. Webb, *The Book of Judges: An Integrated Reading* (Sheffield: Almond Press,
1987) 75.

"And He could not bear the 'amal of Israel": Divine Compassion, Resignation, or Rejection?

Most commentators, medieval and modern, have understood the final phrase of the censure narrative—"and He could not bear the *'amal* of Israel"—to be one of compassion.[15] While God had rejected their initial cry in 10:10, their removal of the foreign gods as reported in 10:16a-b, according to this view, engenders a change in God's disposition to one of compassion. The change of heart here is seen to be similar to other episodes where divine wrath ultimately gives way to compassion as in Jonah 3:10 and Jer 26:10, where God feels remorse concerning his intent on account of a change in human behavior (cf. also Exod 32:14; Jer 18:7-8; 26:3; Joel 2:13-14; Amos 7:3-6).[16] The JPS translation is representative of this interpretation: "He could not bear the miseries of Israel." עמל, "suffering," "travail," is taken to refer to the miseries of Israel. Within this understanding of 16c as an expression of divine compassion, Israel's claims of "we have sinned" (vv. 10, 16) are taken to reflect sincere contrition.[17]

Polzin, and in his wake, Webb, have challenged this understanding of 16c on a number of lexical grounds.[18] In other passages of divine remorse, the term used to indicate a change in heart is usually נחם while the word used to refer to that which is being overturned or cancelled is רעה, as in, "The Lord renounced (וינחם) the punishment (הרעה) He had planned to bring upon His people" (Exod 32:14). Here, however, the term expressing the purported divine remorse is קצר נפשו ב. Elsewhere this implies not "remorse," but "impatience" as in Zach 11:8—"My patience with them was at an end" (ותקצר נפשי בהם) and in Num 21:4, "the people became impatient with the journey (ותקצר נפש העם בדרך)"[19] (cf. Judg 16:16, where the phrase appears, but without the prepositional *bet*).[20] Accordingly, Polzin and Webb

---

[15] Rashi; Qimḥi; Moore, *A Critical*, 282; Richter, *Die Bearbeitungen*, 23; Soggin, *Judges*, 203; James D. Martin, *The Book of Judges* (CBC; Cambridge: Cambridge University Press, 1975) 135; Elitzur, *Book of Judges*, 118; Amit, *Book of Judges*, 191.

[16] cf. Webb, *Book of Judges*, 45.

[17] Richter, *Die Bearbeitungen*, 23; Boling, *Judges*, 193; Soggin, *Judges*, *203*; Martin, *Book of Judges*, 135.

[18] Robert Polzin, *Moses and the Deuteronomist* (New York: Seabury Press, 1980) 177; Webb, *Book of Judges*, 46.

[19] The translation is my own, and accords with Rashi's understanding of the verse, that they were impatient *with* the journey, and not as most modern translations render, that they became impatient while along the journey.

[20] Cf. the use of the similar phrase קצר רוח as "impatient" in Mic 2:7 and Job 21:4 (although it seems to have other meanings in Exod 6:9 and Prov 14:29).

reject the notion that God here sees Israel's actions, and, as it were, melts in compassion and sympathy, as would be clearly expressed by the verb נחם. Rather, God's mood here is one of *impatience*.

However, Polzin and Webb diverge concerning the object of God's impatience, namely, עמל ישראל. For Polzin the word עמל does not refer to Israel's sufferings, but rather to Israel's continuous pestering to convince God to deliver them.[21] He translates the entire phrase, "and he grew annoyed [or impatient] with the *troubled efforts* of Israel."[22] Within this understanding, Israel's claims of contrition are deemed suspect by God, who sees Israel as a recidivistic offender seeking only deliverance, but not truly desirous of repairing the ruptured covenantal bond with God. For Polzin the phrase represents divine rejection, and a further solidification of what God had said in verse 13, "No, I will not deliver you again."

Polzin's interpretation of 10:16c, may be strongly challenged. On lexical grounds, one is hard pressed to find another instance in which the term עמל is used in the sense that he suggests.[23] Moreover, it may be challenged when seen within the context of the larger narrative unit of the battle against the Ammonites—for, in fact, God does save them, as Scripture states explicitly in 11:32. Thus, to summarize to this point, two positions have been advanced concerning the meaning of 10:16c. The interpretation of divine compassion conforms with the information supplied concerning the divinely granted victory later in the story, but strains the normal lexical implications of the phrase ותקצר נפשו ב. Conversely, Polzin's suggestion of divine impatience accords with the lexical implications of the phrase, but runs counter to the information supplied later in the narrative unit.

A middle strategy of interpretation of 16c that straddles the two understandings examined so far is found in the medieval commentary of Gersonides:

> The Almighty had repeatedly delivered them from their oppressors, as they would cry to Him and return to Him, and turn away from serving other gods. Now, however, He would no longer be prepared to deliver them (cf. v. 13). Israel was greatly distressed by this and removed the

---

[21] Polzin, *Moses*, 177.

[22] See in a similar vein, the first explanation of Gersonides to the phrase in his commentary to v. 10:16.

[23] There is similarly no lexical support for Gunn and Fewell's reading that God "grew impatient with the *troubler* Israel." See David M. Gunn and Danna Nolan Fewell, *Narrative in the Hebrew Bible* (Oxford: Oxford University Press, 1993) 113.

foreign gods from their midst, and served God. Yet now, God had become impatient with the idea of granting them *a full deliverance* as He had done on earlier occasions on account of the '*amal* of Israel… which means lies and deceitfulness, as in the phrase "mischief and evil" (עמל ואון).[24] The meaning of the sentence is that on account of the path of lying and deceit embarked upon by Israel, by worshipping foreign gods, God became impatient with them, and did not desire to grant them a full deliverance … and this is why Scripture does not write here, "And the Lord raised up a champion for them."

Like Polzin and Webb, Gersonides understands ותקצר נפש to mean impatience. Yet Gersonides differs from Polzin concerning the conclusions that God draws in light of the situation. For Gersonides, God's displeasure will express itself, not through an outright refusal to intercede on Israel's behalf, but by withdrawing another step along the continuing path of decreasing salvation. He will not grant Israel "a *full* deliverance." Israel will indeed be saved—and saved by God himself—as indicated in 11:32. The parameters of the salvation, however, will be markedly different from those of Israel's recent past. Israel's request for a leader (10:17) produces no results. God does not "raise up a champion." While the salvation indeed brings victory over the Ammonites, it is immediately marred by the tragedy of Jephthah's daughter (11:34-40), and itself engenders Israel's first civil war, as the tribe of Ephraim challenges Jephthah's handling of the campaign (12:1-6).[25]

To summarize, the account of 10:6-16 is one of a relationship which suffers from betrayal and insincere pronouncements of loyalty. Israel has betrayed her covenantal partner. Enduring Ammonite oppression, Israel calls to her covenantal partner in a tone of contrition, and asks to be delivered. God, for His part, is rightfully indignant and is suspicious of Israel's true motives, suspecting insincerity. When Israel appeals a second time, God yields reluctantly. Tired of their appeals, He brings about salvation in a manner less direct and less full than in any of the previous salvation episodes in the book.

---

[24] See the word עמל in this sense of "mischief" in the construct state (as in the present case), Ps 7:17; Prov 24:2; Job 16:2.

[25] See here, in a similar vein, Webb, *Book of Judges*, 48.

10:17-11:11—Jephthah: Reluctant Hero or Sly Opportunist?

The synchronic readings of Jephthah's ascendance to the leadership
of the tribes of Gilead have produced highly contrasting readings of
the character of Jephthah. The interpretations of his negotiations
with the elders of Gilead have given forth to portrayals of Jephthah,
variously, as a reluctant and appropriately modest hero and alternatively as a self-interested opportunist. The debate is found within
both medieval rabbinic and modern critical scholarship. The passage
is an exegetical quagmire as it bears seeming internal contradictions
and numerous points at which even the simple meaning is unclear,
particularly concerning the precise terms offered to and asked for
by Jephthah throughout the negotiation. To bring the passage into
conversation with the divine reproach pericope of 10:6-16, we must
attempt to clarify the issue of Jephthah's characterization here and
not rest our comparison on a possible reading, but rather on a preferred reading of the negotiation narrative. For the sake of brevity
I shall offer my reading of the passage in the main body of the text
and refer to the counterarguments in the notes.

My reading of Jephthah as reluctant, perhaps even modest, assumes,
to begin with, that in 10:18, the public offer made by the elders of
Gilead is this: whoever takes the initiative to fight the Ammonites,
will be *immediately* designated the *rosh* of all of Gilead.[26] The language
of the verse מי האיש אשר יחל להלחם ... יהיה לראש implies that the
conferral is not dependent upon victory but upon having the courage and initiative to accept responsibility for waging the campaign,
to begin with.[27]

The issue of leadership is taken up again in 11:5, as the elders seek
to retrieve Jephthah from exile in the land of Tob and to offer him
the position of *qatzin*, which is taken to mean a military commander,
and in some form and fashion, a lesser title than that of *rosh*. It is commonly accepted that whereas *qatzin* implies military leadership, *rosh*
implies broader powers of civil leadership.[28] When the elders made

---

[26] Abarbanel to 10:18; Amit, *Book of Judges*, 194.

[27] Elitzur (*Book of Judges*, 119), by contrast, sees the title of *rosh* as a *reward* for victory.

[28] Lillian Klein, *The Triumph of Irony in the Book of Judges* (JSOTS 68; Sheffield:
Almond Press, 1988) 86-88; Martin, *The Book of Judges*, 138; Timothy Willis, "The
Nature of Jephthah's Authority," *CBQ* 59 (1997) 35-36; Amit, *The Book of Judges*, 193.
On *rosh* see further J.R. Bartlett, "The Use of the Word ראש as a Title in the Old

their offer of *qatzin* in v. 6, they did so on the assumption that Jephthah would be only too happy to be welcomed back into the fold of Gilead. There would be no need, the elders thought, to offer Jephthah what any person had been offered earlier in the crisis, namely appointment to the position of *rosh* (10:18). Jephthah could be had, as it were, "at a discount."[29]

To their great dismay, however, he rejected their offer (11:7). From his caustic tone and reference to his banishment, they then understood correctly that Jephthah had rejected not the offer of *qatzin* per se, but of any reunion with them outright. They understood that he was incensed by the expulsion and possibly also by the act of disinheritance (11:2). They perhaps also realized that they had misplayed their hand. Certainly now, after no one had risen to the challenge put forth in 10: 18, and now with the Ammonites poised for attack (11:4), the very least they could have done is to offer Jephthah terms equal to those offered others in good standing in Gilead. Having offered *anyone* the position of *rosh* in 10:18, they had only added insult to injury by now offering Jephthah the relatively lowly title of *qatzin* at this juncture. Jephthah's caustic response in 11:7 engenders a radical rethinking on the part of the elders. "We thought he would be happy to be let back in the fold; instead we see that we have only added to the depth of his injury. But what to do? The Ammonites are poised to attack!" The elders now perform an about-face in order to ensure that Jephthah joins them, as he is their only hope. It is now that they offer him either a) the same offer originally made public, namely immediate appointment to the position of *rosh*[30] or b) an even better offer, namely that in reward for

---

Testament," *VT* 19 (1969) 1-10. On *rosh* vs. *qatzin* see H.N. Rösel, "Jephtah und das Problem der Richter," *Biblica* 61 (1980) 251-55. See also Kenneth M. Craig, Jr., "Bargaining in Tov (Judges 11:4-11): The Many Directions of So-Called Direct Speech," *Biblica* 79 (1998) 81 n. 9; Amit, *The Book of Judges: The Act of Editing*, 81 n. 57. David Marcus has contended that in this passage the two terms are synonymous and mean, broadly, "leader" ("The Bargaining Between Jephthah and the Elders [Judges 11:4-11]," *JANES* 19 [1989] 95-100). To support his contention from textual witnesses, Marcus states (p. 96) that the Peshitta version of the passage makes no distinction between the two terms. Yet the Peshitta version of v. 11 reveals that this is not so. The fact that the two terms appear in parallel stichs of verse (Micah 3: 1, 9), does not, *perforce*, imply that the terms are identical, as Marcus claims here (p. 97). In some instances parallel terms are fully synonymous, but in many instances are related, yet distinct from one another. See James L. Kugel, *The Idea of Biblical Poetry* (New Haven: Yale University Press, 1981) 8; Robert Alter, *The Art of Biblical Poetry* (New York: Basic Books, 1985) 3-26.

[29] Webb, *Book of Judges*, 52.

[30] As per Abarbanel in his second approach; Kaufmann, *Book of Judges*, 219.

his courage he will be appointed *rosh* after the battle, win or lose.[31]
Surely, they reasoned, Jephthah would not refuse such a generous
offer. They even make protestations of their sincerity in welcoming
him back (11:8): *"Honestly, we have now turned back to you. If you come
with us and fight the Ammonites, you shall be our commander over
all the inhabitants of Gilead."*

To their utter dismay and consternation, the response they get from
Jephthah is less than enthusiastic. When Jephthah says (v. 9) "[Very
well], *if* you bring me back to fight the Ammonites, and the Lord
delivers them to me, I am to be your commander," the elders become
alarmed; Jephthah is highly wary. Beyond wanting God's imprimatur
(i.e. victory granted him on the battlefield), Jephthah, they correctly
perceive from his words in 11a, wants to see just what type of reception
he is to receive from those who disinherited, nay, *exiled* him from his
father's house.[32] Questions of tactics rise to paramount importance.
Will he back out? How can his commitment to fight the Ammonites
be augmented? This brings us to the interplay of vv. 9-11. The elders
work within the narrow, technical limits of what Jephthah had said,
namely, of making his appointment conditional on the outcome of the
battle, while getting him to agree to assume the full position of *rosh*
immediately. Jephthah had demurred and asked not to be appointed
unless granted victory. The flip side of this, as they see it, is that the
thought uppermost in Jephthah's mind is that if he does not win, he
has no business presiding as *rosh*. To this the elders vow, *in affirmation*, that indeed, his word will be honored: "If you claim that you do
not want to reign as *rosh* in the wake of defeat, then very well; if and

---

[31] R. Joseph Kara; Boling, *Judges*, 198: Klein, *The Triumph of Irony*, 87.

[32] Those that see Jephthah as an opportunist in this passage find their greatest
obstacle in this verse, which reads without difficulty within the paradigm of Jephthah
as reluctant. Many attempts have been made to coax out of this verse extortion or
manipulation through varying strategies of syntactic surgery. All, however, require
reading into the verse words that are not there. See Abarbanel; Kaufmann, *Book of
Judges*, 219; Webb, *Book of Judges*, 52. Amit (*Book of Judges: The Act of Editing*, 81), in her
earlier work, agrees with this reading and places herself firmly within the Jephthah as
Opportunist camp, characterizing him as "manipulative and extortionist." In her more
recent work (*Book of Judges*, 193), however, she appears to have adopted the interpretive
paradigm of Jephthah as Modest and Reluctant. Here she writes that "Jephthah did
not exploit the despair of the elders and averred that he would accept the post of *rosh*
only in the event of victory on the battlefield... Jephthah is a positive character... who
earns the regard of the reader. His faithfulness to God, exhibited both in the negotiations with the elders of Gilead and in the negotiations with the king of Ammon, serves
as a harbinger of the divine support that he will ultimately receive."

when that transpires, "*we will do just as you have said.*" In the meantime, however, you have not been rejected; not by Gilead and not by God, and so we intend to appoint you *rosh*. To all of their extreme measures of importuning, Jephthah agrees and is appointed *rosh*.

A comparative examination of the tone and tenor of 11:11 supports our characterization of Jephthah as reluctant. Verse 11:11 tells us of the assumption of power by Jephthah and consists of three state-ments:[33] a) "Jephthah went with the elders of Gilead" b) "and the people appointed him as *rosh* and *qatzin* over them," and c) "Jephthah spoke his words before God at Mizpah." Note the diminutive nature ascribed to Jephthah here; he does not *lead* the elders in 11a, but rather goes with them. He does not *rule* over the people (as would be suggested by an active verb such as וימלך, "and he reigned," or, וימשל, "and he ruled"), but rather is installed by them. He is not actor, but rather is acted upon. Finally, upon his installation, he seems to go off by himself to Mizpah to convene with God before embarking on his mandate. An analysis of similar "installation" phrases elsewhere in the Bible is revealing. While the act of one person joining another is com-monplace, the reporting of this commonplace activity within biblical narrative, is not. The phrase "and X went with Y (וילך .. עם...)," as we have here in 11a, is found only concerning Deborah who goes with Barak (Judg 4:9) and concerning Balaam who goes with the chieftains of Moab (Num 22:21, 35, and with Balak, 22:39). In these two cases, the act of "going with" implies acquiescence after an initial episode of refusal. Deborah had not wanted to accompany Barak to battle but following his importunity, relented. The same is true regarding Balaam. Early in the narrative Balaam expresses hesitation about joining the chieftains of Moab. The phrase "And Balaam went with the men" is indicative of a shift from refusal to acquiescence. Seen in this light, 11a may be read to indicate that it was in wariness that he acceded to the demands of the Gileadites and now joined them.[34]

The positive portrayal of Jephthah is further strengthened by a reading of 11:29:

---

[33] Because the foregoing remarks compare the language of 11:11 to the language of similar passages elsewhere, I have opted to employ my own translation here, in an attempt to preserve the most literal meaning of each word, rather than defer to exist-ing translations which attempt to convey a sense of context.

[34] Positive readings of Jephthah in this account are likewise rendered by Soggin (*Judges*, 208) and by Hertzberg (Hans Wilhelm Hertzberg, *Die Bücher Josua, Richter, Ruth* [Göttingen: Bandenhoech & Ruprecht, 1953] 214), though with less attention to the ambiguities presented by the text.

Then the spirit of the Lord came upon Jephthah. He marched through Gilead and Manasseh, passing Mizpah of Gilead; and from Mizpah of Gilead he crossed over [to] the Ammonites.

The bestowal of the spirit of the Lord (רוח יהוה) is found with regard to seven other biblical characters, all of whom are cast without blemish at the time of this bestowal (Othniel—Judg 3:10; Gideon- Judg 6:34; Saul- 1 Sam 10:6; David- 1 Sam 16:13; Ezekiel- Ezek 11:5; Micah- Mic 3:8; Jahaziel the son of Zechariah the Levite—2 Chr 20: 14). Two instances, in particular, underscore the correlation between good spiritual standing and the bestowal of the spirit of God. While in his youth, Saul merited the spirit of the Lord resting upon him. Conversely, once he fell out of favor, the spirit left him (1 Sam 16: 14). The only questionable character upon whom the spirit of the Lord rests is Samson (Judg 13:25; 14:6, 19; 15:14). Yet the case of Samson is the exception that proves the rule. Scripture itself is aware that Samson's behavior—chasing after Philistine women—is not what is expected of a hero of Israel. Scripture therefore offers the unusual interjection of explaining how such a licentious figure came to be granted such great divine gifts: "His father and mother did not realize that this was the Lord's doing; *He was seeking a pretext against the Philistines*, for the Philistines were ruling over Israel at that time" (Judg 14:4). Two verses later, the spirit of the Lord descends upon Samson for the first time, with the attack of the lion. Samson receives the spirit of the Lord in explicitly exceptional circumstances, in spite of his behavior. The dynamics of the resting of the spirit of the Lord are clear: across the entire Bible the spirit of the Lord descends exclusively upon meritorious figures; when such figures fall from grace (e.g. Saul), they may be denied the spirit of the Lord. When a person of questionable character is endowed with the spirit of the Lord, Scripture explains the reasons for such.[35]

We may now summarize our reading of 10:17-11:11, the narrative of Jephthah the Reluctant, and now include the verses to which we have not attended thus far, 11:1-3. In 10:18 the elders of Gilead offer the position of *rosh* to anyone willing to lead the campaign against Ammon. While the question is left open with no takers, Scripture intimates in the very next clause that a worthy candidate was, in fact, readily available: "right under their noses," as it were, is Jephthah, who is introduced in immediate juxtaposition to 10:18 in 11:1, as "a

---

[35] For more on the spirit of the Lord, see *EB* 7.330-36.

man of valor."[36] But, of course, the elders of Gilead had not thought to turn to the spurned Jephthah on account of the story told in 11:1-3. It is significant that the chronology of these verses is out of order. Jephthah was born and expelled prior to the advance of the Ammonites in 10:18, yet Scripture wishes us to see Jephthah as the logical choice to the call of 10:18, and hence the juxtaposition of 10:18 and 11:1a.[37] Much controversy has centered around the question of the legality of the actions of Jephthah's brothers and the elders of Gilead in disinheriting him.[38] Yet, it is clear that even if the move to disinherit Jephthah was legal and just, the *expulsion* of Jephthah from his father's house to the land of Tob was not.[39] In 11:5, with the situation truly dire, due to the advance of the Ammonites, the elders find themselves with no other option but to send an expedition to the land of Tob to retrieve Jephthah. Their offer of *qatzin* constitutes less than what they had offered in their public declaration of 10:18, where the initiator of the campaign against Ammon was offered the bait of receiving the title of *rosh* immediately. Their offer of *qatzin* in v. 6, in effect, adds insult to injury. Having expelled him (and perhaps

---

[36] Moreover, as Jacobs (Jonathan Jacobs, "The Story of Jephthah," M.A. thesis, Bar-Ilan University, 1997, 23 [Hebrew]) points out, Jephthah is identified straight away as a Gileadite, which stands in stark contrast to the way in which they relate to him: as an outcast and not part of the clan.

[37] This comment accords with the claim made by Yair Zakovitch that the formulaic introduction of a character "and so and so was a…," as we have here, never represents the opening of a new section, but implies a continuation of the preceding narrative. He cites Gen 3:1, Exod 3:1, and 2 Kgs 5:1 as illustrations of the phenomenon in addition to the verse here at hand. See Yair Zakovitch, *"Every High Official Has a Higher One Set Over Him": A Literary Analysis of 2 Kings 5* (Tel Aviv: Am Oved, 1985) 19 (Hebrew).

[38] Gersonides, Abarbanel, and Kaufmann *Book of Judges*, 218 all see the action of disinheriting Jephthah as having no basis in ancient Hebrew law, though their respective arguments are predicated on several varying assumptions. Others however, have argued that the elders of Gilead were within their rights to disinherit Jephthah on account of his lineage, though again varied approaches are taken to substantiate this claim. See I. Mendelsohn, "The Disinheritance of Jephthah in Light of Paragraph 27 of the Lipit-Ishtar Code," *IEJ* 4 (1954) 116-19 who claims that once Gilead's legal wife had children Jephthah became disinherited. Other scholars have claimed categorically that any son of a prostitute has no legal standing whatever in inheritance (E. Neufeld, *Ancient Hebrew Marriage Law* [London: Longmans, Green, 1944] 127; Martin, *The Book of Judges*, 137; Gray, *Joshua, Judges, Ruth*, 332. David Marcus has suggested that Jephthah was disinherited because he was the adopted son of a prostitute and that the brothers were challenging the legality of his adoption (D. Marcus, "The Legal Dispute Between Jephthah and the Elders," *HAR* 12 [1990] 105-15). Most recently, Joseph Fleishman has reviewed and challenged each of these views, (to this writer's mind, successfully so) in his "The Legality of the Expulsion of Jephthah," *Dine Israel* 18 (1995-96) 61-79, concluding that the disinheriting of Jephthah had no legal basis.

[39] Fleishman, "The Legality," 77-78.

also having disinherited him) unjustly, the elders now make Jephthah
an offer lower than the "going rate" that had been offered earlier,
and at a time when their predicament vis-à-vis Ammon had in the
meantime worsened. Jephthah's response in v. 7 registers his sense of
personal injury and intimates a desire to detach himself from them
rather than to manipulate himself into a leadership position over those
who scorned him.

From here, the negotiation proceeds along the lines suggested above.
The elders, desperate to secure his return, turn to importuning. They
profess their sincere desire to retrieve him into the fold of Gilead, and
make him an improved counter-offer to entice him (v. 8). Jephthah, still
wary of the abuse he suffered at their hands, does not fully acquiesce
(v. 9). He will fight on their behalf but does not want the title of *rosh*
until he sees that he has been fully accepted by the tribes of Gilead and
that God has given His imprimatur to this through battlefield victory.
The elders are disturbed by the degree of his injury and failure to grab
at such a generous offer. Eager to galvanize Jephthah's commitment
to them, they appoint him to the positions of *rosh* and *qatzin*, leaving
him the proviso that in the event of defeat he would be permitted to
abdicate the position of *rosh* (vv. 10-11).

The Reproach Narrative of Judges 10 and the Negotiation
Narrative of Judges 11:1-11

From here we proceed to bring the narrative of the divine reproach
of 10:6-16 and the account of the negotiations between the elders
of Gilead and Jephthah into conversation. In their respective studies, both Polzin and Webb have attended to many of the structural
similarities between the two juxtaposed accounts, and a review and
critique of their work is in order. Both Polzin and Webb have identified similarities in form and motif between the two accounts, yet the
interpretations they give their findings are based on readings that I
have questioned in the earlier parts of this chapter.

Polzin[40] draws the main lines of equivalence between the two episodes:

1) Both may be characterized as "confrontatory dialogues." God
confronts Israel in dialogue in chapter 10, while Jephthah confronts

---

[40] Polzin, *Moses*, 178.

the elders in dialogue in chapter 11. Israel, notes Polzin, had rejected God, just as the elders of Gilead had rejected Jephthah, and banished him to the land of Tob.

2) Threatened by the Ammonites, the elders of Gilead reached out to Jephthah, just as Israel cried out to God for help in response to the Ammonite oppression in chapter 10. 3) In each episode, Polzin remarks, the savior responds in bitterness, and he compares Jephthah's rejection of 11:7 with God's rejection of Israel's pleas in chapter 10.

In spite of these motival and structural similarities, Polzin sees the stories as ultimately divergent, and addresses the rhetorical aim of the author in establishing what he sees as the contrastive equivalence between the two plots:

> The elders of Gilead now repeat their offer of the prize by which they hope to insure their own success: the promise of the lordship of Gilead to Jephtah. Unlike Yahweh with respect to Israel, however, Jephtah is influenced positively by the Gileadites offer: *the test has now become a trap.* (ital. Polzin)… If God refuses to be used by Israel, Jephtah has no such hesitation with respect to Gilead.[41]

Polzin builds upon two assumptions questioned earlier in this chapter. The first concerns the characterization of Jephthah. Polzin sees Jephthah as an opportunist, a stance which we suggested should be rejected in favor of the interpretation that sees Jephthah as reluctant. Second, Polzin interprets 10:16c, ותקצר נפשו בעמל ישראל, to mean that God had tired of Israel's insincere pleas, *and therefore did not grant them salvation.* Yet, on the basis of 11:29-33 we suggested that God does, in fact, save Israel here, albeit in a less direct and less complete fashion than in earlier episodes. In other words, contrary to what Polzin says, God is, in fact, ultimately swayed by Israel in the reproach narrative, and Jephthah does makes a deliberate attempt to forestall his appointment as *rosh* in chapter 11.

Yet, even if we assume all of Polzin's assumptions here, a fundamental weakness is still inherent in his reading. What, according to Polzin, is to be derived from the equivalence established between the two episodes? Polzin here answers: "If God refuses to be used by Israel, Jephthah has no such hesitation with respect to Gilead."[42] For Polzin, the author has gone to great rhetorical pains to underscore the fact

---

[41] Ibid., 178.
[42] Ibid..

that Jephthah, unlike God, is given to desires of power. Put differently, Jephthah is mortal and God is not. To the present writer, the point seems a relatively trivial and obvious one, one that hardly warrants bringing two episodes into intricate equivalence with one another.

Webb, following Polzin, develops an alternative meaning of the analogy between the two chapters. On the structural level, Webb sees several stages common to the two dialogues that Polzin had not. The added strata that Webb sees are particularly evident in elements 3 through 5 of the following scheme:

1) In each episode, Israel appeals to the rejected savior (God, Jephthah, respectively) out of an inability to cope with the Ammonites.
2) Each initial request is met with a rebuttal, namely God's rejection of Israel's pleas in 10:11-14, and Jephthah's rejection of the first offer of the elders in 11:7. These first two stages were identified by Polzin.
3) In each episode, notes Webb, the begging party presses its case with importuning. This may be seen in Israel's second plea, that of 10:15, and the second offer of the elders to Jephthah in 11:8.
4) In each account, the begging is not only a plea for salvation, but an expression of repentance, if only professed. Israel expresses a desire to restore her bond with God in 10:10 and 10:15 and the same sentiments are implicit in the elders' opening words of 11: 8, where they respond to Jephthah's expression of injury with the words, "Honestly, we have now turned back to you."
5) In each, concludes Webb, the begging party ultimately acknowledges the sovereignty of the previously aggrieved party. Israel fully acknowledges God in 10:15-16, while the elders of Gilead are moved to appoint Jephthah both *rosh* and *qatzin* prior to the battle (11:11).

From here, Webb, like Polzin, determines that the stories ultimately conclude on divergent notes, and speculates as to the meaning of the equivalence between the two passages:

> Where the two episodes differ sharply is in the final response given by Yahweh and Jephthah respectively. Yahweh can no longer tolerate the misery of Israel; Jephthah manifests only self-interest... The episode displays... the calculating way in which [Jephthah] goes about achieving his personal ambitions.[43]

The comments here need to be understood against the larger backdrop of Webb's approach to the entire Jephthah narrative of 10:6-12:7. Throughout his comments to these stories (divine dialogue narrative 10:6-16; ascension of Jephthah to power, 10:17-11:11; negotiation with the king of Ammon, 11:12-28; battle and vow, 11:29-40; civil war with Ephraim, 12:1-7) Webb seeks to identify a common theme: the "tendency to accommodate religion to political norms."[44] Webb sees these stories as illustrative of the fact that the service of God is not for its own sake but as a means toward achieving some material end. Webb rightly identifies this theme of the politicization of religion in a number of the episodes. It is an accurate characterization of Israel's importuning in seeking God's deliverance in chapter 10; it is likewise an accurate reading of Jephthah's vow, which seems an attempt to "buy off" God with promises of sacrificial gifts, if only he will grant victory on the battlefield. Webb is also correct that insincerity and manipulation are seen in the stance of the elders vis-à-vis Jephthah in the negotiation narrative. While paying lip service to sincerity and their desire to close ranks with him (11:8), they are ultimately driven by self-preservation: they need Jephthah in order to overcome the Ammonites. Yet it is this search for a meta-theme that leads Webb to assess Jephthah's character incorrectly in the narrative under study:

> [Jephthah] has debased religion (a vow, an offering) into politics. It is the sequence of dialogues in episodes 2-4 (i.e. negotiations with the elders, negotiations with the king of Ammon, battle and vow—JB) which gives the point its dramatic force. The same point is made by the 'parallel' dialogues of episodes 1 and 2 (i.e. the divine reproach narrative and the negotiation narrative—JB). Israel has debased repentance into negotiation.[45]
> This then I propose, is the major theme of the narrative in its finished form. It is about the tendency to accommodate religion to political norms. It shows this happening at both the national *and the personal level* (ital. JB).

By characterizing Jephthah's negotiation with the elders as opportunism, Webb gets to register another incident of manipulation in the tally of such episodes that he finds across the Jephthah narrative. While the search for themes that cut across an entire unit is in itself admirable, it runs the risk of blurring distinctions between the com-

---

[43] Webb, *Book of Judges*, 54.
[44] Ibid., 74.
[45] Ibid., 74.

posite sub-units, and of looking for similarities where they may not exist. Thus, Webb's preference for reading Jephthah as opportunist here may not be based solely on his interpretation of the ambiguous verses of 11:6-11 (which, as noted, more strongly support the reading of Jephthah as Reluctant). Rather, it would seem that Webb sought to read Jephthah as an opportunist as it conforms to the meta-theme that he sees across the five episodes of the Jephthah narrative.

I would now like to present my interpretation of the evidence at hand by enumerating what I see as the analogical elements between the two stories, and describing what may be the message implicit in the equivalence. Fundamentally, I concur with all of Webb's findings concerning the parallel between *Israel* in chapter 10 and the *elders* in chapter 11. The elders of chapter 11, like Israel in chapter 10, are motivated by self-interest, and are driven to behave by importuning. Where I take issue with Webb and add to the equivalence formed between the two chapters is in what I identify as a much stronger equivalence between *God* in chapter 10 and *Jephthah* in chapter 11. This view of the analogy furthers lines of interpretation first suggested by Gunn and Fewell.[46] The full list of equivalences between the two narratives is, I submit, as follows:[47]

1) The equivalence begins with the observation that in both passages, Israel suffers oppression at the hand of the Ammonites and *fails* to appeal to the obvious savior who is available, and yet is not appealed to because he has been rejected. This is evident in chapter 10 vv. 6-8. Had Israel properly returned to God, perhaps He would have delivered them. But for 18 years they failed to do so and thus continued to suffer. In like fashion the chieftains of Gilead search in vain for a leader to lead the campaign against Ammon (10:18), when an obvious candidate, "Jephthah—a man of valor" (11:1), is close by, as conveyed by the literary juxtaposition of 10:18 and 11:1. Like God, however, in chapter 10, Jephthah is not considered, because he has been rejected.

2) The second equivalence takes us back to the opening point of the comparison as had been noted by Polzin and Webb: In each episode an appeal is made to the rejected, yet potential, savior (God, Jephthah, respectively) out of an inability to cope with the Ammonites.

---

[46] Gunn and Fewell, *Narrative*, 114.

[47] Within the following seven-point scheme, one can find a skeletal version of it (elements 1, 2, 4, and 5) in highly abbreviated form in Gunn and Fewell (*Narrative*, 114).

3) As Webb noted, initial pleas are made to the savior (10:10, 11:6). Yet, what should be further noted is the *inadequacy* of each plea. As we noted earlier, Israel's contrition of 10:10 indicates a professed desire to renew their relationship with Yahweh. Yet it is not categorically clear that they are prepared to sever all ties with the Baalim, as witnessed by the fact that it is only later, in 10:16, after they have received a tongue lashing from God, that they actually "removed the alien gods from among them." Their appeal in 10:10, therefore, is lacking not only because it is motivated by self-interest; it lacks even more fundamentally because even if taken at face value as sincere, it is insufficient in terms of the necessary change it fails to promise.

The same inadequacy is seen in the offer of the elders to Jephthah. In 10:6 they offer Jephthah the post of *qatzin* and to lead the campaign against Ammon. Yet, in 10:18, the chieftains of Gilead had made a public offer that anyone who was prepared to undertake the campaign against Ammon would be appointed *rosh* on the spot. Like Israel before them, the elders are motivated by self-interest, and make an offer to their savior that is insulting in its inadequacy.

4) The pleas are rejected by the savior, who experiences an appropriate sense of wound and betrayal, as had been noted by Polzin and Webb. It is important to recall that while the disinheriting of Jephthah may have been on questionable legal grounds, the expulsion had no legal basis whatever. Jephthah's claims against the elders are as strong as God's are against Israel in chapter 10; in each a deep, wounding injustice has been perpetrated. Noteworthy here are the lexical similarities between God's rejection of Israel and Jephthah's rejection of the elders:

הלא ממצרים ומן האמרי... לחצו אתכם... <u>ואתם</u> עזבתם <u>אותי</u>... לכו וזעקו אל האלהים אשר בחרתם בם המה יושיעו לכם <u>בעת צרתכם</u> (10:11-14).

<u>הלא אתם</u> שנאתם <u>אותי</u>... ומדוע באתם אלי <u>עתה</u> כאשר <u>צר לכם</u> (11:7).

Each begins with the exclamatory הלא (10:11; 11:7) and each pointedly highlights the insincerity of the plea by using the term "time of distress" (צר). God states caustically (10:14): "Let them (i.e. the foreign gods) deliver you in *your time of distress* (בעת צרתכם)." Jephthah likewise asks rhetorically, "Why do you come to *me now when you are in trouble* (עתה כאשר צר לכם)?" Each claim likewise bears an accusation of personal injury utilizing the words אתם ("you" pl.) and אותי ("me"). God

charges Israel, "you have forsaken Me (ואתם עזבתם אותי)" (10:13), while
Jephthah charges the elders, "You rejected me (אתם שנאתם אותי)"
(11:7).[48] These linguistic markers establishing equivalence between
Jephthah and God were not noticed by Webb. Neither, however,
would they have fit his model. Jephthah the opportunist cannot be
equated too closely with God. When Jephthah speaks, according to
Webb, it is with self-interest alone in mind; when God speaks it is with
justified indignation. Yet, as we propose, when Jephthah is seen as
reluctant and wounded as opposed to power-hungry, the equivalence
between Jephthah and God comes into greater focus.

5) Second offers are made to the savior, offers that are meant to
be more enticing. Whereas in 10:10, Israel had fretted about the idols
they served, they now remove them in 10:16: "They removed the
alien gods from among them and served the Lord." In other words,
this second gesture by Israel is the gesture they should have made
in the first place. The same dynamic is seen in the second offer of
the elders to Jephthah. Here, in 11:8, they offer him the title of *rosh*
immediately.[49] In other words, they offer him the same status that
had been offered to any other member of Gilead in good standing in
10:18. Finally, they have made the offer that they should have been
making all along, so as to accord Jephthah the recognition that he
deserves as a full-fledged member of Gilead.

6) These offers, as Webb noted, reflect a sense of wanting to repair
the breach in the relationship between the savior and his would-be
subjects: in a word, they profess "repentance." Israel says as much in
10:10 and 10:15, and the same sentiments are implicit in the elders'
opening words of 11:8, where they respond to Jephthah's expression
of injury with the words, "Honestly, we have now turned back to
you." What may be added, though, is that what is manifestly exhibited
through equivalence of motif, is also supported through an indirectly
common lexical field. The penitent claims of Israel in 10:10 and 10:
15-16, do not actually use the verb ש.ו.ב.. Nonetheless, the double
act of removing alien gods from within their midst (ויסירו את אלהי
הנכר), and of worshipping God (ויעבדו את יהוה) is the very definition
of the term "to return" in 1 Sam 7:3: "If you mean to *return* (שבים)
to the Lord with all your heart, *you must remove the alien gods* (הסירו את)

---

[48] Jacobs, "The Story of Jephthah," 27.
[49] Abarbanel, in his second explanation; Kaufmann, *Book of Judges*, 219; Amit, *Book of Judges*, 196.

אלהי הנכר) and the Ashtaroth from your midst and direct your heart to the Lord and serve Him (ועבדהו) alone."

7) Webb concluded his observations of similarity by noting that in each story the supplicant ultimately acknowledges the sovereignty of the savior; Israel returns to the exclusive worship of God, while the elders of Gilead appoint Jephthah to be *rosh* and *qatzin*. Yet, the more significant point, to my mind, is the equivalence established between the disposition of each savior in light of the second offer, or plea, by the supplicant. Each savior is left torn; each supplicant is finally taking the appropriate steps of action (i.e. Israel abolishes the foreign gods and worships Yahweh; the elders offer Jephthah what everyone else had been offered). Each supplicant is stating a desire to promote the relationship along the terms through which it should be conducted. Yet, for each savior a nagging question persists: are they sincere? Will their protestations of fealty last beyond the immediate moment of crisis? The ambivalence is reflected in the final stance taken by each savior. For God, it is reflected in the expression ותקצר נפשו בעמל ישראל. God feels wearied by Israel's importuning. He indeed suspects their professed sincerity. But in the end he relents, and indeed does ultimately offer Israel deliverance from the Ammonites.

The same is true of Jephthah. He is wary of their offer of 11:8 and conditions his acceptance of the title of *rosh* not only on God's sanction of the appointment through victory in battle, but also upon his own determination of the welcome that he receives in Gilead: "If you bring me home again to fight with the Ammonites, and the Lord gives them over to me, I will be your head" (RSV). The term *if you bring me home* (אם משיבים אתם אותי) employs the same root of .ש.ו.ב that the elders had used to indicate their stance of rapprochement and appeasement in v. 8: "Honestly we have now turned back to you" (ועתה שבנו אליך). Jephthah's choice of words seems to indicate that he wishes to monitor carefully the extent to which they have indeed "returned" to him, and whether he can count on this as an enduring stance. Jephthah, therefore, like God in chapter 10, agrees to deliver Israel, but with no small degree of wariness.[50] The motival equivalence between the two narratives may be summarized in structural terms whereby a common

---

[50] For Gunn and Fewell (*Narrative*, 114), Jephthah is a figure driven by opportunism, and thus this ultimate point of the analogy is omitted by them. Indeed, even as they come close to identifying several of the common elements that I propose, they

sequence of actions dictates the plot of both stories:

1) The savior is unjustly rejected.
2) The oppressed people fail to appeal to the savior in time of distress because he has long since been rejected.
3) The supplicants make an inadequate and insincere appeal to the savior in order to address the Ammonite problem.
4) The savior rejects the appeal out of a sense of betrayal (lexical markers אותי - אתם, עת צרה, הלא).
5) Desperate, the supplicants make a second round of offers to woo the savior.
6) Though wary of the insincerity of the supplicants, the savior elects to grant salvation.[51]

I believe that the extended string of analogous elements that I have delineated bears directly on the message of the comparison. Webb indicated that the equivalence between the negotiation narrative of chapter 11 and the rebuke dialogue of chapter 10 demonstrates to us the political nature of Israel's character at this time; the same self-interest and insincerity that manifest themselves in chapter 10, reappear vis-à-vis Jephthah in chapter 11. I would like to take the equivalence a step further and suggest that it exists not only between Israel and the elders in the two respective narratives, but between the rejected savior in each as well. The message for the reader is not only about the nature of Israel, but about the nature of God.

Recall that we stated that the God-Israel dialogue-like encounter of chapter 10 is nowhere else found in the Bible. This rhetoric, we suggested, was employed to underscore God's sense of wound and injury in human terms so that the reader could more easily relate to the sense, not only of sin, or transgression, but indeed of betrayal and pain. The analogy between the two narratives achieves the same objective. In chapter 10 God's pain and Israel's disloyalty are concretized, rendered human, through the rhetoric of the rebuke dialogue. In chapter 11, God's pain, sense of mistrust, and betrayal are dramatized through the metaphor analogy of Jephthah's experience with the elders.

---

offer the analogy no interpretation. The features common to the reproach narrative of chapter 10 and the ascension narrative of chapter 11 simply demonstrate artistry; a common plot. Yet Gunn and Fewell seek in this no didactic message.

[51] It should be noted that even though I have questioned Marcus's suggestion that the words *rosh* and *qatzin* are interchangeable in this passage this schematic summary works equally well according to his reading of the passage.

In the previous chapter, the narrative of the rape of the concubine and the battle narrative of the demise of the tribe of Benjamin were seen to comment on each other. The rape of the concubine, we saw, was cast in terms that reflected a hostility reminiscent of battle; the brutality through which the tribes avenged the Benjaminites was reminiscent of the gang rape perpetrated against the concubine. The question of proleptic and analeptic tendencies was not definitively resolved, for their relationship was intertextual and bilateral.

The present analysis, however, displays no such mutuality. One must ask why Scripture chose to tell of Jephthah's rise to power in the first place. Othniel, Ehud, Barak and Deborah, not to mention the minor judges of the Book of Judges, are all introduced without any comment concerning their ascent to power. Indeed, the narratives of Gideon and Samson do supply such information, but in a manner that directly influences the accounts of their actions as saviors of Israel. Gideon needed to overcome his sense of inferiority. The series of signs that he is given slowly weans him of this, with the result of his sweeping victory over the Midianites. Samson's birth is recorded, but, here again, the fact of his Nazirite status is part and parcel of the entire Samson narrative; one could hardly imagine the Samson narrative bearing the same integral meaning without the annunciation narrative of chapter 13.

Can the same be said of the negotiation narrative of 10:17-11:11? It would seem that the subsequent episodes of the Jephthah narrative (i.e. the negotiations with the king of Moab, the victory account and the vow story) could all have remained intact even if Jephthah had been introduced in a highly cursory fashion, as are the other major figures of Judges mentioned above. The detail of his political ascent, however, becomes charged with valence when it is seen as a foil against which to understand Israel's disposition toward God at this time. As Webb said, it highlights Israel's self-interest and insincerity; moreover, we might add, it underscores the sense of divine pain, injury and mistrust. Indeed the passage of 10:17-11:11 is not primarily concerned with the insult and snubbing accorded a local chieftain, Jephthah. The focus of the passage is, however, cast on a central biblical theme: assessing and concretizing the strained relationship between God and his wayward covenantal partner, Israel. The very real and concrete dimension of Jephthah's abuse stands as a metaphor for Israel's treatment of God in chapter 10.

The equivalence drawn here entails, however, a theological hazard, or danger: the equation of human and God. In a similar comparative study, E.L. Greenstein has shown Samson to stand in equivalence to Israel;[52] midrashic sources already saw elements in the life of Abraham as parallel to later events to befall the children of Israel;[53] the present writer has argued elsewhere that the events experienced by Moses in Exodus 2 bear a striking resemblance to those to be experienced by the liberated Hebrews later in the book.[54] The lives of great figures are made to stand in equivalence to events that are the experience of the nation as a whole. Here, however, the contention is of a different order: here the contention is that a leadership figure stands in equivalence, not to another human, or even an aggregate of humans, but indeed in equivalence to God himself. The proposition, for all of its textual basis, would seem to violate the principle of the unbridgeable gap that the Bible generally promotes between the human, fraught with weakness, and the sovereign God of history depicted in the Book of Judges.[55]

In point of fact, however, the narrative of Judges 11 poses no such problem. For at the same time that Jephthah stands in rhetorical equivalence to God he is the paradigm of the humble leader who understands that his power exists only for the grace of God. Offered leadership, he rejects it (11:7). When urged by way of the importuning of his would-be subjects, he demurs and conditions his acceptance of

---

[52] Edward L. Greenstein, "The Riddle of Samson," *Prooftexts* 1 (1981) 237-60. See also, Kenneth R.R. Gros Louis, "The Book of Judges," in Kenneth R.R. Gros Louis and James Ackerman (eds.), *Literary Interpretations of Biblical Narratives* (2 vols.; Nashville: Abingdon Press, 1974) 1.161.

[53] *Bereshit Rabbah* 40:8. See further in rabbinic sources, Naḥmanides Genesis 12: 10.

[54] Joshua Berman, "The Analogy Between Moses and Israel in the Book of Exodus and its Meaning," unpublished seminar paper, Bar-Ilan University, 1997.

[55] Amit (*Book of Judges: The Art of Editing*, 350-51) has questioned the notion of absolute divine sovereignty in the theology of the author of Judges on the basis of Jephthah's statement to the king of Moab, "Do you not hold what Chemosh your god gives you to possess?" (11:24). Yet, as Kaufmann (*Book of Judges*, 24) and Elitzur (*Book of Judges*, 127; cf. Boling, *Judges*, 205) have argued, Jephthah may simply be adopting a diplomatically shrewd stance. To avert the ensuing conflict, he speaks to the King of Moab in his own theological language. Alternatively, we may suggest that Jephthah really meant what he said, and that this is further evidence of his waywardness, from the overall perspective of the Deuteronomistic history. In any event, one should not conclude that the voice of a (particularly problematic) character such as Jephthah necessarily represents the voice of the author of the book.

the post upon the de facto receipt of God's approval through victory on the battlefield. After receiving the post, he prefaces his efforts against the Ammonites by appealing to God at Mizpah. The course of his negotiation with the King of Moab displays the same sense in Jephthah as one who is aware that his own power is granted only by God. Nowhere in the 17-verse negotiation does Jephthah suggest the superiority of his forces over those of Moab. Rather he suggests that the King of Moab acknowledge the justice of Israel's possession of the disputed territory as he does: as a product of divine decree. Jephthah mentions God's role in the acquisition of this territory at four junctures (11:21, 23, 24, 27). Jephthah concludes his appeal to the King of Moab solely by crediting the God of Israel: "May the Lord, who judges, decide today between the Israelites and the Ammonites" (11:27). The author allows himself to set Jephthah in equivalence with God because Jephthah is a humble leader of flesh and blood acutely aware of his standing before the sovereign God of Israel.

To summarize, we may reflect upon some of the methodological issues raised in this chapter concerning the establishment of the metaphor analogy. The equivalences established in the previous chapters relied heavily on semantic similarities between terms in the narratives under comparison. The present case study reveals virtually none. With the exception of the terms הלא , עת צרה and אתם—אותי, we identified no semantic parallels between the two narratives. What serves as the basis of this metaphor analogy is the sequence of similar plot actions sustained across a nearly identical structure. Yet, because actions in a plot, or motifs, are less easily identified than lexical markers, it took some effort to build upon the observations of earlier scholars and to arrive at our final common structure.

We also saw a good example of how even the very identification of the lexical bases of an analogy is but a function of the interpretation given to the equivalence. For Webb, who perceives Jephthah as an opportunist, the common terms of עת צרה, הלא, and appositive words אתם—אותי here go unnoticed. As they are oft-found terms, Webb presumably saw in them no significance. Yet a different interpretive model, that of Jephthah as reluctant, suddenly allows previously undetected signals to be received and interpreted. The strong rhetorical congruence established by the narrative between Jephthah and God suddenly casts these otherwise commonplace terms in a bright comparative light. We also see here the manner in which the identification

of additional elements of the analogical base can alter the meaning
ascribed to the analogy as a whole. These shared terms indicate that
the equivalence here is not only between the elders and Israel, but
between Jephthah and God as well.

CHAPTER FIVE

TWO DAYS OF FEASTING (ESTH 5:1-8) AND TWO DAYS OF FIGHTING (ESTH 9:1-16) IN THE BOOK OF ESTHER

In the present chapter I seek to discern a latent meaning of the battle narrative of Esther 9 by demonstrating an analogy between this narrative and the account of the two days of feasting in Esther chapter 5. Before turning to the task of establishing this analogy, a pause is in order to first establish that the narrative of chapter 9 can indeed be categorized as a battle story. Several oft-found features of many biblical battle reports are absent here. The locale of the battle is not specified; the leaders of the armies are not named. Indeed, Israel's foes here are listed solely as such—"the enemies of the Jews" without a definite national identity. As noted in our introduction, however, the biblical battle story does not have a set form; rather, it is recognized by typical features—themes, phrases and motifs that recur in many battle narratives. Many of these typical features are evidenced here, so much so that it creates a strong impression that the author of Esther 9 desired to cast his narrative in a manner that would classify it within the battle-report tradition.

The clash is not spontaneous between groups of rabble, but between organized battalions. The enemies that the Jews face are organized regiments (חיל) (8:11) and the Jews themselves began to prepare for the 13th of Adar with the dispatch of the communiqué, some nine months in advance (8:11).[1] Fear grips the enemy (8:17) in anticipation of a calamity (Exod 15:16; 1 Sam 11:7; Ps 105:38; Job 13:11).[2] The battle account of chapter 9 attends to the issue of booty taking at numerous points (8:11; 9:10, 15, 16), and offers a breakdown of casualty figures at different stages in the conflict (9:6, 15, 16). It describes the foe as "unable to stand before" Israel, a common motif in the battle reports of Joshua (10:8; 21:44; 23:9).[3] The MT graphically arranges the names

---

[1] C.A. Moore, *Esther* (AB 7B; NewYork: Doubleday, 1971) 80.
[2] Adele Berlin, *Esther* (JPS Commentary; Philadelphia: Jewish Publication Society of America, 2001) 81.
[3] Frederic W. Bush, *Ruth, Esther* (WBC 9; Dallas: Word Books, 1996) 461.

of Haman's sons in a vertical list of vanquished foes, the likes of which
are found elsewhere in the list of vanquished kings in Joshua 12.[4] It
incorporates the motif of fear gripping the enemy (על + פחד) (8:17; 9:
2, 3) as Israel emerges victorious in a nearly effortless manner, which
is particularly reminiscent of the battle stories of Chronicles (1 Chr
14:17; 2 Chr 14:13; 17:10; 20:29; cf. Josh 2:9, 24).[5]

Our analysis of the battle report of Esther 9:1-16 opens with an
observation. The narrative documents events that transpired over two
days of fighting. The actual achievements of the second day (9:15),
however, pale in comparison with those of the first, seemingly on every
scale of significance. On the first day the Jews killed 75,500 of their
enemies while on the second day they added another 300 to that figure.
On the first day they killed the ten sons of Haman in Shushan, who,
perhaps, were affiliated with the leadership of the campaign against
the Jews. Those killed on the second day, however, seem entirely
nondescript. Historicist perspectives have averred that chapter 9 is
to be seen as an etiology, a later attempt to bolster observance of
the two-day festival of Purim.[6] The etiological aspect of this text is
undeniable. Nonetheless, even when the text is probed as a literary
construct, the equality underscored between the two days of fighting
seems unwarranted.

I would suggest, however, that, in its description of the 14th of Adar,
the narrative is only secondarily concerned with the actual events and
achievements of the second day of fighting. Note that the fighting and
its results are reduced to a single verse, 9:15. The narrative's interest
in the second day is not in its results but rather in its genesis—how
it came to be that the Jews received a second day to retaliate against
their enemies within the city of Shushan. To this subject, the narrative devotes four verses, 9:11-14, a detailed account of the discussion
between Esther and the king. A key to understanding the narrative's
interest in the second day, I would submit, is to see it as a milestone
in the development of the character of Esther. I will contend that the
meaning of the analogy between the two days of fighting and the two

---

[4] Ibid., 475.
[5] Gillis Gerleman, *Esther* (BKAT 21; Neukirchen-Vluyn: Neukirchener-Verlag,
1982) 131. See the same motif in non-narrative sections: Exod 15:16; Deut 2:25;
11:25; Ps 105:38.
[6] David J.A. Clines, *The Esther Scroll* (JSOTSup 30; Sheffield: Sheffield Academic
Press, 1984) 48; Gerleman, *Esther*, 134; Moore *Esther* 91; Michael V. Fox, *Character
and Ideology in the Book of Esther* (Columbia, SC: University of South Carolina Press,
1991) 112.

days of feasting concerns the characterization employed by the scroll in its casting of the figure of Esther.

The present chapter, like all of the case studies in this work, is primarily concerned with the interdependence between the battle narrative and the account that precedes it. My working assumptions about Esther's character, however, differ fundamentally from conventional understandings that have been offered. A grid of understanding concerning the figure of Esther, therefore, must first be established. Before embarking on a close study of the battle narrative of chapter 9 in conversation with the feast account of chapter 5, I first set out to provide a detailed accounting of my understanding of the characterization of Esther in the Book of Esther.

Several commentators have claimed that Esther is the only character in the scroll that experiences growth and development; and that, unlike other figures, her character is not built around a single trait.[7] Most of the attention to Esther's development has focused around the events of chapter 4 and the transition from her initial reluctance to her ultimate acquiescence to appeal before the king on behalf of her people. It is this writer's contention however, that the events of chapter 4 constitute only the initial stages of her evolution and that in Esther we are witness to a process of inner struggle and growth that extends all the way through the scroll's final verses. The present study draws heavily upon the work of Simone de Beauvoir concerning gender relations in a patriarchal society. Moreover, it employs studies of the psychology and sociology of persons who endure the process of disclosing their true, stigmatized identity in an inimical environment as a lens through which to understand the figure of Esther. The process of coming out among gays and lesbians has been of sustained academic interest for over thirty years and offers, *mutatis mutandis*, a comprehensive model with which to analyze Esther's own "coming out" as a hitherto hidden Jew.[8]

---

[7] See, for example, Clines, *The Esther Scroll*, 145; Fox, *Character and Ideology*, 196; Bush, *Ruth, Esther*, 319.

[8] Throughout his earlier work on Esther, Timothy Beal employs the term "coming out" to refer to the moment of Esther's disclosure in 7:1-3 (*The Book of Hiding: Gender, Ethnicity, Annihilation and Esther* [London: Routledge, 1997]). The implication is that "coming out" is fundamentally an *event*. The social scientific studies cited here suggest otherwise: that coming out is a *process*. The same, I believe, is true for Esther as she struggles to disclose her stigmatized identity. I have developed these ideas more fully in an adapted version of this chapter, "Hadassah bat Abihail: From Object to Subject in the Character of Esther," *JBL* 120:4 (2001) 647-69.

My characterization of Esther is intimately bound to the question of the scroll's comment concerning Jewish identity in a Diaspora setting. The issue has engendered much discussion and I should like to state my position within this discussion at the outset. One position maintains that the scroll heralds the rich and creative possibilities of leading an integrated identity as a Jew who fully participates in the life and leadership of the host-culture.[9] A second camp adopts a more sanguine approach to the question. Jewish survival and even success are available to the Diaspora Jew. The scroll's message, however, is that this is achieved only through clever, careful, and clandestine manipulation of the powers that be.[10] A third view explores the issue of Jewish identity in a Diaspora setting, not in terms of the possibilities of survival and success, but in ontic and existential terms: what becomes of Jewish identity and the self-concept as Jew under the strains of Diaspora existence? It is on this score that Greenstein and Bach have written that the scroll accentuates the inherent tensions engendered by dual loyalty to Jewish tradition on the one hand and temporal authority on the other.[11] This position has been argued in expansive fashion by Timothy Beal in his two recent works on Esther.[12] My contribution here is an attempt to broaden further the avenues opened by Beal in this regard.

My characterization of Esther opens by exploring her actions as a woman in a highly patriarchal society, particularly in chapter 2 and the first half of chapter 4. From there, I probe the manner in which she embarks upon the process of revealing her stigmatized identity as a Jew to those around her (the latter half of chapter 4), and how she

---

[9] See, for example, W. Lee Humphreys, "A Life-Style for Diaspora: A Study of the Tales of Esther and Daniel," *JBL* 92 (1973) 216; John Craghan, *Esther, Judith, Tobit, Jonah, Ruth* (Wilmington, Del.: Michael Glazier, 1982) 9.

[10] See, for example, Sidnie Ann White, "Esther: A Feminine Model for Jewish Diaspora," in Peggy L. Day (ed.), *Gender and Difference in Ancient Israel* (Minneapolis: Fortress Press, 1989) 167; Susan Niditch, "Esther: Folklore, Wisdom, Feminism and Authority," in Athalya Brenner (ed.), *A Feminist Companion to Esther, Judith and Susanna* (Sheffield: Sheffield Academic Press, 1995) 41; Lilian Klein, "Honor and Shame in Esther," in *idem.*, 175.

[11] Edward L. Greenstein, "A Jewish Reading of Esther," in Jacob Neusner, *et al*, (eds.), *Judaic Perspectives on Ancient Israel* (Philadelphia: Fortress Press, 1987) 234-37; Alice Bach, *Women, Seduction, and Betrayal in Biblical Narrative* (Cambridge: Cambridge University Press, 1997) 192. On Jewish Diaspora stories in the biblical period, see Berlin, *Esther*, xxxiv-xxxvi.

[12] Timothy K. Beal, *The Book of Hiding: Gender, Ethnicity, Annihilation and Esther* (London: Routledge, 1997); *idem.*, *Esther* (Berit Olam; Collegeville MN: Liturgical Press, 1999).

evolves through this process across the narrative of the scroll (chapters 5-9). Through these examinations we will attempt to delineate the scroll's message concerning the complexity of Jewish identity in a Diaspora setting. Finally, this analysis of Esther's character will provide us with a framework against which we will explore the manner in which the battle narratives of chapter 9 form a narrative analogy with the drinking narratives of chapter 5. The analogy, I will claim, contributes to an understanding of Esther's evolution through the chapters of the story.

Esther 2:1—4:11: Simone de Beauvoir and the Notion of the Other

My characterization of Esther begins with a probe of Esther chapter 2. The process by which young virgins are conscripted for the king situates Esther in a milieu that has been characterized as patriarchal in the extreme.[13] What may we say of Esther's personality throughout this? What indications does the text offer as to what Esther has *become*? Fox, among others, has said that Esther here is passive and indeed the syntax of much of chapter 2 underscores this.[14] She is *taken* in the round-up of virgins (2:8) as she is *taken* to the king's palace (2:16). In preparation for her night with the king she is, as Beal puts it, "utterly deferential," asks for nothing and takes only what Hegai advises her.[15]

Esther may have been, simply, a passive person. Turning to Simone de Beauvoir's typology of the "Other," however, I would like to suggest that her passivity be understood as an outgrowth of situation. To be Other, suggests de Beauvoir throughout her work, is not only to be *treated* as object, but ultimately to submit—in mind and in temperament—to *becoming* an object. In a strongly patriarchal culture the woman who wishes to survive has no choice but to accord and accede to Otherness, and thereby forgo subjectivity, transcendence, and a will of her own. She must adopt a posture of submissiveness and complicity.[16] Her very femininity, from the perspective of the One male, is predicated upon these traits. Only by making herself object

---

[13] See, for example, Beal, *Book of Hiding*, 24-37; Fox, *Character and Ideology*, 34, 197; Jon D. Levenson, *Esther* (OTL: London, SCM Press, 1997) 63.

[14] Fox, *Character and Ideology*, 198.

[15] Beal, *Book of Hiding*, 69.

[16] Simone de Beauvoir, *Le Deuxième Sexe* (2 vols.; Paris: Gallimard, 1976) 1.17.

and prey can the Other woman realize her femininity in the eye of the absolute, essential male.[17]

The observation of Esther's otherness has acute implications for the narrative of Esther 2. In the wake of Vashti's banishment Ahasuerus sought a new wife who would be beautiful, but who would also be prepared to be what Vashti was not: the consummate Other; a wife prepared to surrender entirely her own subjectivity and will. The passivity discerned in Esther's behavior reflects an adaptation strategy fitted to the realities of her situatedness. In order to survive and rise above the seraglio, Esther assumes the mind and temperament of the objectified, inessential Other.

De Beauvoir asserts that the Other woman gains value in men's eyes "by modeling herself upon their dreams," and that in readying herself she must "repress her spontaneity and replace it with the studied grace and charm taught by her elders," as self-assertion diminishes her femininity and attractiveness.[18] The comment is illuminating of 2:15-17. In contrast with the virgins who preceded her, Esther asks for no special aids, and accepts only what Hegai suggests. It is this expression of Esther's yielding and conformity that immediately precedes the phrase in 2:15, "and Esther won the admiration of all who saw her."[19] They admired her for her beauty. No less, however, did they apparently see in her that trait that Vashti so critically lacked: the capacity to "model herself in others' (viz.: Ahasuerus's) dreams."

The evolution of Esther's otherness is attested through the numerous appellations ascribed to Esther in 2:15: "When the turn came for Esther daughter of Abihail—the uncle of Mordecai, who had adopted her as his own daughter—to go to the king...." What is most significant about these appellations is their inclusion at this juncture. Esther has already been introduced in 2:6 and her adoption by Mordecai already reported. The repetition of these details of identity and relation, the mention of her patronymic name here and *not* earlier in verse 2:6 all signify that Esther stands at a threshold of identity. She enters the king's palace as the daughter of Abihail, as the adopted daughter

---

[17] Ibid., 2.600.

[18] Ibid., 2.101.

[19] This, in contrast to the JPS translation, which reads, "*yet* Esther won the admiration." I would claim that the word *yet* is out of place. It was her deference and submission that contributed to her femininity as Other in the world of Ahasuerus' palace. Cf. also, Berlin *Esther*, 28.

of Mordecai. But she will emerge from those chambers with a new designation: *Esther, the king's wife.*[20]

The years of conforming to the king's notion of consummate Other continue to influence the next phase of her evolution, the events of chapter 4. White notes that at this point in the narrative Esther has already been queen for five years.[21] Put differently, six years have elapsed since the daughter of Abihail, who became daughter of Mordecai, was taken from home on her path to becoming the consummate Other, as the king's wife. The manifold effects of this extended period of otherness are keenly exhibited in Esther's refusal (v. 11) to comply with Mordecai's request. What is most significant in her refusal, perhaps, is what is *not* said. Rejecting Mordecai's proposal, she offers no alternative. With sackcloth not an option for the king's wife, we might have expected her at least to join in the act of fasting (as she only later will). Failing that, she might have openly bewailed the fate of her people, in empathy and commiseration. Her comment, in contrast, relates neither to the Jews, nor to Mordecai at all. She does, to be sure, relate to herself but above all else her comment centers around the person of the *king.* No other verse in the MT version of Esther bears the word "the king" as many times as does v. 4:11:

> All the *king's* courtiers and all the people of the *king's* provinces know that if any person, man or woman enters the *king's* presence in the inner court without having been summoned, there is but one law for him—that he be put to death. Only if the *king* extends the golden scepter to him may he live. Now I have not been summoned to visit the *king* for the last thirty days.

Note that Esther herself recognizes that the mission could be successful—if she is fortunate enough to be offered the golden scepter. Why does she lack the courage to make the heroic effort undertaken by the common soldier in battle: to risk one's life for the sake of the greater good? Fox claims that she is "simply concerned for her personal safety."[22] Alternatively, however, Esther's absorption with the

---

[20] I render the word מלכה here as "king's wife," as opposed to the conventional "queen," in accordance with the translation of Edward L. Greenstein ("The Scroll of Esther: A New Translation," *Fiction* 9/3 [1990] 52-81). "Queen" implies an autonomous degree of authority that Esther never displays. The term "king's wife" on the other hand, appropriately stresses her subservience to him.

[21] White, "Esther: A Feminine Model," 170.

[22] Fox, *Character and Ideology*, 62.

king and failure to grasp the moral imperative of the moment are well explained by de Beauvoir. Because woman is fully dependent upon what she terms, "Man the One" for her material protection, she is easily inclined to forfeit the moral justification of her existence as she becomes a thing.[23] The deep-seated tendencies toward complicity endemic to her otherness deprive her of the transcendence necessary to attain the loftiest human attitudes: heroism, revolt, disinterestedness, imagination, creation.[24] De Beauvoir is quick to point out, however, that the Other woman who fails to act heroically is hardly to blame for her failure. The fact that her station is defined as a function of the male power structure, perforce limits her horizons: "Her wings are clipped, and it is [unfairly] found deplorable that she cannot fly."[25] Seen in this light, Esther is unjustly accused by Levenson of, "allowing the queenship to go to her head."[26] Nor should Esther be judged as, "too busy with her make-up and other skin-deep activities," as charged by Fuchs.[27] Esther is not spoiled. Esther is the victim of the ravages to the self-concept suffered through the subjugation of six years of Otherness.

Here, for the first time, we see that the subjectivity denied Esther through becoming an Other is associated not only with a loss of self and of transcendence. Rather, and significantly for the scroll's message concerning Jewish identity in the Diaspora, Esther's Otherness is coupled with an implicit attenuation of her Jewish identity. In 4:13-14 Mordecai will censure her, engendering within her intense dissonance. De Beauvoir characterizes the nature of her struggle: stabilized as an object, the Other woman finds herself conflicted between her aspirations as a subject, and the compulsions of a situation in which she is inessential. [28]

Esther 4:12-16: The Overcast Dawn of Esther's Emergent Self

As we proceed from here through the closing verses of chapter 4, the prism of de Beauvoir's work becomes insufficient. Liberation for de

---

[23] de Beauvoir, *Le Deuxième Sexe*, 1.21.
[24] Ibid., 2.518.
[25] Ibid., 2.493.
[26] Levenson, *Esther*, 80.
[27] Esther Fuchs, "Status and Role of Female Heroines in the Biblical Narrative," in Alice Bach, (ed.), *Women in the Hebrew Bible* (New York: Routledge, 1999) 80.
[28] de Beauvoir, *Le Deuxième Sexe*, 1.31.

Beauvoir would simply be to overcome all of the handicaps of being the Other woman. She would become, instead of object, subject; instead of immanent, transcendent; instead of inessential, essential. The emergence from Otherness is an emergence into the sunlit world of being the One with all its attending benefits for the psyche and the persona. Yet as Esther begins slowly to shed her status as the consummate Other woman within Ahasuerus's power structures the identity that she is beckoned to take on is anything but a sunlit, serene status as the One. To be sure, Mordecai calls upon Esther to adopt a subjective identity more fully and publicly. Yet it is an identity that is highly stigmatized; indeed, it is an identity marked for death.

To assess the evolution of Esther's character, therefore, we must appreciate that at play here are social and psychological processes of integrating a new and *stigmatized* identity. Before engaging the narrative of Esth 4:12-16, I pause for a moment to consider issues raised in the social scientific literature concerning the establishment of a positive minority identity and the complexities involved in the disclosure of a stigmatized identity in an inimical environment.

In her study of Jewish identity and self-esteem, Klein confirms general theories by Lewin that the concealment of one's identity correlates with low self-esteem.[29] Klein found that respondents who agreed with the statement, "when dealing with certain Gentiles it is best not to advertise the fact that one is Jewish," were found likely to display other markers of low self-esteem.[30] Thus, Mordecai's call to Esther to act on her Jewishness challenges her to marshal the self-esteem and assertiveness that have been severely diminished through not one, but two concomitant experiential processes in the king's palace. First, as stated, her self-esteem had been eroded through the six-year adaptation of her self-concept as Other woman. Her self-esteem had been further challenged, however, through the vigorous efforts of concealment and attendant fear of exposure that she had endured concerning her true identity as a Jew. For Esther to *act* on Mordecai's call (as opposed to merely acceding to it verbally, as she does in 4:16) she will need to engage in measures that will foster her diminished self-esteem.

The inner tasks that await Esther are well-understood through

---

[29] Kurt Lewin, *Resolving Social Conflict* (New York: Harper, 1948).

[30] Judith Weinstein Klein, "Jewish Identity and Self Esteem," Ph.D. dissertation, The Wright School, 1977, 110.

McDonald's comments concerning the tasks involved in the process
of coming out concerning a stigmatized sexual identity:

> Coming out involves adapting a non-traditional identity, restructuring
> one's self-concept, reorganizing one's personal sense of history, and alter-
> ing one's relations with others and with society... all of which reflects
> a complex series of cognitive and affective transformations as well as
> changes in behavior.[31]

Applied to Esther, *mutatis mutandis*, McDonald's comments suggest that
disclosure of her stigmatized identity (let alone an identity that marks
one for annihilation) comprises several psychological processes. She
must consider which of the many contradictory labels available to her
currently shade and color her identity: Is she a Jew or a Persian? Is
she marked to be annihilated, or by extension through Ahasuerus an
accomplice to the act of annihilation? Is she the wife of Ahasuerus
or the adopted daughter of Mordecai? Is she the king's wife or is she
an orphan in exile?

Finally, one may deduce from McDonald's portrayal that the disclosure of a stigmatized identity marks a point of no return. With the
truth out, one perforce must alter a spectrum of relations with others
and with society. Even if she is granted the golden scepter, Esther faces
an uncertain future. The dynamic of her relationship with Ahasuerus
and the court will perforce be altered as a result of her disclosure and
of the now exposed efforts of concealment and, perhaps, even decep-
tion that she had undertaken.

In light of these reflections concerning the difficult inner task that
awaits Esther, the present writer finds unpersuasive her depiction
here by many commentators. Esther's affirmative response (4:16) to
Mordecai's call is widely cast as a near metamorphosis; the change in
her is characterized as "abrupt"[32] and engenders a strategic plan carried
out with "determination"[33] and "firm conviction,"[34] and heralds the
emergence of "a strong and clever royal woman."[35] The notion that
inner processes of struggle are resolved in Esther instantaneously is
open to serious challenge. Such sanguine assessments are incongruent
with intonations found in Esther's own statement at the end of 4:16:
"Then I shall go to the king, though it is contrary to the law; *and if I*

---

[31] G.J. McDonald, "Individual Differences in the Coming Out Process for Gay
Men: Implications for Theoretical Models," *Journal of Homosexuality* 8 (1982) 47.

[32] Fox, *Character and Ideology*, 199; Bush, *Ruth, Esther*, 321.

[33] Fox, *Character and Ideology*, 199.

[34] Bush, *Ruth, Esther*, 320; cf. White, "Esther: A Feminist Model," 170.

[35] Berlin, *Esther*, 50.

am to perish, I shall perish!" Contrary to Mordecai, who expresses faith that her mission will succeed and that it is explicitly for this that she has risen to the crown, Esther seems quite pessimistic.[36] Resolved to accede to Mordecai, she is torn asunder by her six-year subjugation as the consummate Other on the one hand, and by her experiment with a nascent sense of subjectivity on the other. Far from heralding the emergence of a confident heroine, Esther's last words in this chapter underscore feelings of inner turmoil and dissonance as she commits to a plan of action for which she lacks the necessary inner resources.

Against this backdrop her call for a public fast at the opening of 4:16 needs to be closely scrutinized. On a primary level Esther's call for a fast in the face of doom is in line with a well-established biblical tradition of intercessory fasts in circumstances of crisis (cf. 1 Kgs 21: 27; Jonah 3:5-8; Neh 9:1). Yet, as the king's wife takes the first steps toward reconnecting with her subjective, essential, Jewish identity, the social implications of her call to fast are enormous as well. Bush has written here concerning her call for the fast, "she... issues commands that the *local community... should join her* and her maids in a three-day twenty four hour fast (ital. mine)."[37] Her declaration to Mordecai, however, implies strangely that it is *she* who will be joining *them*: "Go, assemble all the Jews who live in Shushan, and fast on my behalf; do not eat or drink for three days, night or day. I and my maidens will observe the same fast." Esther's fast expresses *her* solidarity with the Jews, at least as much as it does *their* solidarity with her.

Moreover, fasting at this juncture in the narrative of Esther 4 has a well-developed history. Esther is calling upon the Jews to fast, when they *have already fasted*, as attested in 4:3. Fasting constitutes behavior that has been marked in our story as the Jewish response to impending doom. In calling for a new fast, Esther is embarking upon a mode of behavior that is paradigmatically Jewish, and in so doing joins ranks with her fellow Jews.

Esther could have expressed other symbolic gestures of allegiance with her people. Fasting, it would seem, was chosen in a highly deliberate manner. She could not don sackcloth (4:2), nor offer *verbal* supplications for those would be visibly discernible. By joining ranks with the Jews of Shushan through fasting she experiences solidarity

---

[36] Cf. Sandra Beth Berg, *The Book of Esther* (SBLDiss. Series 44: Missoula, Montana, 1979) 39.

[37] Bush, *Ruth, Esther*, 400, and in a similar vein, Berlin, *Esther*, 49.

with them while still maintaining her spatial and social distance from them and from Mordecai. At the same time that she fosters a sense of solidarity that is highly palpable for her (i.e. through the ceaseless and deepening experience of hunger) she does so in a fashion indiscernible to the observer. This allows her to continue to "pass" publicly as the queen of Persia while establishing inner distance from her identity as object, as Ahasuerus's Other woman. Cass has observed within the context of coming out that passing allows individuals time to absorb and manage an ever-growing commitment to a new self-image and that this can prove a relatively easy task because it entails simply continuing in old patterns of behavior.[38] Note the extreme duration of the fast—three days. No doubt, the Jews of Shushan understood this as indicative of the need to achieve maximum intercessory efficacy. Yet, considering her inner struggle, the extended period of time also buys Esther a stay in which to assimilate her commitment to her newfound identity within the security of modes of behavior that will arouse no suspicion. Concerning the balance between her Persian and Jewish identities, she embarks on an inner journey whereby she is outwardly "in" even as she is increasingly moving inwardly "out."

A third and final component of Esther's fast is deserving of our attention and that is the company in which she carries out her fast: "I *and my maidens* will observe the same fast." The maidens will be the first group to which Esther, in effect, confesses her true identity. Coleman's study of the social aspects of the coming out process illuminates the vital role played by the maidens at this juncture. Seeking external validation, homosexual individuals risk disclosure to others. The vulnerability of the self-concept during the coming out stage mandates that such individuals choose carefully to whom they disclose their homosexual identity. It is important, Coleman writes, that these first persons be people who will accept the client's homosexuality, so that the existential crisis can begin to resolve in a positive direction.[39] Esther's ultimate test, of course, will be at the moment she reveals her identity to Ahasuerus. But that is a step she is not yet equipped to take: witness the three-day interval of fasting and the delays that she takes during the two days of feasting in chapter 5, to which we

---

[38] V. Cass, "Homosexual Identity Formation: A Theoretical Model," *Journal of Homosexuality* 4 (1979) 226.

[39] E. Coleman, "Developmental Stages in the Coming Out Process," *Journal of Homosexuality* 7:2-3 (1981/82) 34.

will attend shortly. When Esther drafts her maidens to join her for a 72-hour intercessory fast, one can only assume that she shared with them the cause for and purpose of this monumental undertaking. In so doing she created for herself a coterie of confidants who accept her disclosure that she is a Jew, a sisterhood of solidarity that remains faithful to her throughout the process.

The first step of the disclosure process, then, has been successfully navigated. The maidens' implicit acquiescence bolsters Esther's self-concept as both a legitimate person and an accepted Jew. The step is a crucial one, for as Davies has written, disclosure and the emergence of a strong self-identity interact in a reciprocal relationship: disclosure bolsters self-esteem, and in turn, greater self-esteem paves the way for the process of even wider disclosure to continue.[40] Esther may now embark upon the process of disclosure to the king himself: the events that unfold in chapter 5.

Esther 5:1-8: Milestones Along the Road to Denouement

Verse 5:1 relates that on the third day of the fast Esther donned royal apparel in preparation for her entree to the king. Her royal clothes indicate, as Beal suggests, that she wished to look her best for the king, which is to say she wished to appear the consummate Other in his ogling male eye.[41] Even as she is defiant of the king and his laws through her trespass, she seeks ways to visually counterbalance that impression, by donning robes that accentuate her fidelity to the throne.

Bach has correctly written that Esther here senses the power of her beauty over the king.[42] Returning to de Beauvoir, however, we can see an interpretation of the "hold" of beauty that tempers that sense of power, with an interpretation more in line with the spirit of Esther's highly tentative advance toward the king. De Beauvoir writes that in the relation of master to slave the master has the capacity to satisfy his need of the slave at will. Because of his dependence, however, the slave will always be conscious of the need he has for his master. Even if

---

[40] P. Davies, "The Role of Disclosure in Coming Out Among Gay Men," in K. Plummer (ed.), *Modern Homosexualities: Fragments of Lesbian and Gay Experience* (London: Routledge, 1992) 76.

[41] Beal, *Book of Hiding*, 77-78.

[42] Bach, *Women and Seduction*, 197.

the need is at bottom equally urgent for both, it always works in favor of the oppressor and against the oppressed.[43] Ahasuerus can remain in this scene relatively relaxed. Esther, ever the consummate Other, has always been available upon request. By contrast, Esther here is in dire need of Ahasuerus. The encounter spawns not empowerment but awe in Esther's heart. Esther, then, overcomes the first hurdle when the king extends the scepter. She asserts herself and her subjectivity by crossing the threshold of his chamber uninvited, and lives to move on to the next moment. Her courageous act emboldens her to take the next—small—step.

Ahasuerus effectively offers her carte blanche in 5:3, yet Esther demurs and asks only that he attend the drinking feast that she has prepared. Commentators, rabbinic and modern, have assessed her demurral on a tactical level.[44] Yet I would suggest that the risks involved in passing up the king's offer suggest a need for interpretation from psychological perspectives. Esther cannot yet bring herself—in spite of the king's offer—to divulge her true, stigmatized identity and to fully assert herself as a subjective being. She cannot muster the temerity to look him in the face and state: "I am a Jew." She therefore takes another small, yet significant step. Until now Esther, as the consummate Other, has always been the one who *is called* (nay, not even that —4:11!). Now, for the first time, she experiments with the mode of subjectivity in her direct, verbal relationship with the king: she is now the one who is doing the calling. The position of transcendence and of control over him is alien and is by itself an enormous step in the promotion of her self-concept. Esther therefore issues an innocuous request, one that will be easy for the king to grant: attendance at a banquet in his honor. Esther's first disclosure was carefully orchestrated so that it would be in front of a receptive audience, the maidens. In like, deliberate, fashion, Esther, in her first stance as subject in front of the king, poses a request that will likewise be met with receptivity, slowly nurturing her emerging subjectivity and self-esteem.

The invitation advances Esther's growth in a second fashion. She moves the venue of encounter with the king to her own turf. Unlike the throne room, the (unidentified) venue of the drinking banquet will be a space not nearly as rigidly organized by the king's royal power

---

[43] de Beauvoir, *Le Deuxième Sexe*, 1.20.
[44] Cf. *b. Meg.* 15b and the recent discussion by Levenson, *Esther*, 90.

structures.[45] It will be a space defined by Esther's will rather than Ahasuerus's authority.

From here, we proceed to a crucial, if enigmatic, episode in the saga of Esther's development: her request at the drinking party that the king and Haman attend yet a second party, to be held the next day. Within our larger characterization of Esther, the passage is of particular importance, as 5:7-8 will constitute the analog narrative to the battle account that we will encounter later in chapter 9. Commentators have given varying explanations of this request. Some have sought to recover the tactical calculations that may have led to this step, while others have ascribed it to Esther's reticence and continued inability to make her ultimate move. A full hearing, then, is in order to clarify the relationship between tactical and emotional bases for the deferral, and call for a second drinking party.

Some commentators, particularly those working within the rabbinic tradition have suggested that the second party is designed to arouse the king's jealousy (cf. *b. Megillah* 15b). These commentators[46] point to the difference in language employed between Esther's two invitations. On the first day Esther invites the king and Haman to "the feast that I have prepared for *him*" (5:4). When she extends the invitation to the second feast, however, Esther describes the affair as "the feast which I will prepare for *them*" (5:8). Esther, it is claimed, gives the impression that she is taken with Haman, and desires to see him again. The move, these commentators claim, may be the cause of the king's insomnia that night (6:1) and predisposes the king to suspect Haman of adultery when he returns from the garden to find him lying on the queen's bed (7:8).

Two counter-claims however, may be raised. Clines has argued that the difference in language between the two invitations is better explained as a function of Esther's audience at the time of each invitation, and as an issue of etiquette and politeness. The invitation to the first banquet is extended in the throne room, in the presence of the king alone. The second invitation, however, is extended at the banquet in the presence of both the king and Haman. Esther must refer to both of them in this invitation at the risk of offending Haman. Given these two alternative explanations, this writer finds a close reading of

---

[45] Cf. White, "Esther: A Feminine Model," 171.

[46] E.g. Amos Hakham, *Esther* (Daat Miqra; Jerusalem: Mossad Harav Kook, 1990) 37 (Hebrew).

the passage inconclusive; both options make sense within their own internal spheres of logic.[47]

The scales of judgment here, however, may be tipped, nonetheless. The notion that Esther intended to arouse the king's jealousy is difficult on the grounds of plot structure. Underlying this assessment of Esther's move is the assumption that it was entirely planned. Esther, according to this reading, invited both the king and Haman to the first party, with full intent of deferring her request. She then invites them to a second party, this time implicitly accentuating her esteem of Haman by throwing a party in *their* honor, and not *his* (i.e. the king's) alone. On the surface of Esther 5, this assumption is entirely tenable. It has difficult consequences, however, for the meaning of the structure of the ensuing plot in chapters 6 and 7. According to this theory, Esther—at the juncture of 5:8—fully planned to reveal her request at the second banquet, as she in fact does in 7:1-4. Put differently, the events of 5:8-6:14—Mordecai's reward and Haman's humiliation—are of no causal relevance whatever to the main plot of Esther's plan to reveal her identity at the second banquet. Even if the entire story of Mordecai's recognition had not occurred, Esther would have been prepared to reveal her secret at the second banquet, in accordance with her plan. To this writer, however, the story seems crafted in such a way that it seems vital that the events of 5:8-6:14 transpire precisely when they do, in order for the main plot to advance. Those who interpret the second party invitation as a deliberate tactical move can only claim that the impeccable timing of Mordecai's recognition and Haman's humiliation constitute a wonderful coincidence, perhaps even a sign of divine providence: just as Esther was about to spoil the day for Haman, it happened on its own anyway. The two motions of plot, however, according to this reading, are causally unrelated.

Other commentators have taken a different approach to 5:7-8. Esther's request that they return for a second banquet is not born out of tactical considerations, and was not part of her original plan. Rather, on the spot, at the first banquet, she lost her nerve.[48] Bush,[49] following Bardtke,[50] has found syntactic evidence for this approach.

---

[47] Clines, *The Esther Scroll*, 179 n. 6.
[48] Levenson, *Esther*, 91; Ibn Ezra 5:8.
[49] Bush, *Ruth, Esther*, 404-05.
[50] H. Bardtke, *Das Buch Esther* (KAT 17/5, Gütersloh: Mohn, 1963) 339.

Most translations of 5:7 end the verse with a colon, and read the transition of 5:7-5:8 as does the RSV:

> But Esther said, "*My petition and my request is:* If I have found favor in the sight of the king, and if it please the king to grant my petition and fulfill my request, let the king and Haman come tomorrow, to the dinner which I will prepare for them, and tomorrow I will do as the king has said.

Bush and Bardtke, however, identify 5:7 as an *anacoluthon* (a sentence that breaks off and begins anew without syntactical or logical completion), in line with the reading of the new JPS translation:

> "My wish," replied Esther, "my request… if Your Majesty will do me the favor, if it please Your Majesty to grant my wish and accede to my request—let Your Majesty and Haman come to the feast which I will prepare for them; and tomorrow I will do Your Majesty's bidding."

For these commentators, the strategy of reading v.7 as an anacoluthon is apparent. According to the reading of the RSV, the term "my petition and my request" bears contradictory meanings in the two verses. In v.7, her "petition and request" is that they attend the second banquet. In v. 8, however, her petition and request is that secret which she is yet hiding, and promises to reveal on the morrow. According to Bush and the JPS translation, however, the term bears a single consistent meaning. In v. 7, Esther begins to enunciate the words, "My petition," "my request" and intends to make her great disclosure. Alas, however, she is overwhelmed by the enormity of the task, and is unable to rise to it. She stammers, and instead invites them to a second banquet a day later, at which time, she assures the king, she will reveal her petition and her request.[51]

While we have adopted Bush's proposition that 5:7 should be read as anacoluthon, the meaning that we have ascribed to the passage is not dependent on that reading. We may assume that verse is to be read as the RSV proposes, namely that the verse represents a fully articulated introduction of her desire that they both attend a second drinking party on the morrow. Within this reading, however, we need not adopt the position that this was done as part of a fully deliberate plan which Esther had had in mind from the moment she entered the throne chamber on the first day. We may read 5:7 as a fully articulated

---

[51] See Bush (*Ruth, Esther,* 405) and Bardtke (*Das Buch Esther,* 339) for alternative approaches as to the meaning of the anacoluthon.

sentence and still ascribe to it reticence. When asked by the king to
state her petition and request, Esther fails to summon the courage and
self-esteem necessary to divulge the whole truth and so, instead, invites
them to the second party in a composed and articulate fashion. To
summarize, the difference between a reading of 5:7 as anacoluthon
and full sentence is only one of degree. If the verse is interpreted as
anacoluthon, then Esther's hesitation overcomes her only at the very
last moment. Fully intending to state her appeal, she literally chokes
as the words come out of her mouth. If the reading of a full-sentence
is preferred, then the hesitation is a less jolting one, one that Esther
has recognized before she begins to speak. Either way, Esther here
has failed to seize the moment and make her appeal while the king is
receptive and with Haman present for the kill. Either way, a setback
has been suffered.

She had thus far taken five constructive steps in reclaiming her
subjectivity and self-image. She had resigned herself to carry out
Mordecai's bidding, and had verbally committed herself to him to do
so. She then won the approval and legitimization of the maidens, as
they joined her in her arduous fast. She further mustered the temerity
to cross the threshold of the inner chamber and win the king's grace.
From there, she verbally asserted her subjectivity and made an initial
request of him. Finally, she maneuvered events in such a way that the
party would transpire at a location of her choosing, further neutralizing
to some extent the sense of abject Otherness that had once been the
signature of her disposition toward the king.

Yet, at the same time that Esther has sustained growth, she has all
the while maintained her outer role as the consummate Other. She
dons royal garb to show her fealty to the king; she touches the head of
the scepter in deference and submission. She invites him in a gesture
whose ostensible purpose is to demonstrate her esteem and veneration
for him. The modalities of behavior, her conception of self, of the "old
Esther"—the consummate Other—suddenly loom large indeed as she
stands before the king face to face. The entire passage, therefore, finds
Esther in a stage of "passing," and passing is a double-edged sword.
On the one hand, as mentioned before, it allows the individual the
opportunity to absorb and manage a new identity, while maintaining
the outward modalities of the old one and thus avoid external conflict.
On the other hand, however, passing engenders tremendous internal
conflict, as the individual experiences cognitive dissonance, that feel-

ings and behavior are not consistent with self-definition.[52] Esther in 5:7-8 is in a state of crisis. Hers is the dissonance of being outwardly "in" and inwardly "out."

Esther 7: The Failure of Esther's Disclosure

Esther's disclosure would seem to mark a clear victory on a number of scores. The divulgence of her identity and her appeal are highpoints in the emergence of her self-esteem. Haman's execution marks a clear victory in her crusade to save her people. Nonetheless, in terms of the dynamics of how one expresses Jewish identity in the Persian court, the narrative of chapter 7 points to at least as many failures—on the personal and public fronts—as achievements.

I begin my analysis of the chapter with what is *not* written. Note how the argument from Mordecai's heroics is conspicuously absent from Esther's appeal. Esther could have said, "See! The Jews are loyal citizens—they are the *most* loyal citizens!" She realizes, however, that the key to her success here will be to play the card that she has played all along: the card of the consummate Other. "If I have found favor in your sight, O king, and if it please the king, let my life be given me at my petition, and my people at my request" (RSV). Indeed, not only does Esther cast herself as the Other woman, but also the Jewish people by extension become the Other nation; they are not referred to by name, but merely as an extension of her. If they will be spared, it is because she is the king's consummate Other.[53] Her people, she claims in collective self-deprecation, have no great worth. Had the decree been a sentence of forced labor, she wouldn't have troubled the king.

Tactically, all this may have been wise, and even necessary. But there are also implications of this strategy for Esther's emerging self-image as a Jew. Even at the moment of her great disclosure, Esther does not say, "I am Jewish." Only after she responds to the king's query in 7:5 as to the identity of the perpetrator does she indicate her identity, and this only obliquely, by implicating Haman, but not by labeling herself as Jewish.[54] The Jews, as a named, identifiable

---

[52] B.M. Dank, "Coming Out in the Gay World," *Psychiatry* 34 (1971) 192.

[53] Cf. Berlin, *Esther*, 66.

[54] This, in spite of the fact that she already knew Haman to be a semi-vanquished foe. The textual basis for this presupposition is found later on, in 8:1, when Mor-

people, in fact, go entirely unmentioned.[55] Thus, Esther grows in her subjectivity: for the first time, she makes a plea that has nothing to do with honoring the throne (as was ostensibly the case with the banquets), but is exclusively expressive of her own agenda. Conversely and paradoxically, however, Esther achieves this by accentuating her status as object.

Beal has effectively summed up the status of Esther's self-concept as Jew following the disclosure. While she has disclosed her Jewishness, she does not return—neither here nor at any point throughout the rest of the story—to a state of being solely Jewish,[56] or, I would add, fully Jewish. This, says Beal, is evident in the epithets given the main protagonists. Whenever Esther and Mordecai are mentioned together, they are set apart by their appellations. Mordecai is always Mordecai "the Jew," Esther, "the king's wife" (8:7, 9:29, 31). Dank has written, concerning the process of coming out, that the public expression of identity disclosure signifies to the individual the end of the identity search.[57] Yet, even following disclosure, Esther is neither fully Persian nor fully Jewish, for she has made her disclosure in half-hearted fashion. As Lewin has written, minority members suffer loss of self-esteem not because they belong to two identities, but out of an *uncertainty* of "belongingness."[58]

She is now the "outed" Jew, who in her behavior and mentality remains the consummate Other. The challenge now facing her is shifted. The question is no longer "Will she tell, or won't she?"; "Will she appeal on behalf of her people, or won't she?" The question that now confronts our analysis of Esther's character is a subtler one. What role will her newly revealed Jewishness play in her overall persona? Alternatively, to borrow a contemporary idiom, the question may be phrased, will the necklace bearing her Star of David rest prominently over her royal garb, or will it be tucked away underneath, for no one to see, except when necessary?

---

decai presents himself before the king, "for Esther had revealed how he was related to her." The king is introduced to Mordecai in light of his heroic deeds, and is at least familiar with his name. Esther merely fills in the still hidden details, that they are, in fact, cousins. This episode transpires on the same day as the second banquet and thus implies that already at the banquet Esther was aware of Mordecai's rise and Haman's fall.

[55] Berlin, *Esther*, 66.
[56] Beal, *Book of Hiding*, 100.
[57] Dank, "Coming Out," 190.
[58] Lewin, *Resolving Social Conflict*, 179.

The ensuing events of chapter 7 offer Esther no secure setting in which to work out these tensions. As many commentators have pointed out, while her life has been spared, the king has yet to say a word that would indicate that he intends to revoke the decree; indeed, he has not related to the decree at all.

This brings us to the first three verses of chapter 8. It is now—and only now—that Esther reaches for "the Mordecai card," and makes the introduction. The reasons are clear. She has played her best hand, her status as consummate Other in her appeal of 7:1-3, and has come up short; she is redeemed but not a word has been said of her people. In fact, as Levenson points out, the king has even taken measures beyond those she requested, but they are not the ones that Esther stipulated. She requested clemency for her people. The king, however, chooses to bestow special favors as he sees fit. To Esther, he gives Haman's estate (8:1).[59] It is precisely now that she subtly introduces Mordecai; perhaps the king will see the two of them as representative: if both Esther and Mordecai are Jews, then perhaps the Jews aren't so demonic after all. The introduction of Mordecai to the king is not carried out in a spirit of celebration, a happy denouement. Rather, it is a tactical ploy initiated by Esther under the duress that will spill out into the open in her plea of hysteria in 8:3.

But the hoped-for gesture never comes. The king never translates his affinity for Esther the (new) Jew and Mordecai the (well-known and trusty) Jew into a generalization about the Jews as a whole and the decree to annihilate them. Instead, the king deals with them solely on an individual basis. Having spared Esther, he now grants Mordecai the ring taken from Haman, signifying the transfer of high office.

In their study of coming out, Weinberg and Williams identify a crucial distinction in the process of disclosing a stigmatized identity: the distinction between *mere tolerance* on the one hand, and *genuine acceptance* on the other. Genuine acceptance will correlate with a stronger self-concept and induce individuals to freely label themselves in terms of the disclosed identity, in light of their acceptance.[60] In the narrative of Esther 7:1-8:2, Esther and Mordecai have been saved. Still, the question looms large, particularly for Esther: has she been merely tolerated as a Jew or genuinely accepted? The king's total obliviousness to the

---

[59] Levenson, *Esther*, 107.
[60] M.S. Weinberg and C.J. Williams, *Male Homosexuals: Their Problems and Adaptations* (New York: Penguin, 1974) 155.

plight of the doomed Jews suggests for Esther that her Jewishness has
been overlooked, excused, but not more than that. Perhaps the king
perceives a hierarchy of Jews. Jews are a threat, as Haman claimed.
But then there are some good Jews, like Esther and Mordecai: Jews
by descent who nonetheless display fealty to the throne and hence
demonstrate behavior not typologically "Jewish." Esther can only
conclude, then, that she has been merely tolerated. It should be of
no surprise to us, as we begin the next episode at 8:3, that we see
Esther rushing headlong back to her posture as consummate Other
in order to save her people.

Esther 8: Esther's Misconception of Her Otherness

Esther's plea to the king at this point is without rival in terms of its
expressions of Otherness. In previous appeals she uses a maximum
of two introductory supplications; here, crying and stumbling, she
uses four (8:3-5 RSV):
  1)   if it please the king,
  2)   and if I have found favor in his sight,
  3)   and if the thing seem right before the king,
  4)   and I be pleasing in his eyes

She concludes in singular fashion, linking her request to the king's
desire, or, care for her: *and I be pleasing in his eyes*.[61] They will be spared,
assumes Esther, only if the king deems it pitiful for his prized object
to have to witness the obliteration of her people and her kindred.

The king's response in 8:7 is dramatic both in terms of the psycho-
dynamics of Esther's Otherness and in terms of the process of reading
and interpreting Esther. Thus far, the king has done much but in a
fashion that has been consistently open to multiple interpretation. Here,
the king will explain in his own words the actions that he has taken.
His statement will enable us to discern retroactively whether Esther
correctly interpreted his behavior thus far, or not. The construction
of the verse is critical, and is quoted in full:

> Then King Ahasuerus said to Queen Esther and Mordecai the Jew, "I
> have given Haman's property to Esther, and he has been impaled on
> the stake for scheming against the Jews."

---

[61] Moore, *Esther*, 78; Bush, *Ruth, Esther*, 445.

Notice, first, to *whom* the king addresses himself. Esther had thrown herself down in tears and had based her supplication on her status as consummate Other. When the king addresses Esther *and* Mordecai *the Jew*, jointly, it is a sign that, perhaps, both Esther and we as readers who have perceived the action through her eyes have misinterpreted the king's initiatives in chapter 7. His address to both Esther and Mordecai attests to the fact that he recognizes Esther not only because of her status as consummate Other. He addresses them as the joint protagonists of the Jews, as he goes on to say in the next verse, "And you (pl.!) may further write with regard to the Jews as you see fit." Moreover, the steps already taken that he enumerates and their order are highly significant. From Esther's perspective, the most significant move taken by the king has been that he has spared her life. Yet the king does not even mention this in his list of activities on their behalf. This suggests that the king never contemplated considering Esther as marked for annihilation. He therefore, does not mention it within his list of graces to the Jewish people. Instead, he mentions the supererogatory step taken to transfer Haman's estate to Esther's possession. Finally, and most essentially, we derive from the king's own comments the reason he had Haman impaled. Haman was impaled because he schemed against—not "her people and her kindred"—but against "*the Jews*." The delayed revelation of the king's inner thoughts is stunning and poignantly underscores the poetics employed by the scroll. Narrative perspective in Esther has taken us through the scroll with Esther's eyes, and with Esther's psyche. Esther has moved from step to step with a deep-seated sense of Otherness and attendant lack of self-concept as a subjective being and as a Jew. All of her attempts to assert her own subjectivity, agenda and transcendence are fraught with tension for her. Finally, here in chapter 8, a mask has been removed and it is the *king's*. We didn't recognize his true face because we beheld it through the eyes of an object, denied her own identity.

What is striking about the sudden realization that it is, colloquially speaking, "cool to be Jewish" in Ahasuerus' kingdom, is what becomes of Esther in the remainder of this chapter. The king mandates both Esther and Mordecai to compose royal communiqués (8:8). Only Mordecai, however, participates in this effort (8:9).[62] As the com-

---

[62] Thus, we may challenge Berlin's contention (*Esther*, 75) that "it is they who author the proclamation that will save the Jews." *They* were commissioned, but only *he* took initiative.

muniqués begin to disseminate, Mordecai triumphantly exits to the streets of Shushan. Esther, we would expect, should join him in what could be described in contemporary terms as Mordecai's ticker-tape parade, yet Esther is strangely absent here as well.

Nothing, however, is strange at all about Esther's absence in these roles. Nowhere in the scroll (to this point) is Esther ever seen outside of the palace, or in communication with the wider public outside the palace.[63] Esther, it would seem, is absorbed in Otherness; her vision of self is, and still remains, an object of the king. Mordecai carries no such baggage. When the king issues ordinances that nearly celebrate the public legitimacy of Jews and Judaism, Mordecai comfortably maximizes the opportunity. Esther, however, is reluctant to flaunt her Jewishness, lest she be perceived as retreating from her commitment to her role as consummate Other. Mordecai the Jew is the hero of "Salute to the Jews Day" in 8:15; Esther the king's wife cannot even allow herself to attend.

At this juncture in the narrative a new set of circumstances has emerged: Jews and Judaism are not only merely tolerated as we may have suspected in chapter 7. Nor are they even genuinely accepted. They are held in awe (8:17). The question that still remains is this: can a Jew who has over many years adopted a pronounced posture of otherness vis-à-vis the dominant culture, now shift gears? To return to an earlier idiom, will Esther ever wear her Star of David with public pride or, will she recede into the familiar stance of Otherness now that a crisis has been averted? This is the tension that awaits the reader in the ninth chapter of the Scroll of Esther.

In the discussion to this point, I have attempted to outline what I believe to be the development of a major theme within the scroll of Esther: the innate connection between Esther's emerging subjectivity and the development of her self-image as a Jew across the entire narrative. I have done so in great detail because I believe that the narrative analogy between the battle report of chapter 9 and the feasting narrative of chapter 5 that I shall now proceed to develop plays upon this very issue.

---

[63] This includes her call for the Jews to fast in 4:16. Unlike every other public call in the scroll, Esther's call is never written down, lest her cover be blown. Rather, as the verse itself suggests, Esther told Mordecai that he should initiate and promulgate the fast on her behalf. As far as the public knew, this was Mordecai's call for fasting, and not a directive from Esther: "Go, assemble all the Jews... and Mordecai went about and did just as Esther had commanded *him*." *Him* and not *them*.

The Second Day of Fighting and the Second Day of Feasting:
A Narrative Analogy

We next encounter Esther at the interval between the first and
second day of fighting in 9:12-13. In v. 12 the king invites Esther to
express her additional desires following the news of the Jews' success
in the fortress of Shushan. The king, and only the king, learns of
the casualty figures in Shushan. Esther's deferential posture seems to
this point maintained, as she learns of what has transpired through
him. Following his report, the king asks a rhetorical question, "how
much more have they done in the rest of the provinces?" On the
level of plot advancement, the question signals to Esther that the king
is quite comfortable with what the Jews have done—"the king has
joined the Jews' cheering section," as Berlin writes[64]—and this will
embolden her to make her request. The king's question, however,
represents a delicate play of poetics in the structure of the narrative.
The answer to the question, "in Shushan they have killed 500, how
much then have they killed in the provinces?" has a definite answer:
75,000. That answer, however, is revealed only in the summary of
the battles, following the events of the second day, in v. 16. That
figure could well have appeared as a concluding comment to the
detail of what transpired in the provinces, perhaps at the end of v.
5. When the king asks, "in Shushan they have killed 500, how much
then have they killed in the provinces?" the reader is given no extra
vantage-point over the story's internal characters, Esther and the
king. Had the casualty figure appeared, say in v. 5, all of the tension
would have dissipated from the story, and the events of the second
day would have seemed as little more than a footnote. By deferring
the detail of the casualty figure to the end of the account, the narrator has maintained tension in the story. We, like the king and like
Esther, can only imagine what is happening across the width and
breadth of the 127 provinces. By delaying the report of the casualty
figure, the narrator still leaves us within the momentum of the story.
The second day will not be a footnote to the first, but rather will
attain a significance of its own. That significance, however, is not in
the battlefield results but rather in the decisions taken by Esther that
engendered them and what those decisions signify.

Esther's response reveals a figure who has begun to blossom into

---

[64] Berlin, *Esther*, 86.

full subjectivity. Esther makes two requests: that the Jews be granted
another day to pursue their enemies within the city of Shushan, and
second, that the (already executed) sons of Haman be publicly impaled.
Beal has astutely noted that, "execution is not so much concerned with
death but with the publication of death, including a public claim of
responsibility for that death."[65] Esther's double request manifests and
reveals a pro-active confidence in her dealings with the king that we
have yet to encounter in her. The spirit that comes through in the
content of her request is mirrored by the language that she chooses.
Her only introductory plea is, "If it please your Majesty," which is
used by every character in the scroll when addressing the king (1:
19; 3:9; 5:4, 8; 7:3; 8:5, 9:13). Absent here are any of the distinct
terms of Otherness that have permeated her dialogue with the king
throughout the story (cf. 5:2, 8; 7:3; 8:5). No more does Esther cast
herself as a voyeuristic image of the male ogle.[66] Esther has evolved
into her essential, subjective self. And, as we have claimed throughout, subjectivity for Esther in the scroll is equated with a positive
self-concept of Jewishness. Previously, Esther allowed herself to refer
to the Jews only as extensions of her Otherness vis-à-vis the king. No
longer appealing on behalf of "her people" or "her kindred," she now
accords them an essential identity within her palace discourse as *the
Jews* of Shushan.

At this point I would like to arrive, finally, at the purpose of this
chapter for our study of the biblical battle report. I would like to
demonstrate the manner in which the second day of fighting and the
second day of feasting in chapter 5 stand in relation to one another as
narrative analogies. On the first day of feasting the king asked, "What
is your wish? It shall be granted you. And what is your request? Even
to half the kingdom, it shall be fulfilled" (5:6). On the first day of fighting, he asks similarly, "What is your wish now? It shall be granted
you. And what else is your request? It shall be fulfilled" (9:12). In each
instance, Esther asks that the next day (מחר) witness a repetition of
the events of the first. In chapter 5 she asks that the king and Haman
again the next day (מחר) attend a drinking party that she will make
for them, and in chapter 9 she asks that again the next day (מחר) the
Jews be allowed to take revenge on their enemies.

Sternberg notes that repetition can function as "an index of a

[65] Beal, *Esther*, 113.
[66] Bach, *Women and Seduction*, 199.

change in the state of affairs."[67] Modifying that statement slightly, I would claim that in the present instance the repetitions of form, as witnessed between the second day of feasting and of fighting, function as an index of change in the state of Esther's self-concept. The similarities in form displayed highlight the contrastive differences in the valence of the formal elements. The same word, "tomorrow," conveys vastly different inferences about Esther's self-image in each. Esther's call to repeat the action of the first day for a second time, is likewise reflective of the transformation that she has undergone in the interval between the two passages. In chapter 5, the king's query, "What is your wish? It shall be granted you. And what is your request? Even to half the kingdom, it shall be fulfilled" (5:6), should have been met by an Esther ready to capitalize upon the ideal confluence of circumstances. With the king nearly begging for a second time to do her bidding, and with Haman standing right there, Esther could not have asked for a more perfect opportunity to assert her agenda and save her people. Ensconced however, in Otherness, marginalized and emptied of her own sense of transcendent self, Esther instead fails to seize the opportunity. Her call for a repetition of the event of the first day, namely to re-stage an event that honors the king demonstrates her inability to engage the king except as an othered, inessential being. The postponement of her true request represents the squandering of an opportunity, a procrastination born of inferiority, with no certainty that circumstances will present themselves again. Esther loves "tomorrow," to corruptly paraphrase Little Orphan Annie, because tomorrow is a whole, entire day away.

The contrast with the battle narrative of chapter 9 could not be greater. When Esther responds to the king's query, "What is your wish? It shall be granted you. And what is your request more, it shall be fulfilled," she seizes the moment. The repetition of the events of the first day will endow the Jews with an even more heightened status of honor and dominion. Esther has blossomed into full subjectivity and affirmation of her essential, Jewish self. Esther loves "tomorrow," to again corrupt Little Orphan Annie, because the heady developments tomorrow will bring, are *only* a day away.[68]

---

[67] Sternberg, *Poetics*, 438.

[68] Many scholars have noted the extensive use of doubling in syntax, language, motif, and structure throughout the scroll, in a manner more prevalent than in other biblical narratives. See Athalya Brenner, "Looking at Esther Through the Looking Glass," in Athalya Brenner (ed.), *A Feminist Companion to Esther, Judith, Susanna* (Shef-

I offer one final comment on the role of the word "tomorrow" in each of the two passages, and that concerns the contrastive positioning of the word within the syntax of each passage. In 5:8, the word "tomorrow" is situated at the end of Esther's request:

> If Your majesty will do me the favor, if it please Your Majesty to grant my wish and accede to my request—let Your Majesty and Haman come to the feast which I will prepare for them; *and tomorrow I will do Your Majesty's bidding.*

Embarrassed by the importuning nature of her deferral, Esther attempts to redeem the postponement in the king's eyes, by embedding the notice of the delay in the part of the response likely to please the king most. Tomorrow is not expressed at the beginning of the verse, in conjunction with her desire for them to conform to her wish and attend the second party. Tomorrow, rather, is expressed at the end of the verse, when she communicates the hour at which she will dutifully do the king's bidding. In 9:13, however, the words "Also tomorrow" (גם למחר) are the very first words she utters in responding to the king's invitation. The words so embody the full statement of what she requests, that their force almost would allow them to stand on their own. "Tomorrow" in chapter 9 calls forth no apology. "Tomorrow" is seized with impunity. The victories in the city of Shushan are matched by Esther's personal victory in the assertion of her essential, Jewish self, in the presence of the king.

The Metaphor of Fighting and of Feasting

In our introduction we drew attention to the distinction between a standard narrative analogy and a specific subset of narrative analogy to be the focus of this study—the metaphor analogy. The examples of narrative analogy cited in this study thus far have all been illustrations of this convention, the metaphor plot. Joshua 7 depicted the trial of Achan, while Joshua 8, the conquest of Ha-Ai. The analogous relationship of the stories was essentially metaphoric. We claimed that through the establishment of an equivalence plot between the two narratives, we could effectively refer to Joshua 7, not only as the *trial* of Achan, but indeed as the *conquest* of Achan. The same metaphoric

---

field: Sheffield Academic Press, 1995) 71; Greenstein, "A Jewish Reading," 237-38; Levenson, *Esther*, 6-10.

quality was true of the other two battle stories that we have probed until now. In Judges 19-20 we were able to speak of the "Rape of Binyamin," while in Judges 11 we interpreted the importunity of Israel vis-à-vis Jephthah as a metaphor for Israel's importuning behavior vis-à-vis God in Judges 10.

May we rightly term the narrative analogy between the second day of feasting and second day of fighting a metaphor analogy? The examination carried out thus far would suggest not. It would seem that the narrative analogy at hand is one of common subject matter. In both instances the king asks Esther to state her request, and in each instance she asks for a repetition of the day's activity on the morrow. The analogy, as we suggested, is drawn as an index of the change in Esther's character. Nevertheless, I would like to examine the material under study from a different angle and consider the possibility that the analogous elements between the fighting of chapter 9 and the feasting of chapter 5 do, in fact, stand in metaphoric relationship, and may be properly termed as metaphor plots.

To do so, I would like to first inspect the evidence that the drinking of wine and massacre by the sword stand in metaphoric relationship to one another across the Bible. The evidence suggesting this relationship is both explicit and widespread. Thus we find in Jeremiah:

> For thus said the Lord, the God of Israel to me: 'Take from My hand this cup of wine—of wrath[69]—and make all the nations to whom I send you drink of it. Let them drink and wretch and act crazy, because of the sword which I am sending among them.' (25:15-16).
> And if they refuse to take the cup from your hand and drink, say to them, 'Thus said the Lord of Hosts: You must drink!... I am summoning the sword against all the inhabitants of the earth—declares the Lord of Hosts.' (25:28-29).

Elsewhere, Jeremiah refers to impending destruction as jars full of wine (13:12-14); the destructive force of Babylon is referred to as her wine (51:7). God causes the Babylonian kings to drink at their drinking parties (משתיהם) to the point that they are easily slaughtered (51:39).

The Psalmist also saw wine as a metaphor for devastation by the sword. Referring to military defeat, he writes:

> You have made Your people suffer hardship; You have given us wine that makes us reel (60:5).

---

[69] Some read here יין חמר as a variant of יין חמה. For discussion, see Robert P. Carroll, *The Book of Jeremiah* (OTL; Philadelphia: Westminster Press, 1986) 498-99.

Elsewhere, we likewise find wine as an image of punishment for the wicked:

> There is a cup in the Lord's hand with foaming wine fully mixed;
> From this He pours; all the wicked of the earth drink, draining it to
> the very dregs (75:9).

Elsewhere, the drinking of intoxicating beverages is similarly equated with desolation by sword (Isa 51:17-19; Ezek 23:32; Obad 16; Hab 2:16).

I would like to suggest that the biblical metaphoric equivalence between the cup of wine and destruction is implicit in the feasting narratives of chapters 5-7. Noting that Esther draws from many other biblical texts, such as the Joseph narratives, Samuel, Deuteronomy and the Wisdom Literature, Beal has understood Esther to be contextualized within the dialogical space of canonical Scripture.[70] That Esther would employ an oft-found metaphor and draw a metaphoric association between wine and sword, then, is in keeping with the author's eclectic engagement of terminology and imagery found elsewhere in the Hebrew Bible.

On one level the drinking parties accentuate Esther's impoverished self-concept as Other. They honor and glorify the guests of honor, the king and Haman, and as regards Esther, these parties underscore that she is not yet up to the task. The biblical metaphor connecting drinking wine and suffering death offers a counter-valence to the meaning of the wine consumed in chapter 5, and at the second banquet itself in chapter 7 (RSV 7:2—"And on the second day, *as they were drinking wine*, the king again said to Esther, 'What is your petition…'"). Even as Esther hesitates and stalls, her focus remains one: to maneuver Haman toward his own demise. The wine that she serves up, ostensibly for his honor, is in fact a trap through which to destroy him. Like the wine mentioned by the prophet, the wine that she serves the wicked is the wine of staggering, the wine that brings devastation.

The metaphor of the cup of wine as representative of destruction may shed further light on the narrative analogy between the two days of feasting in chapter 5 and the two days of fighting in chapter 9. To return to the elements of the narrative analogy that have been noted thus far, we may present our findings graphically:

---

[70] Beal, *Book of Hiding*, 117.

Esther 5	**Esther 9**
A one-day event (feasting)	A one-day event (fighting)
King queries during the event: "What is your request, and it shall be granted; what is your petition and it shall be fulfilled."	King queries during the event: "What is your request, and it shall be granted; what is your petition and it shall be fulfilled."
Esther asks for the event (feasting) to be repeated tomorrow	Esther asks for the event (fighting) to be repeated tomorrow

Note that this formulation of the analogy obscures the particulars of the event in each narrative. In order to cast feasting and fighting—highly dissimilar activities—as analogous elements, we had to define them abstractly, as events defined solely in terms of their chronology. They each emerge in the analogy, therefore, simply, as episodes initially conceived as one-day affairs (i.e. in ch. 5 the king initially thought he was going to attend one party, not two, while in ch. 9, the license to take revenge against their enemies was granted to the Jews for only a single day, the 13th of Adar), which are later repeated the next day as per Esther's request.

Thus far, I have referred to the analogous elements here as "fighting" and "feasting," admittedly, in part, to capitalize on the alliteration between them in the English language. If we wish to label each of the corresponding elements with a single semantic marker, we would be more correct to attend closely to the language of the text. Following this methodology, the terms "fighting" and "feasting" should rather be substituted with the terms "sword" and "wine," respectively. In chapter 9, Esther asked that the Jews be allowed to wield the *sword* as they did on the first day: "So the Jews struck at their enemies with the *sword*, slaying and destroying" (9:5). This is not to say, of course, that the Jews slay their enemy exclusively by use of swords. Rather, the word "sword," beyond its literal meaning, is also a semantic marker that encapsulates the entire narrative of destruction, generally.

Opposite the word 'sword" in the narrative analogy at hand, is the word "wine" as a referent to Esther's banquets. Both feasts are explicitly labeled "wine feasts" (5:6; 7:2). Haman's "happy and lighthearted" spirit (5:8) should not be seen solely as a result of the honorable invitation extended him. Rather, it should also be seen in combination with the drinking of wine that went on that day at the first banquet.[71] The eunuchs hurriedly bring Haman "to drink" with Queen Esther (6:14).

The proposed analogy between the sword of chapter 9 and the wine of chapter 5, underscores the meaning of the wine consumed in chapter 5. Even as Esther hesitates and stalls, the wine that she serves the wicked is the wine of staggering, the wine that brings devastation.

In summation, the narrative analogy between the second day of fighting and the second day of feasting, underscores the development of Esther's concept of self. It effectively contrasts a stage of intense inner struggle in chapter 5, and an episode that signals a pinnacle in the search for a secure, assertive identity as a Jew and as a subjective being in chapter 9. The evidence that we see here of a metaphor plot, in which the analog stories stand in metaphoric association, is suggestive. That wine may serve as a metaphor for the sword is well-documented across many biblical texts. The analogy between fighting in chapter 9 and feasting in chapter 5 may serve to underscore that the wine feasts hosted by Esther can be understood as occasions at which the cup of wrath is served to the wicked Haman.

---

[71] Indeed, the term "lighthearted" (טוב לב) is used to connote intoxication even without express conjunction with the word wine. See Isa 65:13-14; 1 Sam 25:36.

CHAPTER SIX

THE BATTLE AT BAAL PERAZIM (1 CHR 14:8-12) AND THE ACCOUNT OF PEREZ UZZAH (1 CHR 13:1-14)

The final two case studies of this work examine battle stories from the Book of Chronicles. The contribution of these accounts to my thesis is twofold. The first is their contribution to the aggregate of accounts in which a battle report forms a metaphor plot of the story that precedes it. Two more such examples make the validity of the proposition that much stronger. Yet, these examples add a unique dimension to the documentation of my thesis precisely because they are drawn from the Book of Chronicles. The Chronicler's version of these two battle stories will be compared with the parallel versions found in the apparent *Vorlage* in Samuel-Kings. In each instance we will see that the version of the *Vorlage* does not reveal the battle story to be a metaphor plot of the preceding narrative and that in subtle ways the Chronicler has reworked the material by means of this convention as an overarching principle of design. In each instance we will highlight salient aspects of the version of the story found in the *Vorlage* and their rhetorical implications. We will then document the relevant differences in the Chronicler's version of the story and proceed to analyze closely that account and the new readings that it generates.

This chapter explores the intertextual relationship between two episodes within the ark narrative of 1 Chronicles 13-16: David's victory over the Philistines at Baal Perazim (1 Chr 14:8-12) and the unsuccessful attempt to bring the ark from Kiriath Jearim to Jerusalem and the debacle at Perez Uzzah (1 Chr 13:1-14). Both accounts are also found in 2 Samuel 5-6 where their order is the reverse. We will contend that it is only within the ark narrative of 1 Chronicles, however, that the battle account of Baal Perazim stands as a metaphor analogy to the account of Perez Uzzah.

Our study is executed in three stages. There are competing interpretations of the nature of the failing that led to the debacle of Perez Uzzah. These interpretations, in turn, bear upon the meaning of the interrelationship between the account of Perez Uzzah and that of Baal

Perzaim. Our first order of business, then, is to clarify the Chronicler's view of the deficiency that resulted in the debacle of Perez Uzzah. While the two accounts are arranged in close proximity, they comprise but two elements of the larger ark narrative of 1 Chronicles 13-16. Their interrelationship, then, should not be discussed in a vacuum but rather in terms of the meaning of the larger structure of the narrative unit. Before bringing the two pericopes into comparison, therefore, our second order of business will be to assess the organizing principles guiding the Chronicler's structure of the ark narrative. Finally, we will perform a close reading of the two pericopes, noting the Chronicler's reworking of the stories found in the *Vorlage*. We will interpret the evidence to suggest that the Chronicler reworked the material in a fashion that casts the story of David's victory at Baal Perazim as a contrastive metaphor analogy that parallels the account of the fiasco of Perez Uzzah.

Perez Uzzah: An Anatomy of the Failure

Sara Japhet has correctly noted that the Chronicler's account of the ark narrative witnesses a shift of onus for the debacle at Perez Uzzah from Uzzah to David.[1] The moment of failure in the first attempt to transport the ark is not solely at the moment that Uzzah touched the ark. His trespass represents only the final improper act of a string of missteps. David's self-incriminatory remarks in 1 Chronicles 15, as he prepared to transport the ark a second time, offer a view onto the chain of missteps:

> Because you (i.e. the Levites) were not there the first time, the Lord our God burst out against *us*, for *we* did not show due regard for Him... The Levites carried the ark of God by means of poles on their shoulders, as Moses had commanded in accordance with the word of the Lord (1 Chr 15:13-15).

It is now, and only now, in 1 Chronicles 15 that David turns to Levites to perform the task of the ark's transport. Whereas David acknowledges the Pentateuchal law that specifies that Levites should

---

[1] Sara Japhet, *The Ideology of the Book of Chronicles and Its Place in Biblical Thought* (Frankfurt: Peter Lang, 1989) 475.

transport the ark, those entrusted with the ark's transport originally, Uzzah and Ahio (1 Chr 13:7 = 2 Sam 6:4), were priests.[2] Moreover, whereas Pentateuchal law states that the ark was to be borne upon the shoulders, here, a cart was brought (1 Chr 13:7 = 2 Sam 6:3). David was undoubtedly aware of the decision to employ Uzzah and Ahio and the decision to draw the ark in a cart. Neither priest nor prophet censures David in the wake of the failed attempt, and David arrives at the remedy on his own (15:2). It is no surprise, then, that as he commissions the Levites in 1 Chr 15:13, he states that the onus of the debacle was not solely, or even primarily upon Uzzah, but, rather, "the Lord our God burst out against *us*, for *we* did not show due regard for Him."[3]

We note along with Japhet[4] that "for all that David is cast in a positive light in Chronicles, certain components of the portrayal suggest a figure who is far from ideal," and that "it cannot be said that the desire to praise the son of Jesse dominates the book as an all-embracing principle."[5] The Chronicler retains the episode of the census (1 Chronicles 21 = 2 Samuel 24) in which David is censured and severely punished through the plague that strikes Israel. Moreover, while the *Vorlage* account of 2 Samuel 7 is ambiguous about David's disqualification concerning the building of the Temple, the Chronicler is explicit: David is unfit to build the Temple because of the blood that he has shed (1 Chr 22:7-8). Fewer good kings are compared to David in Chronicles than are in Kings.[6] It is interesting to note that all three episodes in which the Chronicler finds fault with David highlight some aspect of cultic worship in Jerusalem. David is labeled a man of war in the context of his disqualification to build the Temple. The story of the census concludes with the revelation of the site of the Temple (1 Chr 21:24- 22:1). The present focus of study, the ark narrative, reveals a fault in David's handling of the transport of the ark. For all the veneration that the Chronicler displays toward David, the Chronicler remains

---

[2] Compare with 1 Sam 7:1, and see discussion in P. Kyle McCarter, *II Samuel* (AB 9; New York: Doubleday, 1984) 169. Indeed the inappropriateness of these two for the task is alluded to in their patronym: they are sons of Abinadav. Greenstein (Edward L. Greenstein, "Deconstruction and Biblical Narrative," *Prooftexts* 9 [1989] 62) has rightly claimed that the patronym is a conflate of the names Nadab and Abihu, earlier priests who also violated Temple protocol (Lev 10:1-7).

[3] Sara Japhet, *I & II Chronicles* (OTL; Louisville: Westminster, 1993) 301.

[4] Japhet, *The Ideology*, 473.

[5] Ibid., 478.

[6] Ibid., 477.

prepared to sacrifice David's reputation for the sake of conveying vital information concerning the Temple and proper worship there.

While the Chronicler's implication of David in the ark narrative of 1 Chronicles 13-16 is clear, what is less clear is the root of the fault: why did David fail to observe proper protocol in the first attempt? Japhet's claim[7] that David exhibited "carelessness" seems questionable in light of the enormous efforts expended by David to gather the whole of Israel for this momentous event. It seems untenable to claim, simply, that David never bothered to learn the proper procedure, or had known of it, only to allow his memory to lapse at the critical moment. If we assume that David was aware of these laws, the question we must ask, therefore, is this: can we posit a view of the ark that would have led David to ignore these laws, not out of "carelessness," but out of an ideological or motivational flaw? That some attitudinal error was at play is evident from David's self-incriminatory remarks: "for we did not seek it as ordained" (כי לא דרשנהו כמשפט). On one level David clearly refers to the procedural errors that were committed. Yet, as Japhet notes, the word דרשנהו bears a clear antecedent—1 Chr 13:3: "for we did not seek it (דרשנהו) in the days of Saul."[8] The failure in the time of Saul had no connection to the process of transporting the ark and was reflective of an errant attitude. In like fashion, therefore, we may see the debacle of Perez Uzzah as a failure in attitude as well.

The importance of proper attitude, of purity of intention, within the Chronicler's world-view should not be underestimated. Along with Rudolph,[9] Japhet cautions us against seeing the Chronicler as representative of legalistic religiosity.[10] Phrases such as "seeking God with all one's heart," or "setting one's heart" abound in Chronicles. Indeed, the root ד.ר.ש., through which David described his failure vis-à-vis the ark, appears six times in Chronicles as an action accompanied by some intent of the heart (1 Chr 28:9): "And you, my son Solomon, know the God of your father, and serve Him with single mind and fervent heart, for the Lord searches all minds and discerns the design of every thought; if you seek Him He will be available to you, but if you forsake Him He will abandon you forever" (cf. 2 Chr 12:14; 19: 3; 22:9; 30:19; 31:21). In at least one instance, improper inaction is

---

[7] Japhet, *I & II Chronicles*, 293.
[8] Ibid., 301.
[9] W. Rudolph, *Chronikbücher* (HAT; Tübingen: Mohr, 1955) 303.
[10] Japhet, *The Ideology*, 252.

accepted because it is redeemed by piety of the spirit: "For most of the people… had not cleansed themselves, yet they ate the paschal sacrifice in violation of what was written. Hezekiah prayed for them, saying, 'The good Lord will provide atonement for everyone who set his mind on worshipping God… even if he is not purified for the sanctuary.' The Lord heard Hezekiah and healed the people" (2 Chr 30:18-20). Proper and pure intent is presented in contradistinction to cultic norms.[11]

A close reading of David's initiative (1 Chr 13:1-5) is revealing. Long before the ark is loaded onto the wagon (v. 7), the Chronicler marks this initiative as a failure by using a distinctive semantic flags. In verse 2 David propositions the officers: "let us send far and wide (נפרצה נשלחה על אחינו) to our remaining kinsmen throughout the territories of Israel… to transfer the ark of Our God to us." The phrase "let us send far and wide" is a loaded one, in that it bears multiple echoes of the sin of Uzzah. The root of the word נפרצה is the root that dominates David's lament of Uzzah's fate (13:11), "because the Lord had burst out against Uzza (כי פרץ יהוה פרץ בעזא); and the place was named Perez-Uzzah" (ויקרא למקום ההוא פרץ עזא).

Moreover, as Galil and Garsiel have rightly asserted, the word נשלחה also represents a colored term within the context of the narrative of Perez Uzzah.[12] Uzzah extended his hand (וישלח את ידו) to touch the ark (v. 9), and God smote him on account of the fact that he had extended his hand (על אשר שלח ידו) (v. 10). In both, David's act of "sending" and Uzzah's act of "extending" Scripture's uniform choice of preposition is unusual. David proposes sending "'to' our remaining brethren," where the common preposition אל is replaced with על. Uzzah, likewise, is said to extend his hand "to" the ark (v. 10), where, again, the more common preposition אל is replaced with על. The usage of the root ש.ל.ח. is entirely conventional within each respective context, and hence not *prima facie* evidence of a basis to claim that this contributes to the analogical link. The Chronicler underscores the semantic association he creates between them by appending the less conventional preposition על to each action prior to the direct object.

---

[11] Ibid.. See a broader discussion on wholeheartedness in devotion in the thought of the Chronicler in idem., 247-65, and in Yehuda Kiel, *1 Chronicles* (Daat Miqra; Jerusalem: Mossad Harav Kook, 1986) 111-12 (Hebrew).

[12] Gershon Galil and Moshe Garsiel, et. al. (eds.), *The Book of First Chronicles* (Olam HaTanakh; Tel-Aviv: Davidson-Eti, 1995) 174 (Hebrew).

He negatively judges David's initiative by expressing it in terms that anticipate and foreshadow Uzzah's trespass.

This exercise in close reading suggests that even the initial decision to bring the ark was in some fashion tainted. This is surprising, for the very act of bringing the ark to Jerusalem is, in itself, a worthy undertaking: witness the conclusion of the narrative, with the bringing of the ark to Jerusalem in 1 Chronicles 16. Before pushing forward in the text of 1 Chronicles 13, I would like to develop a theological thesis concerning the ark that I believe can then be shown to suffuse the Chronicler's version of the two attempts to bring the ark to Jerusalem.

The theological point in question here is well-illustrated through another ark narrative—that of 1 Samuel 4.[13] There, the elders call for the ark to be brought to the battlefield in the effort against the Philistines (v. 3). To be sure, bringing the ark to the theater of battle is considered not only a legitimate action, but commonplace and normative (cf. Num 10:35; 2 Sam 11:11). It is an expression of God's commitment to the covenantal bond in Israel's hour of distress. Moreover, it serves as a reminder that wars are won only because God desires to grant Israel victory and not because of the military prowess of Israel's army. Nonetheless, as Fokkelman and others have aptly commented, in this particular instance the desire to bring the ark emerges as theologically tainted. Proper action is invalidated by improper intention. Although the elders correctly understood the defeat suffered to be divinely decreed (v. 3), no soul-searching takes place nor is God consulted via the oracle.[14] As Fokkelman expresses it, the elders maintain a flawed theology:

> As long as the ark reaches the troops [the elders believe] then all will be well. This is the magical organization of one's own certitude, a kind of superstition based on the metonymy that the owner can be replaced by his footstool… It is understandable that representatives of a chosen

---

[13] Since Rost's initial proposition (Leonhard Rost, *Die Überlieferung von der Thronnachfolge Davids* [Stuttgart: W. Kohlhammer, 1926]) of an independent ark narrative comprised of 1 Sam 4-7, and 2 Sam 5, an entire field of scholarship has emerged concerning the redactional history of these narratives and their interrelationship with the larger works within which they are found. For two recent studies, see John W. Wright, "The Founding Father: The Structure of the Chronicler's David Narrative," *JBL* 117:1 (1998) 45-59; A. Stirrup, "Why has Yahweh Defeated Us Today Before the Philistines? The Question of the Ark Narrative," *Tyndale Bulletin* 51:1 (2000) 81-100.

[14] J.P. Fokkelman, *Narrative Art and Poetry in the Books of Samuel. Vol. 4. Vow and Desire (1 Sam 1-12)* (Assen: Van Gorcum, 1993) 201.

people appeal to the covenant relationship, but this does not relieve them from behaving properly, and the covenant does not imply that mortals automatically have God's aid at their disposal. This would thoroughly disturb the balance and the mutuality of responsibilities and rights.[15]

Fokkelman's interpretation echoes earlier sentiments expressed on the episode of 1 Samuel 4 by Abarbanel:

> When the ark of the Covenant of the Lord arrived in the camp they cheered in exaltation as do victors, for they presumed that the covenant with God would surely provide them with salvation. They did not however, cry out to God nor did they return to Him. Rather, they presumed that the ark was a cameo (תחבולה) for victory in battle.[16]

Fokkelman marshals several semantic cues within the text to substantiate his argument. The cohortative נקחה, followed—not by the object, the ark—but with the predicate, אלינו, stresses their motivation to organize the ark in accordance with their own program, and to reap its beneficiary effects. Moreover, as Fokkelman points out, the subject of 3b is tenuously ambiguous. Who is it, or, what is it, that will "be present among us and will deliver us from the hands of our enemies"? The syntax of ויבוא בקרבנו following the object, ארון ברית יהוה leaves room to wonder whether the elders themselves are capable of distinguishing between God's presence as covenantal partner and savior, and the ark as a kind of magical cameo.[17] Garsiel[18] and Elitzur[19] maintain that the appellation, ארון ברית יהוה צבאות ישב הכרובים in v. 4 is an elaborate one to underscore the misperception of the ark as a cult-object that delivers guaranteed results.

In contemporary idiom, the form "x-abuse" is employed in refer-

---

[15] Ibid., 201-02.

[16] Don Isaac Abarbanel, *Commentary to Former Prophets* (Jerusalem, 1955) 192, at 1 Samuel 4:5. See in a similar vein, K.A.D. Smelik, "The Ark Narrative Reconsidered," in A.S. van der Woude (ed.), *New Avenues in the Study of the Old Testament* (Oudtestamentische Studiën 25; Leiden: Brill, 1989) 135-36 and 141, who decries the transformation of the ark into a "cult-object." The notion that the bringing of the ark was a proper action invalidated by improper intention has been widely accepted. See Yehuda Kiel *1 Samuel* (Jerusalem: Mossad Harav Kook, 1981) 48 (Hebrew); Shmuel Abramsky and Moshe Garsiel (eds.), *1 Samuel* (Olam HaTanakh; Tel-Aviv: Davidson-Eti, 1993) 66 (Hebrew); Moshe Zvi Segal, *The Books of Samuel* (Jerusalem: Kiryath Sefer, 1956) 45 (Hebrew); Yehuda Elitzur, "Eben-ha-Ezer," in E. Elinor, et. al (eds.), *Zeidel Memorial Volume: Essays in Biblical Studies* (Israel Society for Biblical Studies Publications 11; Jerusalem: Kiryath Sefer, 1962) 115-18 (Hebrew).

[17] Fokkleman, *Narrative Art*, 4: 202.

[18] Abramsky and Garsiel, *1 Samuel*, 66.

[19] Elitzur, "Eben-ha-Ezer," 116.

ence to a sentient being, as in "child-, spouse-, or, animal- abuse."
The violation of the ark's paramount purity, may, in similar fashion,
be seen in 1 Samuel 4 as an illustration of "ark-abuse." A somewhat
more muted form of "ark-abuse" is at the core of the ark narrative of 1
Chr 13-16. That something went wrong here is evidenced by David's
self-incriminatory remarks seen earlier, and by the series of missteps
that culminated in Uzzah's trespass. Perforce, we are beckoned to
identify a failing here. That the offense was less grievous than that of 1
Samuel 4 is evidenced by the outcome. It is true that Uzzah is struck
down and that David suffers a setback. Yet, this is an outcome far
less severe than the total defeat at the hand of the Philistines suffered
there and the loss of the ark. Therefore, we must identify a failing of
a subtler and less severe nature than the "ark-abuse" of rendering the
ark a mere "cult-object," as per the failing at Eben ha-Ezer.

For whose sake was the ark being relocated to Jerusalem? From
one standpoint the relocation of the ark may be said to be good for
God's image. His sovereignty is certainly more apparent when his
"footstool" rests in the capital of his chosen people, rather than in a
rural storehouse. Yet, the transfer of the ark to Jerusalem stands to
benefit other parties as well. The positioning of this pericope within
the narrative of David's rise is suggestive. Following the ascendance
narratives of 1 Chronicles 11-12, David's effort may be seen as a move
to consolidate his nascent coalition by engaging in a national effort to
solidify and centralize his regime through the transfer of the ark.[20] It
promises to bolster David's standing in the eyes of the people. It stands
to cement Jerusalem's status as a capital city, as it now will become the
cultic as well as national center of the country. God's presence in the
midst of the new capital of Israel proffers greater divine providence.
All of these attendant benefits—for God's image, for David and for
Israel—are implicit in the ark's relocation, without distinction. Yet, the
motivation and intent of the individual who initiates this endeavor must
express the clearest distinction. The endeavor to move the ark must be
undertaken with a primary sense of the glory of God being brought
to its rightful place. If the ark is moved without an appropriate sense
of its transcendence and with an excessive eye toward what it means
for the sovereign who moves it, or what it means for the stature of

---

[20] Mordechai Cogan, "Royal City and Temple City: The History of Jerusalem
From David to Josiah," in Shmuel Ahituv, Amihai Mazar (eds.), *The History of Jerusalem:
The Biblical Period* (Jerusalem: Yad Ben-Zvi Press, 2000) 72 (in Hebrew).

the city that receives it, then—as in the narrative of 1 Samuel 4—the ark will have been abused.

A contemporary socio-religious example will serve to elucidate the point. The Code of Jewish Law (*Shulḥan ʿArukh*) specifies the criteria desired for a man to lead Jewish prayer services on behalf of the congregation.[21] The person appointed, particularly on occasions such as the High-Holy Days, bears a great responsibility, and must see himself humbly, solely as a representative of the people before God. At the same time his choice confers great honor, for it publicly signals that the nominating body felt him worthy of such a responsibility. If such a person is nominated several years running and begins to see this honor as his right, or if he leads services in accordance with own tastes rather than out of a sensitivity for the congregation's tastes, then he will have abused his privilege. These would be grievous offenses. Yet even if the nominee performs his task to the full satisfaction of his congregation, his endeavor is undermined if he dwells upon the esteem afforded him by the nomination. Moving the ark poses such an attitudinal tightrope for David. To move the ark is a worthy task, for all the reasons enumerated above. Yet in it there is an inherent danger—the danger that David will too strongly sense his own interests as a young king in the success of the endeavor.

We proceed now to investigate the terms of discourse employed within the narratives of the two attempts to relocate the ark. In the following argument I shall contend that in the account of the first attempt to transfer the ark the language of discourse reveals that David's motivation to transfer the ark was tainted with undue self-interest. While ostensibly looking to honor God and His ark, David imbues the transfer with an undue intimacy with the ark, and a keen, yet, inappropriate sense of the attendant benefits for himself and for Israel. By contrast, the account of the second attempt to transfer the ark reveals a language of discourse in which the ark's transcendence is properly respected, and in which the motivation to relocate the ark is entirely for the sake of God. The examination is carried out via a comparison along several semantic fault lines that distinguish the two accounts. It should be noted that by and large, these differences have not been noted in the critical literature to Chronicles.

The terminus of the ark's journey. Note the language used to describe the place to which the ark is to be taken. In chapter 15 the charac-

---

[21] R. Joseph Karo, *Shulḥan ʿArukh, Oraḥ Ḥayyim*, Section 53.

terization of the ark's terminus takes is identified only with reference
to the ark itself. Thus, in 15:1 we read that David "prepared a place
for the ark of God, and pitched a tent *for it*." The "place" is for "the ark
of God"; the "tent" pitched, is pitched "for it." See, in like spirit, 15:
3: "David assembled all Israel in Jerusalem to bring up the ark of the
Lord to *its place*, which he had prepared *for it*." The same formulation is seen once again in 15:12: "bring up the ark of the Lord God
of Israel to [the place] I have prepared *for it*." This stands in contrast
with the terms of discourse used when David first proclaims the idea
in the first narrative (1 Chr 13:2-3): "let us send far and wide... that
they should gather together to us to transfer the ark of our God *to
us*. Not to "Jerusalem," not to "its place." Indeed, it would seem that
(in contrast to his second attempt) David made no efforts to fashion a
repository "for it" in advance of its arrival. The ark's terminus, instead,
is expressed by David in self-referential terms. It is to be brought "to
us." The attention to the ramifications of the ark's relocation for David
are likewise heard in his frustration following the death of Uzzah (1 Chr
13:12-13): "How can I bring[22] the ark of God *to me*? So David did not
transfer the ark *toward him*, to the City of *David*." The doubled clause at
the end of the verse and, particularly, the appellation "City of David"
are employed here in place of the suppressed name "Jerusalem."[23] It is
worthy of note that in the entire Bible, the complement "to us" (אלינו)
as a terminus for the transport of the ark, occurs exactly twice. Once
in the ark narrative of 1 Samuel 4 referred to above when the elders
call for the ark to be brought to the battlefield (v. 3—נקחה אלינו),
and again here, in the abortive attempt to bring the ark to Jerusalem.
The Chronicler does not include the narrative of 1 Samuel 4 in his
composition. Nonetheless, it would appear that David's call to bring
the ark "to us" is cast in terms distinctly reminiscent of the debacle
of 1 Samuel 4, to further mark the attempt here as shot through with
improper motivations of self-interest and insufficient attention to the
ark's transcendence.

In this vein, it is interesting to see what becomes of the term "the
City of David" in 1 Chronicles 15. 2 Sam 6:12 states that the ark

---

[22] In place of, "How can I bring the ark," the *Vorlage* reads (2 Sam 6:9), "How
will the ark of the Lord come to me?" By stating David's exasperation in the active
form, the Chronicler underscores the dissonance between God's intervention and
David's desire to steer events in accord with his own program.

[23] cf. Fokkelman, *Narrative Art*, 3:190.

was taken "from the house of Obed-Edom to the City of David."
The parallel verse in Chronicles, however (1 Chr 15:25) omits the
terminus, "to the City of David," so as not to underscore the point
rejected in 1 Chronicles 13: the notion that the ark is being brought
for David's sake.[24]

The appellations ascribed to the ark. Throughout the Bible and in both
versions of this story as well, the ark is given several commonplace
appellations.[25] In the most simple form, it is called "the ark" (e.g. 13:
9, 10; 15:23). In most instances, it is referred to as "the ark of the
Lord" (e.g. 13:12, 13, 15:1, 2, 15, 24), or the ark of Yahweh (e.g.15:2,
3, 12). Of all of the 21 occurrences of the word "ark" in 1 Chronicles
13-16, two in particular stand out. The most elaborate name is that
ascribed to the ark as it is being (illicitly!) packed onto the wagon,
in 13:6: "the ark of God, the Lord, Enthroned on the Cherubim, to
which the Name was attached." The elaboration of the name underscores the ark's transcendent nature and stresses the inappropriateness
with which it was being handled.[26] Yet, when David first proposes to
transfer the ark, in his words, "to us," he describes the ark in equally
self-referential terms, "the ark of *our* God" (ארון אלהינו or, perhaps,
"*our* ark of God"), a term found nowhere else in the Bible.[27] In this
context, Eskenazi has astutely noted that the term "the ark of the
covenant of God (ארון ברית יהוה) only appears at the close of chapter
15, in verses 25, 26, 28 and 29 in conjunction with the transport of
the ark by the Levites.[28] The observation is well-explained by the

---

[24] It should be noted however, that the Chronicler does not strike the term "City
of David" from 1 Chr 15:29: "As the Ark of the Covenant of the Lord arrived at the
City of David (עד עיר דויד), Michal the daughter of Saul looked out of the window
and saw King David leaping and dancing, and she despised him for it." The discrepancy may be accounted for as follows: in verse 25, the deletion of the term accords
with other changes noted in this section that underscore that the Ark was not being
transported for David's sake. In v. 29, however, the term "City of David" serves
to imply, not the site of his sovereignty, but to underscore the site of his personal
residence, and is preserved to introduce the episode of his wife's response. We may
further read here, perhaps, a note of irony. The contrast between "City of David"
and his wife's disgust, suggests, to borrow a chauvinistic and anachronistic turn of
phrase, that "the king rules over his city but not over his own home."

[25] For a discussion of the various appellations of the ark, see *ABD* 1:386-87.

[26] Shmuel Abramsky and Moshe Garsiel (eds.), *2 Samuel* (Olam HaTanakh; Tel-
Aviv: Davidson-Eti, 1993) 65.

[27] William Johnstone, *1 and 2 Chronicles. Vol. 2. 2 Chronicles 10-36: Guilt and Atonement* (JSOTSup 254; Sheffield: Sheffield Academic Press, 1997) 169.

[28] Tamara C. Eskenazi, "A Literary Approach to Chronicles' Ark Narrative,"
in Astrid B. Beck et. al. (eds.), *Fortunate the Eyes That See: Essays in Honor of David Noel
Freedman* (Grand Rapids: Eerdmans, 1995) 270-71.

theory advanced here. Vv. 1-24 of chapter 15 detail the preparations undertaken to transport the ark in the proper fashion. Vv. 25-29 depict the actual execution and procession. The ark is identified as the ark of the *covenant* only once Israel relates to the ark properly and herself behaves in good covenantal fashion.

The description of David's merriment. As Israel's covenantal partner and as the authority that has chosen David to be king, God, reasons David, must surely want the preeminent symbol of His immanence in the world to rest in Jerusalem, the newly founded capital of Israel. The plans to bring the ark, then, are initiated in a spirit of covenantal closeness between God and Israel in general, and between God and David in particular. When the wagon sets forth on its abortive journey, David and all present are said to be dancing "before God" (לפני האלהים), implying proximity and therefore intimacy. The comment appears in both the *Vorlage* (לפני יהוה—2 Sam 6:5) and in Chronicles (לפני האלהים—1 Chr 13:8). Yet, when the ark is successfully transported, the Chronicler depicts David dancing while omitting the phrase "before God" found in the *Vorlage*, on two occasions (15:27 = 2 Sam 6:14; 15:29 = 2 Sam 6:16). The ark is transported, within the Chronicler's presentation, amid a heightened air of transcendence. To dance is appropriate. To do so "before God," impinging on the ark's transcendent character, is not.

The same careful comparison of language between the abortive and successful attempts to transport the ark may be seen surrounding the root ע.ז.ז. Whereas the *Vorlage* (2 Sam 5:5) says that David and his company "danced before the Lord to [the sounds of] all kinds of cypress wood [instruments] (בכל עצי ברושים)," the Chronicler (1 Chr 13:8) writes that David and his company danced "before God with all their might—with songs (בכל עז ובשירים)," etc. We have previously seen how the Chronicler takes pejoratively marked roots (ש.ל.ח.; פ.ר.ץ.; על) from the detail of Uzzah's misdeed, and uses them to foreshadow David's initiative, earlier in the narrative. The same trope is at work here.[29] Where the Chronicler writes that David and company danced before God בכל עז, we can hear the association with him, whose very name stems from the root ע.ז.ז—Uzzah. The implication of David dancing בכל עז is that he is doing so "in the spirit of Uzzah," that is,

---

[29] Alternatively, the difference between the *Vorlage* and the Chronicler's account may be the result of a corruption of the Samuel text here, as the Chronicler's version is supported by the textual witness of 4QSam. For discussion, see Japhet *I & II Chronicles*, 279.

in a way that fails to display proper distance and reverence for the ark.[30]

Just as dancing לפני האלהים was a feature of the first narrative in Chronicles and deliberately omitted from the second, so is the case with the term עז. The *Vorlage* does not hesitate to write that in the second attempt to transfer the ark David "whirled with all his might before the Lord (מכרכר בכל עז לפני יהוה)." We have already seen the Chronicler's aversion to expressing David's merriment "before the Lord" in this scene of ostensibly proper conduct. It is within this vein that the Chronicler writes here, "And David was wrapped in robes of fine linen (ודויד מכרבל במעיל בוץ). The Chronicler chooses to omit that David danced בכל עז because that term has already been negatively tagged earlier in the narrative of 1 Chronicles 13, and is therefore inappropriate for the account of David's proper conduct in 1 Chronicles 15.[31]

The root ע.ז.ז., by contrast, finds its proper expression, from the Chronicler's perspective, in 1 Chronicles 16, in which the word עז appears three times within the amalgam created here between Psalm 105 and Psalm 96. The word עז here, however, may bear two meanings, both of which stand in contrast to the use of the word as descriptive of merriment in the presence of God's ark. Consider, for example, 16:11: "Turn to the Lord, to His might (עזו)." "Might" here, no longer describes human behavior but is now an attribute of the divine. Yet within the book of Psalms, the word עז is also used as a synonym for the ark, as in "He let His might (i.e. ark) go into captivity, His glory into the hand of the foe" (78:61; cf. 132:8).[32] Set into the ark narrative

---

[30] It is interesting to note that the Judean King Azariah is depicted in 2 Chronicles 26 as having likewise encroached upon holy domain by offering incense in the Temple. Yet, the Chronicler renames Azariah "Uzzah." Is this because he displays "Uzzah-like" behavior? A full accounting of the lines of similarity between the Uzzah account here and the Uzziah account is beyond the scope of this chapter.

[31] For the purposes of the present study I have focused here upon the differences between Chronicles and Samuel with regard to David's conduct in the transport of the ark, for these will be relevant to the narrative analogy that I will later draw between this narrative and the account of the battle against the Philistines. The discussion here is not meant to be an exhaustive study of all of the theological differences between the ark narrative of 2 Samuel 6 and of 1 Chronicles 13-16. For other discussion see Japhet *I & II Chronicles*, 305-06 and Eskenazi, "A Literary Approach," 258-74.

[32] John Day, "Pre-Deuteronomic Allusions to the Covenant in Hosea and Psalm LXVIII," *VT* 36:1 (1986) 8. Other possible understandings of the term עז as a reference to the ark in Psalms are discussed in G.K. Davies, "The Ark in the Psalms," in F.F. Bruce (ed.), *Promise and Fulfillment: Essays Presented to Professor S. H. Hooke* (Edinburgh, T & T Clark, 1963) 51-61.

of 1 Chronicles 13-16, the term עוז takes on a new color. עוז is the province of the ark, and not of its human attendants: Uzzah (through his name, which is metonymic of his trespass) and David (through his action—dancing with עוז —13:8).[33]

The Structure of 1 Chronicles 13-16:
The Consensus of Scholarship Reexamined

While the accounts of Perez Uzzah and Baal Perazim appear in close proximity along the text continuum of 1 Chronicles 13-14, they are but two elements of the larger tapestry that comprises the ark narrative of 1 Chronicles 13-16. It will be instructive, therefore, to discuss their interrelationship in terms of the meaning of the larger structure of the narrative unit. The structure of the ark narrative here is surely a critical issue for the Chronicler, for he has taken great pains to depart from the structure he found in the *Vorlage*. While scholars have noted the linguistic differences, the structural difference between the two versions may be usefully summarized graphically:

2 Samuel	1 Chronicles
David's Enthronement and Conquest of Jerusalem (5:1-10)	David's Enthronement and Conquest of Jerusalem (11:1- 12:41)
Hiram Builds David's Palace (5:11-12)	
David's Wives and Progeny (5: 13-16)	
First Battle Against Philistines (5:17-21)	
Second Battle Against Philistines (5:22-25)	
Failed Attempt to Bring Ark to Jerusalem (6:1-11)	Failed Attempt to Bring Ark to Jerusalem (13:1-14)

---

[33] See similarly 16:27, where עוז, could mean either "His strength," or, equally, "the ark." עוז in 26:28, however, seems to refer exclusively to the Lord's strength.

2 Samuel	1 Chronicles
	Hiram Builds David's Palace (14:1-2)
	David's Wives and Progeny (14:3-7)
	First Battle Against Philistines (14:8-12)
	Second Battle Against Philistines (14:13-17)
	Extensive Preparations to Bring Ark to Jerusalem (15:1-24)
Ark Successfully Brought to Jerusalem (6:12-19)	Ark Successfully Brought to Jerusalem (15:25-16:3)

In the *Vorlage* a series of events precedes David's attempt to bring the ark to Jerusalem. Upon failing, David, within the *Vorlage*, immediately sets out upon his second attempt to transfer the ark, this time with success. By contrast, the Chronicler sets distance between the two attempts to transfer the ark. After the initial failure, the Chronicler lists the same series of events that had preceded David's first attempt in the *Vorlage*. To this, the Chronicler also adds the measures taken by David in preparation for the transfer of the ark that are recorded in 1 Chronicles 15, and which have no parallel in the *Vorlage*.

Why did the Chronicler depart from the *Vorlage* and list the various events that in Samuel precede the first attempt, only after first relating the initial attempt? A consensus exists within the scholarship concerning this question that, I submit, rests on highly questionable grounds. Sara Japhet[34] asserts that the rearranged chronology serves to create the effect of an implicit message to David. In the wake of the fiasco of Perez Uzzah, David was left bewildered. Does God want the ark moved to Jerusalem, or doesn't He? Does the debacle mean that David has lost favor in God's eyes? The events of 1 Chronicles 14, all of which concern blessings bestowed upon David, come to reassure him

---

[34] Japhet, *I & II Chronicles*, 284. Cf. similarly Galil and Garsiel, *The Book of First Chronicles*, 278; R. Mosis, *Untersuchungen zur Theologie des chronistischen Geschichtswerkes* (Freiburg: Heider, 1973) 61, n. 48; Leslie C. Allen, "Kerygmatic Units in 1 &2 Chronicles," *JSOT* 41 (1988) 28; Eskenazi, "A Literary Approach," 266; David A. Glatt, *Chronological Displacement in Biblical and Related Literatures* (SBLDiss 139; Atlanta: Scholars Press, 1990) 58.

that divine grace is indeed with him. To be sure, he must rectify the
technical failings exhibited in the first attempt to transfer the ark, and
to this David attends in 1 Chronicles 15. Yet, by bestowing upon him
a series of blessings in the wake of the debacle, God essentially signals
to David that his basic intention to transfer the ark was acceptable
in the eyes of God. Williamson, in a similar spirit, goes even further:
the blessings bestowed upon David are a reward for having sought to
transfer the ark to Jerusalem.[35]

Inherent in their argument, however, is an assumption that the
Chronicler wishes his audience to read chapters 13-16 chronologically. The building of the palace by Hiram (14:1-2), the birth of the
progeny in Jerusalem (14:3-7), and the two victories over the Philistines
(14:8-17) can all be "reassuring" to David (Japhet) or a "reward" to
David (Williamson) only if they follow in the wake of the debacle
of Perez Uzzah (ch. 13).[36] The Achilles' heel in this assumption is
found in 1 Chr 13:14 (= 2 Sam 6:11): the ark rested in the house
of Obed-Edom for only three months prior to the second, successful attempt to transport it (1 Chr 15:25). That is, only three months
elapsed between the episode of Perez Uzzah and the narrative of 1
Chronicles 15. The events of 1 Chronicles 14, as Williamson himself
has noted elsewhere, could not have happened within this time span.[37]
This is not a comment on the historicity of the events described, nor
of their actual chronology. Rather it is a comment upon the coherence
of the text as perceived through a synchronic reading of the entire
ark narrative.[38] With the greatest of ease, the Chronicler could have
struck the reference to a three-month's stay from the record of 1 Chr
13:14. Indeed, he makes at least four other changes to the verse, yet

---

[35] H.G.M. Williamson, *1 and 2 Chronicles* (NCBCC; Grand Rapids: Eerdmans,
1982) 116.

[36] It should be noted that the material found in 2 Sam 5:11-25 itself is not composed in consideration of chronological order, as David's children could not all have
been born at this time. See discussion in Glatt, *Chronological Displacement*, 58.

[37] H.G.M. Williamson, "The Temple in the Book of Chronicles," in William
Horbury (ed.), *Templum Amicitiae: Essays on the Second Temple Presented to Ernst Bammel*
(JSNTSup 48; Sheffield: Sheffield Academic Press, 1991) 17.

[38] Japhet does not attend to this problem. More remarkably, Galil and Garsiel
(*The First Book of Chronicles*, 178) indicate an awareness of the chronological difficulty,
and still maintain that the events are listed here as a reassurance to David that he
has divine grace even after the debacle. Williamson ("The Temple," 17) attempts,
lamely in our opinion, to account for the breakdown of chronology: "Rather, these
(i.e. Hiram's building, progeny, etc.) are stereotyped markers of divine blessing for
faithful kings."

leaves this chronological marker intact. The retention of the time frame that structures the original sequence of episodes leads us to adopt one of two approaches. The first would be to accuse the Chronicler of sloppy editing; he *should have* omitted the reference so that the passage could read smoothly from a chronological perspective, as proposed by Japhet. Within the present study of the ark narrative of 1 Chronicles 13-16 alone, however, we have seen the deliberation with which the Chronicler labors over his choice of language. To hinge a coherent reading of the narrative upon sloppy editing, therefore, would for us constitute an option only of last resort.

The Structure of 1 Chronicles 13-16: An Alternate Proposal

A second option is to suggest that the Chronicler never wished to imply that the events of 1 Chronicles 14 occurred in the wake of, and as a response to, the debacle at Perez Uzzah. To posit this, however, requires a narratological shift, for it means that we must explain why the Chronicler would present this course of events in non-chronological order.[39]

A rhetorical model may be found in the genre of journalistic coverage of a major political campaign by contemporary news periodicals. Week by week coverage of the campaign details the news as it happens in incremental bits, focusing on the week's gains and losses for each candidate. In the issue following the election, however, retrospective pieces appear. Each candidate's campaign is reviewed and assessed. Here, chronology is not the key, but rather the identification of the trends that emerge by engaging in a highly selective organization of the manifold details of the campaign. It is a process of, proverbially speaking, seeing the forest apart from the trees and of understanding what contributed to the making of a victorious campaign and, alternatively, what confluence of tactics and events contributed to the failure of the losing campaign. A winning campaign may have suffered setbacks along the way. In a retrospective piece, however, a focus could be upon the building of successes that brought the ultimate victory. It

---

[39] Amit (Yairah Amit, "Studies in the Poetics of the Book of Chronicles," in Ben-Zion Luria [ed.], *Professor H.M. Gevaryahu Jubilee Volume: Studies in Biblical Studies and in Jewish Thought* [Jerusalem: Kiryath Sefer, 1989] 284-85 [Hebrew]) has noted that the Chronicler frequently presents events in non-chronological order for the purpose of strengthening his rhetorical claims.

will ignore chronological precision for the sake of thematic unity and development. Conversely, a losing campaign may have had moments of resurgence, yet, in a retrospective piece, these will be down-played, as a new narrative is created which focuses upon the evolution of errors and missed opportunities.[40]

Within individual books of the Hebrew Bible one can also find that the same string of events, or the same period of time is documented twice, from two different perspectives. The opening verse of the Book of Judges tells of the aftermath of the passing of Joshua, with regard to its political and military ramifications. Yet, Joshua's death and its aftermath are retold in Judg 2:6ff, this time focusing upon the degeneration of Israel's conduct vis-à-vis God.[41]

The Chronicler's aim in documenting the events of the early period of David's reign is to address what in his eyes is the most significant event of that period: the transfer of the ark to Jerusalem. David made two attempts to transfer the ark. One failed and one succeeded. Yet, the Chronicler is aware that these were not the only events of the early period of David's career. Indeed, many seminal milestones transpired during this time: the building of the palace by Hiram; the birth of extended progeny; conclusive battles against Israel's perennial foe, the Philistines. Each event has implications for David's understanding of his relationship with God and his interpretation of God's will. Life, however, does not, in actuality, unfold in neat, thematic bundles of experiences. In all likelihood, these events unfolded over time, some contemporaneously, others in isolation. The battles with the Philistines may have been of relatively short duration. The construction of the palace and the birth of eleven children to four wives, certainly were not. With his focus upon the centrality of the transfer of the ark to Jerusalem, the Chronicler seeks to recast the material within a new, thematic narrative. In its first episode, 1 Chronicles 13, the Chronicler details the way in which a newly crowned monarch (1 Chronicles 12) moved to consolidate his nascent coalition by engaging in a national effort to solidify and centralize his regime, through the transfer of

---

[40] See, e.g. *Time* magazine's post-election coverage of the 1996 United States Presidential election (Nov. 18, 1996): Peggy Noonan, "Dole's Long Road," p. 66; Richard Stengel and Eric Pooley, "Masters of the Message," pp. 76-96.

[41] See discussion in Amit, *The Book of Judges: The Art of Editing*, 127-31. David Glatt (*Chronological Displacement*, 1-74) has shown how chronological displacement for the sake of ideological concerns is a shared feature of Mesopotamian royal inscriptions and biblical historiography.

the ark. The pericope may be named, "Moving the Ark I: Story of a Failure."

Chs. 14-16, comprise a second thematic episode of the new narrative, one that may be dubbed, "Moving the Ark II: Story of a Success." The building of the palace by Hiram, the birth of the progeny, the victories over the Philistines, may all have occurred (even within the Chronicler's telling of the history) before the first, failed attempt to move the ark. Yet these events—united by thematic lines we now proceed to draw—are linked together to compose the narrative of the successful attempt to bring the ark to Jerusalem. In restructuring the ark narrative in a way that places these events after the debacle at Perez Uzzah, the Chronicler establishes contrast. 1 Chronicles 14 opens the Chronicler's story of success. Here, rather than witnessing a self-ordained initiative to consolidate power, we see success achieved through human deference to the divine management of affairs. The agenda here is organized by God, not by David. Hiram builds David's palace, while David is a passive bystander, who understands God's grace at work on its own. The victories over the Philistines, in particular, underscore the theme of the submission of human management to divine. In the battle of the Valley of Rephaim, David takes no action until he has consulted with God (14:10). In the second battle, the Chronicler emends the text of the *Vorlage* so as to underscore that David takes no action until he is certain that it is the will of God that he do so (14:14): "David inquired of God *once more*" (cf. 2 Sam 5:23). The account of the second battle against the Philistines continues the theme of conceding the human stewardship of events and deferring to that of the divine. God's statement, "do not go up after them" (14:13) implies that David must sublimate his intuition to pursue an alternative course of action.[42] Moreover, David is told that even as he follows the prescribed course of action, he will not know the moment of attack in advance. He must wait for the divinely appointed sign—the rustling of the trees (14:15). The development of the theme is rounded out in summary statement, that, in fact, "David did as God had commanded him" (14:16). Thematically, 1 Chronicles 14 continues through to 1 Chronicles 15. Having cited in chapter 14 a list of events in which David exhibits deference to God's stewardship of events, the Chronicler demonstrates how these same traits came to bear on the transfer of the ark. Chapter 15 substantiates the great pains that David took

---

[42] Cf. Johnstone, *1 and 2 Chronicles*, 2:177.

to transfer the ark in full accordance with God's design and plan and offers his own recognition that it was in this regard that the earlier attempt had failed (15:12-13).

The explanation offered here affords a coherent synchronic reading of the ark narrative and avoids the difficulties inherent in the chronology proposed by Japhet. The difficulty, of course, in the position being advanced here is that it requires the reader to assume a jump—or, more correctly, a jump back—in time, as chapter 14 returns us to events, some of which transpired already prior to the episode of Perez Uzzah. This narratological step finds justification through a rhetorical device that suggests that the last two verses of chapter 13 and the opening verse of chapter 15 are contiguous in time. These verses are linked in a rhetorical strategy akin to that of resumptive repetition.[43] In a classic case of resumptive repetition, the synchronicity of separate passages is indicated by the repetition of a phrase from the earlier pericope, and attests that the intervening account transpired meanwhile. By repeating the phrase from the earlier passage, the author indicates that he chronologically resumes where he had left off. For example, Gen 39:1 reports that Joseph was taken down to Egypt, even though this has already been reported in 37:36. Through this repetition, Scripture indicates that the events of Genesis 38—the account of Judah and Tamar—happened "meanwhile." Verse 39:1 returns us to the account of Joseph.

In the present instance, the Chronicler bridges the chronological gap created by chapter 14 by linking the beginning of chapter 15 with the end of chapter 13 through the repetition of highly distinct motifs and phrases. When read together, vv. 13:13-14 and 15:1 form a chiastic structure[44] in which the elements stand in parallel, both in theme and in language:

---

[43] On resumptive repetition see Shemaryahu Talmon, "The Presentation of Synchroneity and Simultaneity in Biblical Narratives," in Joseph Heinemann and Samuel Werses (eds.), *Studies in Hebrew Narrative Art Throughout the Ages* (Scripta Hierosolymitana 27; Jerusalem: Magnes Press, 1978) 9-26; Adele Berlin, *Poetics and Interpretation of Biblical Narrative* (Sheffield: Almond Press, 1983) 126-28; Burke O. Long, "Framing Repetitions in Biblical Historiography," *JBL* 106:3 (1987) 385-99.

[44] Isaac Kalimi (*The Book of Chronicles: Historical Writing and Literary Devices* [Biblical Encyclopedia Library; Jerusalem: Bialik Institute, 2000] 162-211 [Hebrew]) has identified chiasmus to be one of the most prevalent stylistic features of Chronicles. Particularly germane here is his discussion of the Chronicler's use of *inclusio* as a way of bracketing off a section. He demonstrates (pp. 282-86) that the corresponding elements that surround the bracketed section are often found to be in chiastic structure, along the lines of the structure that I am proposing here. Generally, there

Both of the C elements exhibit the theme of divine blessing to the protector of the ark, Obed Edom and David, respectively. Moreover, they are semiotically linked through pronominal reference to the ark's protector (לו) and through the focus of the blessing, the "house" (בית). Both B elements refer to the preparation of a place of rest for the ark and are linked semantically by the phrase "ark of the Lord" (ארון האלהים). The A elements both describe an action taken by David in service of the ark, that, while substantively different (A—"he *diverted* [the ark]"; A'—"he *pitched* a tent for [the ark]"), are nonetheless lexical derivatives of the root נ.ט.י.

At the outset we claimed that the accounts of Perez Uzzah and the battle at Baal Perazim needed to be understood within the larger context of the structure of the ark narrative of 1 Chronicles 13-16. We may now bring into comparison these two pericopes that are, respectively, part of the larger narratives of "Moving the Ark I: Story of a Failure" and of "Moving the Ark II: Story of a Success."

The Battle at Baal Perazim (1 Chr 14:8-12)
and the Account of Perez Uzzah (1 Chr 13:1-14)

While these two accounts appear in both the *Vorlage* and in the Book of Chronicles, our focus shall remain, as it has throughout this chapter, on the Chronicler's casting of the narrative. As we compare

---

is growing consensus that Chronicles was composed in a highly literate environment. Frank Polak has noted that texts from the Persian era bear a more elaborate sentence syntax than do texts of earlier periods. See Frank Polak, "The Oral and the Written: Syntax, Stylistics and the Development of Biblical Prose Narrative," *JANES* 26 (1999) 59-105. See also Susan Niditch, *Oral World and Written Word* (Louisville, KY: Westminster John Knox Press, 1996).

the language of the two accounts within Chronicles we will highlight
the innovations found relative to the text of the *Vorlage*. As stated at
the outset, this is done with the purpose of demonstrating that the
intertextuality between the two accounts and the plot equivalence that
emerges between them are a product of the Chronicler's reworking
of the material.

In the introductory chapter on methodology we stated that the
process of identifying base elements of the analogy and the process of
interpreting those common elements were intertwined. Interpretation,
we said, is not a stage subsequent to the identification of the base elements of the analogy. Rather, proposed hypotheses of meaning can
themselves be instrumental in the proper identification of the elements
comprising the analogical base. Conversely, as further analogical elements are identified and incorporated into the hypothesized web of
meaning, they can help us refine, reject or discover different shades
of meaning within the initial hypothesis put forward. That is, once
initial common elements have been identified, a working hypothesis
may be put forth as to the meaning of the analogy. The hypothesis,
in turn, allows other formal aspects of the two narratives to emerge
in a new and analogous light. We proceed now to engage in this
reciprocal process of identifying common forms and explaining their
potential meaning.

The most apparent formal comparison between the two pericopes is
the motif of an etiology surrounding the root .פ.ר.ץ. In each, the word
"burst forth" appears three times, in the generic form of, "the Lord
burst forth a bursting, hence the place is called 'the burst of *x*'":

> And David was vexed because the Lord had *burst* a *bursting* against Uzzah,
> and he called the place *'Bursting* Out Against Uzzah' (13:11).

> David said, "God has *burst* out against my enemies by my hand, like
> a *bursting* flood. Therefore that place is called 'Lord of *Bursting* Out'"
> (14:11 NRSV).

Abramsky explains that the parallel indicates that David's kingship
was checkered with alternating victories and setbacks, determined
from above, not all of which were readily understood to the king
himself.[45] Divine "bursting" can bring good and it can bring disaster.
Abramsky's observation is borne out by the structure of each sentence.
Whereas the etiology is verbally exclaimed by David in victory (14:

---

[45] Abramsky and Garsiel, *2 Samuel*, 65.

11), it is, apparently, only contemplated and suspected by David in defeat (13:11).

Said somewhat differently, the dramatic parallel in form suggests that the two passages are obverses of one another.[46] When seen within the structural context of the ark narrative of 1 Chronicles 13-16, this neat contrast between the two episodes is well understood. God bursts out in hierarchical fashion. Uzzah is stricken down because he encroached upon the realm of the holy in the most palpable fashion—by extending his hand to touch the ark. Accordingly, David named the site "Perez Uzzah." Yet, in 15:13-15, as we saw, David reflects that in fact the "bursting forth" had been "against *us*, for *we* did not seek it as ordained." As we saw, David had encroached upon the ark's sanctity by allowing it to be drawn by cart and attended by Priests, rather than Levites. As we also attempted to demonstrate, this may have been because David had not been sufficiently mindful of the ark's transcendence and was disproportionately focused upon the attendant benefits for him and his nascent kingdom. Uzzah's trespass was the most palpable and hence the most severely punished. While David suffers no corporal punishment, the entire episode marks a setback to his agenda and leaves his leadership tarnished. David himself leaves the episode fearful of the future: "David was afraid of God that day; he said, 'How can I bring the ark of God to me?'"

By contrast, David's campaign over the Philistines is carried out through the sublimation of his own inclination, and through organizing his will in accordance with God's (13:10). The prevailing lack of submission and undue presumption prompt a punitive bursting out by God. Deference, submissiveness and compliance harness that same power toward commensurate recompense: a divine bursting out to David's advantage.

Biblical writers can accentuate a point of significance in the narrative by deviating from a particular aspect of an anticipated convention.[47] The battle story of Baal Perazim is a good case in point. In nearly every facet, its construction and language are textbook examples of typical features of the biblical battle story, as identified by von Rad, Plöger and Richter. The narrative opens with the enemy advancing on Israel (14:8-9). The leader seeks and receives oracular consultation (14:10). The actual engagement is described with little detail, utilizing key roots

---

[46] Fokkelman, *Narrative Art*, 3:190.
[47] Cf. Alter, *The Art of Biblical Narrative*, 62.

such as ע.ל.י. and נ.כ.י. (14:11). The battle site is renamed etiologically
in commemoration of the victory and God's deliverance (14:11). The
author steps out of the grid of convention, however, with the detail of
the abandoned Philistine gods (14:12). While booty reports are also
characteristic of biblical battle stories, attention to the abandonment
of foreign gods or idols is not. Within ancient Near Eastern annals
reports of the taking of enemy idols as a sign of the supremacy of the
victorious divinity are widely found[48] and it is reasonable to suspect
that on occasion Israel's enemies abandoned their idols together with
the other spoils of war. Yet, in no other biblical battle account is there
attention to the abandonment of the enemy's idols.

Several scholars have viewed the significance of the abandonment
of the Philistine idols as a function of its context within the Book of
Samuel. The note, it is said, represents closure. The Israelites had
suffered the loss of the ark at Ebenezer (1 Samuel 4) to the hands of
the Philistines. Now the tables are turned, reversing the fate.[49]

The Chronicler omits the story of the battle of Ebenezer together
with nearly all of the material from 1 Samuel, thus neutralizing the
meaning within his own work of the detail of the abandoned idols.
It may be that he retains the item, simply as part of a broader decision to incorporate the material of 2 Sam 5:11-25 into his work in
wholesale fashion, without substantive deletion. Yet, a comparative
reading of the detail in the two versions suggests that the Chronicler
was dissatisfied with the language in which the *Vorlage* expressed the
incident. According to 2 Sam 5:21, the Philistines abandoned "their
idols" (עצביהם). The Chronicler (14:12), however, emends this to read
"their gods" (אלהיהם). This, it should be noted, in spite of the fact that
elsewhere the Chronicler retains the *Vorlage*'s use of the word עצביהם in
reference to Philistine idols (1 Chr 10:9 = 1 Sam 31:9) and עצבים as a
general reference to foreign idols (2 Chr 24:18). Thus, the adaptation
here cannot be seen as a general Chronistic preference for the word
אלהים over the word עצבים.

While the Chronicler sheds the referent of the captured ark of 1

---

[48] See P.D. Miller and J.J.M. Roberts, *The Hand of the Lord: A Reassessment of the
"Ark Narrative" of 1 Samuel* (Baltimore: Johns Hopkins, 1977) 9-16 and bibliography
on p. 91, notes 69-72.

[49] Kiel, *2 Samuel*, 362; N.L. Tidwell, "The Philistine Incursions into the Valley
of Rephaim," in J. A. Emerton (ed.), *Studies in the Historical Books of the Old Testament* (Leiden: Brill, 1979) 210; cf. P. Kyle McCarter, *II Samuel* (AB 9; New York:
Doubleday, 1984) 154.

Samuel 4, I would like to propose that he reads into the detail of the abandoned Philistine gods at 14:12 a referent of his own making. It refers—within the reworked structure of 1 Chronicles 13-14—back to the abandonment of the ark of the Lord in 1 Chr 13:13. By referring to the Philistine idols—here, and only here—as אלהיהם, the Chronicler creates an equality with the ark of the Lord (ארון האלהים), which had been abandoned by David, following the fiasco of Perez Uzzah.[50] The dual reference to abandoned gods creates a second instance of the "obverse" effect that Fokkelman described regarding the role of the פ.ר.ץ. etiology in the two accounts. When David attempts to appropriate the ark of the Lord within the framework of his own agenda, he is forced to abandon the ark of אלהים near the site of the debacle. When David is submissive to the will of God, as he is in his engagements with the Philistines, it is they who are forced to abandon אלהיהם at the site of their demise.

This motival and semantic parallel has transformative implications for our understanding of the relationship between the pericope of Perez Uzzah and the pericope of Baal Perazim. Were the only formal similarity between them to lie in the etiology surrounding the root פ.ר.ץ., it could suffice for us to understand that the Chronicler wished to contrast the two episodes in a broad, thematic fashion: when a man of power oversteps his mandate and attempts to organize God in accordance with his own agenda, God bursts out, punitively (1 Chronicles 13). When, however, he subjugates his will to divine authority, God will burst out on behalf of his loyal servant (1 Chronicles 14). The com-

---

[50] A note is in order concerning the usage of the various appellations of the ark and their significance. The ark is referred to as the ark of Lord (ארון האלהים) six times in the narrative of 1 Chronicles 13. The first two times (13:3, 5) are in the introductory section that has no parallel in the *Vorlage*. The second two times are in the detail of the loading of the ark onto the wagon (13:6, 7) and the language of ארון האלהים matches that of the *Vorlage* (2 Sam 5:3, 4). In the final two occurrences of the ארון אלהים, in the verses that describe its abandonment and repository (13:12, 14), the Chronicler emends the phrase ארון יהוה found in the *Vorlage*. The Chronicler's use of divine names has been the subject of much interest (cf. Japhet, *Ideology*, 12-41, and with reference to 1 Chronicles 13, p. 29), yet with few solid conclusions. It is difficult to ascertain that the Chronicler emended the phrase ארון יהוה found in 2 Sam 6:9, 11 so as to accord with the word אלהיהם found in 1 Chr 14:12. More cautiously, we could suggest that, for whatever reasons, the Chronicler expressed the *nomen rectum* of the ark as ארון האלהים consistently over the entire narrative of 1 Chronicles 13. The emendation of עצביהם to אלהיהם in 14:12, however, may be understood to be the result of a desire to establish a semantic field between the account of Perez Uzzah and the account of Baal Perazim.

mon item of the "abandoned gods" signifies to us that the comparison
between the two passages is to be seen beyond the level of broad thematic similarity. The common elements of both the etiology and the
abandonment of gods together suggest that the Chronicler may have
wished to create a full narrative analogy between the two accounts in
which the common broad themes may be buttressed by an array of
common details as well. Expressed in geometric terms, the common
item of the etiology establishes a single point of comparison. With the
common theme and language of abandoned gods identified, we may
say that we have here not just isolated points of comparison, but the
suggestion of a line of comparison.

Earlier, we contrasted the language of the first attempt to transfer
the ark (1 Chronicles 13), with that of the second (1 Chronicles 15).
Examining the terminus of the ark's journey, the appellations given
the ark, and the terms of merriment used, we saw how the Chronicler created a negative image of David within 1 Chronicles 13. The
Chronicler, we have now noted, sees the abandoned ark as parallel
to a variant form of a battle story typicality—the despoiled Philistine
idols. This prompts us to re-read the account of Perez Uzzah with an
eye toward other military allusions and references. The effort reveals
that the first attempt to transfer the ark is cloaked in military terms in
a fashion that the second attempt is not. We proceed, first, to simply
document that this is the case. With the evidence in front of us, we
will then attempt to understand the purpose of casting the attempt to
transfer the ark in these terms, through theories of figurative language
developed by Lakoff and Johnson.

We read in the biblical record that David's administration had many
branches and that there were many bodies of authority to whom he
could have turned to execute a large-scale mission. These included
the elders (1 Chr 11:3; 15:25; 2 Chr 5:2, 4; 10:6, 8, 13), the heads of
the tribes and the chiefs (2 Chr 2:1; 5:2), various officers: the officers
of the people (1 Chr 21:2), the officers of Israel or of the tribes of
Israel (1 Chr 22:17; 27:22; 28:1; 2 Chr 12:6), the officers of the holy
and the officers of God (1 Chr 24:5), and the officers of the clans (1
Chr 29:6). Yet his appeal here (13:1) is to the chiefs of the hundreds
and the chiefs of the thousands. While this body is found to perform
civil functions (Exod 18:21, 25; Deut 1:15; 1 Chr 26:26; 27:1, 28:1,
2 Chr 1:2), its predominant domain is military (Num 31:14, 48, 52,
54; 1 Sam 8:12; 2 Sam 18:1; 2 Chr 17:14; 25:5). Priests and Levites
are to participate, it would appear, in only cursory fashion (13:2). In

chapter 15, by contrast, the Chronicler documents by name across 24 verses the Priests and Levites who were charged with the ark's transfer. The chiefs of the thousands are mentioned only in passing (15:25) in an almost titular capacity alone; the chiefs of the hundreds play no role whatever.

Perhaps the most intriguing military term found in the account of 1 Chronicles 13 is the verb used to signify David's embarkation upon the journey. The *Vorlage* states (6:2), literally, "he rose and he went" (ויקם וילך), a standard phrase employed over 30 times in the Bible, and which generally connotes the initiation of an action with eagerness and some degree of anticipation as to the result (e.g. Gen 22:3, Judg 13:11). The Chronicler, however, replaces this with ויעל דוד. Across the Bible, the *qal* form of the word ויעל bears two primary meanings.[51] It can refer to an ascent, whether topographical, or a repositioning from bottom to top (e.g. Gen 19:30; Exod 19:20). In over 30 instances, however it means to set out on a military campaign, to "advance" (e.g. Judg 1:4; 2 Kgs 14:11), even where the topography in question does not suggest ascent. The inference of ויעל דוד is unclear. The traverse from the City of David to Kiriath Jearim is not a continual ascent. Moreover, if it is the Chronicler's intention to indicate a topographical ascent through ויעל, then the meaning of the verse becomes nearly self-contradictory. David "goes up" from Jerusalem to Kiriath Jearim, in order to "go up" from there (להעלות משם)— back to Jerusalem. It is the verbal equivalent of an Escher drawing, in which figures circle to their point of origin, while seemingly in a process of constant escalation. Hence the connotation here of ויעל seems to be a borrowed use of its military undertone, especially in light of the fact that it is the chiefs of the thousands and the chiefs of the hundreds who are leading the endeavor. David, in this sense, "moves out" or "advances" toward Kiriath Jearim. Indeed, in no place in the Bible is the term ויעל used in conjunction with a mass undertaking (as is the case here) where the connotation is anything other than a military undertaking. In 1 Chronicles 15, by contrast, David does not embark upon his mission through the term ויעל; instead, the Chronicler writes of David and the entourage, "who were those who went to bring up the ark (ההלכים להעלות)" (15:25). The term להעלות here refers to the return leg: the traverse from Kiriath Jearim back to Jerusalem.

---

[51] This, in distinction from the *hiphil* form of the word which means "to offer up" in a sacrificial sense (e.g. Num 23:2, 1 Kgs 12:32).

Other terms employed by the Chronicler are found in military contexts, yet not exclusively so. Consider David's call in 13:2 for the people to be summoned "that they should gather together to us ‏(ויקבצו‏ ‏אלינו‏)‎." The gathering of people together through the root ‏ק.ב.ץ.‏ does not bear a specific connotation, and may mean a gathering for any purpose (e.g. Gen 49:2; Deut 30:3; 1 Sam 8:4; 1 Kgs 22:6; 1 Chr 16: 35). Yet approximately one-fourth of the references to the gathering of people is in a specifically military context.[52] Other lexical options existed for the Chronicler here, such as the root ‏ב.ו.א.‏, or the root ‏ק.ה.ל.‏, as in v. 5. When David addresses the chiefs of the thousands and the chiefs of the hundreds for the purpose of "gathering" the people for the purpose of "going up" in a quasi-military sense of the word, the "gathering" takes on undertones of a military draft or mobilization. In 1 Chronicles 15, however, David gathers the people only through the neutral term ‏ויקהל‏ (15:3), a term rarely used in a military context.[53]

The use of military language within the first ark narrative, in what is manifestly not a military undertaking, may be understood through theories of figurative language developed by Lakoff and Johnson.[54] Metaphor, they claim, is not merely the province of rhetoric, or even of language alone. Metaphors are not the *expression* of one thing in terms of another, but rather the *experience* of one thing in terms of another. Metaphors conceptually structure the activities we engage in. The flagship example offered in their work (coincidentally for our purposes) concerns the figurative use of war imagery. Often when we speak of verbal debate, we employ figurative language, or metaphor, taken from the field of battle. Claims are said to be *indefensible*; it is possible to *attack the weak points* of an argument; an argument may be said to be *won* or *lost*; a poor *strategy* can result in all of one's arguments being *shot down*. We view our partner in debate as an opponent. The stances we take on issues are called *positions* that can be abandoned, with new positions taken up. Argument, they stress, is not a subspecies

---

[52] Josh 9:2; 10:6; Judg 9:47, 12:4; 1 Sam 7:5, 6, 7; 28:1, 4; 29:1; 2 Sam 2:25, 30; 1 Kgs 11:24; 20:1; 2 Kgs 6:24; 2 Chr 15:9, 10; 25:5; 32:6.

[53] Only a single occurrence bears a military context, 1 Kgs 12:21 (= 2 Chr 11: 1). Note, however, that within the Persian period we find in Esther that the *niphal* form of the root ‏ק.ה.ל.‏ is used to indicate a military mobilization (Esth 8:11, 9:2, 15, 16, 18).

[54] George Lakoff and Mark Johnson, *Metaphors We Live By* (Chicago: University of Chicago Press, 1980).

of war. Argument, rather, is understood, performed, and talked about in terms of war. In short, the conceptual construct of war structures a significant dimension of our orientation toward oral debate.[55]

Applying Lakoff and Johnson's theories to the ark narrative of 1 Chronicle 13, it would appear that the endeavor to transfer the ark was one highly structured by the experience of military mobilization. This should come as no surprise. David's power base, as elaborately described in 1 Chronicles 11-12, was in the armed forces and it is to its leaders that he turns to execute the mission. The use of the language of battle preparations as indicative of the conceptual orientation of David's experience here, underscores the commentary we offered earlier concerning his first attempt to transfer the ark. David's failing here is in his attempt to appropriate the ark in accordance with his own agenda. David conceived, understood and executed the transfer of the ark as a strategic goal to be achieved. David does not "set out" for Kiriath Jearim, nor "embark toward" Kiriath Jearim. Rather he "advances upon" Kiriath Jearim. This is the import of the military metaphor ויעל.

We have focused thus far upon the military overtones present in the details to transfer the ark, i.e., in vv. 1-6. Similar nuances are carried through in the depiction of Uzzah's trespass and of God's response in vv. 7-11. The Chronicler writes that Uzzah is smitten "because he laid a hand on the ark" (13:10).[56] The idiom chosen here by the JPS translation nicely captures the meaning of the Hebrew על אשר שלח ידו על הארון. To "lay a hand upon" implies violation, even assault.[57]

The same may be seen in the language used to describe God's response. Both the *Vorlage* and the Chronicler describe God's action as ויכהו וימת. Elsewhere, the two verbs together always imply slaying with a sharp instrument (2 Sam 1:15, 3:27, 20:10). Note that all of the occurrences of the phrase appear in 2 Samuel, including, of course, the verse in the *Vorlage* (2 Sam 6:7), the basis for 1 Chr 13: 10. The occurrence of the term exclusively within a single body of

---

[55] Ibid., 3-5.
[56] The *Vorlage* here reads ויכהו שם האלהים על השל (2 Sam 6:7), the meaning of which is unclear. See discussion in McCarter (*II Samuel*, 165) and S.R. Driver, *Notes on the Hebrew Text and the Topography of the Books of Samuel* (Oxford: Clarendon Press, 1913) 267-68.
[57] Japhet *I & II Chronicles*, 280; cf. Ps 138:7. On שלח יד generally, see Paul Humbert, "Etendre La Main," *VT* 12 (1962) 383-95.

literature further suggests a single common meaning.[58] It is perhaps no coincidence that the figurative language of God slaying with a sharp instrument occurs at a site which the Chronicler names the "threshing floor of spear" (גורן כידן).[59]

The etiology offered by David likewise underscores his realization that the glorious transfer of the ark has evolved into a clash with God. Examination of the various uses of the term פ.ר.ץ. is illuminating. The root is used in many contexts, all of which imply "bursting" of one form or another. The appearance of the verb and noun forms together ("to burst a bursting") is found only in the verses under question in this study (i.e., 13:11 and 14:11), and in one other instance, in the Book of Job. There Scripture states, "He breached me, breach after breach (יפרצני פרץ); He rushed at me like a warrior" (Job 16:14; cf. Ps 60:3). The peculiar construct is an explicitly military reference, both in Job, and in the etiology of Baal Perazim at 13:11. This suggests that the phrase "and God burst forth a bursting upon Uzzah," is divine punishment in the semantic cloak of an armed assault. As David himself later remarks, it is not Uzzah alone who suffered a bursting from the Lord, but indeed, "the Lord our God burst out against *us*, for *we* did not show due regard for Him" (1 Chr 15:13).[60]

To summarize, David surely must have had good intentions in his first attempt to transfer the ark. Yet his effort is tainted by his attempts

---

[58] The term is somewhat different than ויך וימת, which, when employed with reference to God implies a plague and is found in several passages (Num 11:33; 1 Sam 5:9; 6:19; 2 Kgs 19:35).

[59] The *Vorlage* here (2 Sam 6:6) reads גורן נכון, while 4QSam[a] reads נודן and LXX[B] of Samuel reads נודב. Different proposals have been given as to the textual evolution of these different forms. See discussions in Japhet, *I & II Chronicles*, 280-81, McCarter *II Samuel*, 164, Driver, *Notes on the Hebrew Text*, 266-67. It is difficult to declare with certainty which of these forms was the original. Moreover, it is difficult to know whether the Chronicler's version, כידן, results from scribal error or as deliberate variation from one of the other forms. Whatever the textual history of this name, our mandate is to execute a synchronic reading of the MT version of the text and to explore the ways in which כידן can be understood within the text before us.

[60] The notion that David and Israel stand as the battlefield enemy of the Lord finds further textual support. In two instances David is characterized in what can only be called distinctly "Philistine" terms. David's call that the ark be transferred is expressed, (ונסבה את ארון אלהינו אלינו 13:3). With reference to the ark, the verb ס.ב.ב. together with the predicate אל- is found elsewhere proclaimed only by the Philistine Ekronites: "They have moved the Ark of the God of Israel to us to slay us" (הסבו אלי ארון אלהי ישראל) (1 Sam 5:10). The procedure of loading the ark upon a "new cart (עגלה חדשה)," is found elsewhere only when the Philistines prepare for the ark's return to Israel (1 Sam 6:7).

to appropriate the ark as a strategic goal. The language of battle-preparations employed in the first part of the pericope is reflective of this. God responds in kind. He meets Israel at the "threshing floor of spear," and figuratively engages Israel in violent confrontation. The key term ויעל was earlier seen to serve as a metaphoric expression of David's experience of "advancing" upon Kiriath Jearim with his officers of thousands and hundreds. Now David's initiative may be seen from an additional perspective. When the Chronicler characterizes David's embarkation through the quasi-military term ויעל, it is also a reflection of God's view of the endeavor. The Lord, however, sees this as "an advance" against the transcendent nature of the ark.

Our findings concerning the metaphor analogy established between the account of Perez Uzzah and the account of Baal Perazim may be expressed graphically. This presentation will bring some of the common elements into bold relief for the first time and further demonstrate the lengths to which the Chronicler has reworked material toward this effect:

	The Account of Perez Uzzah (1 Chr 13:1-14)	**The Account of Baal Perazim (1 Chr 14: 8-12)**
David requests authority	ויועץ דויד עם שרי האלפים והמאות לכל נגיד (13: 1)	וישאל דויד באלהים (14: 10)
ויעל to target—assonance בעל	**ויעל** דוד וכל ישראל **בעלתה** אל קרית יערים (13: 6)	**ויעלו בבעל** פרצים (14: 11)
The controlling hand	וישלח עזא את **ידו** לאחז את הארון (13: 9) ...על אשר שלח **ידו** על הארון (13: 10)	ונתתם **בידי**? (14: 10) עלה ונתתים **בידך** (14: 10) פרץ האלהים את אויבי **בידי** (14: 11)
Smitten "there"	**ויכהו**... וימת **שם** (13: 10)	**ויכם שם** (14: 11)
Etiology פ.ר.ץ.	**פרץ** יהוה **פרץ** בעזא ***ויקרא למקום ההוא פרץ*** עזא (13: 11)	**פרץ** האלהים את אויבי בידי **כפרץ** מים על כן **קרא למקום ההוא** בעל **פרצים** (14: 11)

The Account of Perez Uzzah (1 Chr 13:1-14)		The Account of Baal Perazim (1 Chr 14:8-12)
אלהים	היך אביא אלי את ארון	ויעזבו שם את **אלהיהם**
abandoned	**האלהים**؟ (13:12)	(14:12)
	ולא הסיר דויד את הארון	
	אליו... ויטהו את בית עבד	
	אדם (13:13)	

The graph illustrates two indexes. In graphic tables throughout this study the words in bold typeface have been those that form the semantic basis of the proposed analogy, a convention carried through here as well. Some of the bold typeface common phrases in this graph, however, are also underlined. These are the phrases that appear only in the Chronistic version of the story, while words not underlined are found in the *Vorlage* as well. Even at a glance, one can see that most of the terms common to the two accounts are the Chronicler's innovations. This is highly significant. Analogies of this sort are often considered suspect on account of the fact that the common words are not—in and of themselves—uncommon. It would not be unreasonable, in the present case, for example, to question the conclusions drawn from the appearance of the word "hand" in reference to the Philistines being granted to David's hand (1 Chr 14:10) and, respectively, to Uzzah's trespass (1 Chr 13:10). The use of the word "hand" in each instance is highly conventional, and the claim could well be made that one can therefore make no claims of intertextuality. The parry to such challenges often rests on the contention that the author could have equally as well used other non-matching terms. The parry here, however, is much stronger, because it isn't theoretical, but empirical. The Chronicler began his work with other terms in place—those that he found in the *Vorlage*—and emended them creating a series of common terms between the two passages. While each instance of harmonization, perhaps, could be accounted for with a specific, local answer, the preponderance of the phenomenon within such a limited range suggests that the Chronicler wished to bring the two pericopes into conversation in a way not afforded by the presentation of the *Vorlage*.

The analogy is contrastive, and accords with our earlier contention concerning the structure of the ark narrative, where we termed chapter 13, "Moving the Ark I: Story of a Failure," and chs. 14-16, "Moving the Ark II: Story of a Success." The contrast is evident already in the opening element of the analogy. While oracular consultation prior to battle is typical of the battle story, the Chronicler uses it to great effect by placing it in tension with David's exclusively human consultation concerning the transfer of the ark. Recall that David himself had said to the military chiefs, "If you approve, *and if the Lord our God concurs*, let us send far and wide," etc. (13:2). Yet David never does make the effort to ascertain God's will here. Thus, the opening element of the analogy sets the thematic tone for the entire contrastive equivalence between the two passages. The narrative of Perez Uzzah will be the account of David as he organizes God in accordance with his own agenda. The account of Baal Perazim will be the account of David as he defers and concedes the organization of affairs to the will of God.

Moving forward in the analogy, we have already commented on the overtones of mobilization pregnant in the Chronicler's innovation of the term ויעל at 13:6. What now emerges is that the equivalent term in the analogy, ויעלו בבעל פרצים (14:11) is itself a revision, as the parallel phrase in the *Vorlage* reads, ויבא דוד בבעל פרצים (2 Sam 5:20). Note further, that the item of David's embarkation to transfer the ark reads much more like the advance upon the Philistines than does the corresponding passage in the *Vorlage*. The difference between the two versions is highly pronounced. McCarter in his commentary to 2 Samuel writes that the phrase מבעלי יהודה in 2 Sam 6:2 means that the dignitaries who accompanied David were among "the Lords of Judah."[61] That is, no geographic terminus is stated with regard to this embarkation. The Chronicler, however, revises this to read, "David and all Israel went up to Baalah, Kiriath Jearim of Judah" (13:6). The Hebrew, ויעל דוד וכל ישראל בעלתה, with the term ויעל signifying advance, and the geographic terminus expressed as a derivative of the root ב.ע.ל. parallels the same construct in 14:11. Here the clause ויעלו בבעל פרצים likewise signifies advance through the word ויעל, with the opening of the geographic terminus, the word בעל. The parallel is, again, contrastive. At Baal Perazim, David advances in a sanctioned mission against the Philistines, to a theater whose etiological name is

[61] McCarter, *II Samuel*, 162.

already accessed at the outset of the story. By contrast David's well-intentioned mission to Baalah (Kiriath Jearim) has begun to take on the overtones of the belligerence against the ark that it will ultimately prove to be.[62]

The next semantic element of the analogy reflects the theological issue that stands at the crux of the entire ark narrative, and it does so within a single word, what may be termed, the *"controlling* hand," יד. Earlier we saw that Uzzah's act of "laying a hand," with its suggestion of violation and assault, upon the ark, reflected the tenor of the whole pericope, in which God and his ark were being subverted by the human agenda. Uzzah's hand emerges, not innocently as a steadying and supporting hand, but as a controlling, appropriating one.

When David sublimates his will to God's, however, the motif of the controlling hand is redeemed and is used in his favor. The three references to David's hand (14:10-11) signify his impending domination over the Philistine forces. The use of the term in David's query and in God's response is, of course, highly conventional. Yet, as we noted earlier, the Chronicler's three revisions of the *Vorlage* within these two passages underscores the leitmotif of the controlling hand within the analogy, thereby bringing the conventional uses of the motif into rhetorical play as well.

The final three motifs, that of the enemy being "smitten... there," the etiologies based on the root פ.ר.ץ., and the motif of the abandoned gods (fortified by the Chronicler's semantic revisions), serve the same function as the earlier elements of the analogy. They establish a contrastive picture between David's first attempt to transfer the ark and a formative experience in David's spiritual maturation along the path to the successful transfer of the ark: the encounter with the Philistines in which he sublimates his own inclinations and defers to a scheme entirely organized by God's will.

---

[62] The JPS translation of Samuel reads, "Then David and all the troops that were with him set out from Baalim of Judah to bring up from there the Ark" (2 Sam 6: 2). Baalim, according to this translation, is synonymous with Kiriath Jearim. Notice that within this reading, there is no attention to the journey to Kiriath Jearim, only to the return leg of the venture. For further remarks on textual variants here and in 4QSam[a], see McCarter, *II Samuel*, 162, 168; Kalimi, *The Book of Chronicles*, 69.

CHAPTER SEVEN

THE BATTLE AT RAMOTH GILEAD
(2 CHR 18:28-19:3) AND
THE PRE-BATTLE DELIBERATIONS OF AHAB
AND JEHOSHAPHAT (2 CHR 18:1-27)

Our final battle story is that of the battle to take Ramoth Gilead (2 Chr 18:28-19:3 = 1 Kgs 22:29-40) and the deliberations of Ahab and Jehoshaphat prior to engaging in battle (2 Chr 18:1-27 = 1 Kgs 22:1-28). The account has been the subject of scholarly interest on several accounts. From the vantage point of source criticism and historiography it has been studied in conjunction with 2 Kings 3, which likewise documents a joint venture between Jehoshaphat and the king of Israel.[1] The account documents a prophet, Micaiah, who lies in the name of God, eliciting studies of the nature of prophets and prophecy in light of this.[2] This study is concerned with the interaction between the story's main protagonists, Ahab and Jehoshaphat. In particular, the study seeks to contrast the respective portrayals of Jehoshaphat that arise from the two versions.

Within the account in 1 Kings 22, Jehoshaphat is decidedly a character of secondary importance and serves primarily as a foil through which the figure of Ahab is judged. Before assessing Jehoshaphat's character in the account of 1 Kings 22, therefore, a brief characterization of the figure of Ahab is in order. Ahab's centrality is exhibited through the framing of the story. 1 Kings 22 is the last of three battle stories under Ahab's reign. Ahab's death in the battle (vv. 34-38) constitutes the fulfillment of Elijah's prophecy (1 Kgs 21:19). By contrast, Kings offers no substantive information concerning Jehoshaphat prior

---

[1] See Simon J. De Vries, *Prophet Against Prophet: The Role of the Micaiah Narrative in the Early Prophetic Tradition* (Grand Rapids: Eerdmans, 1978); Burke O. Long, "The Form and Significance of I Kings 22:1-38," in Yair Zakovitch and Alexander Rofé (eds.), *Isac Leo Seeligman Memorial Volume* (Jerusalem: A. Rubinstein, 1983) 193-208.

[2] See Rafael Ha-Levi, "Micaiah ben Imlah: The Ideal Prophet," *Bet Miqra* 12/3 (1968) 102-06 (Hebrew); Robert Goldenberg, "The Problem of False Prophecy: Talmudic Interpretations of Jeremiah 28 and 1 Kings 22," in Robert Polzin and Eugene Rothman (eds.), *The Biblical Mosaic: Changing Perspectives* (Philadelphia: Fortress Press, 1982) 87-103; David Robertson, "Micaiah ben Imlah: A Literary View," in idem., 139-46.

to the story other than the formulaic note announcing his assumption
of power (1 Kgs 15:24) seven chapters earlier.

Ahab emerges from the account in wholly negative terms, most
pointedly apparent in the depiction of his death on the battlefield (vv.
33-40). Since we are primarily concerned with the poetics of the biblical battle story, we now analyze the battle story as it appears in Kings
as a baseline of comparison through which we will shortly engage the
parallel battle story in Chronicles.

The battle commences with Ahab's express decision to enter the
battle theater incognito as he sought to evade the divine decree foretold
by Micaiah (v. 17).[3] Verse 33 makes two salient points: first, that the
archer who felled him shot him at random; and second, that the arrow
entered between the plates of the armor. To dramatize the implications of the details here, we may contrast the episode with a similar
moment—the account of the fall of Josiah (2 Chr 35:23). There, as
here, the king entered the battle arena incognito, and there as well,
the archers felled the king. There, however, the account is told with
economy: "Archers shot King Josiah, and the king said to his servants,
'Get me away from here, for I am badly wounded.'" Each of the two
details of Ahab's demise here highlights a common theme: there is no
evading the divine decree. Ahab succeeded as he had planned; indeed,
he is never identified, nor singled out as a target. Nonetheless, he is
felled by an arrow randomly shot. The same theme emerges in the
detail that the arrow pierced his armor. The chance precision with
which the arrow penetrated the plates of the armor is to be understood
as divinely guided. Note that whereas Scripture could have indicated
where the arrow struck Ahab's body, it instead attends only to how the
arrow pierced his armor. The very clothes with which Ahab sought
to confound the will of God in the end confound him.[4]

---

[3] R. David Altschuler, *Metsudat David* to 1 Kgs 22:30; J. Skinner, *I and II Kings*,
(CBC; Edinburgh: T.C. & E.C. Jack, 1904) 204; Jeffries M. Hamilton, "Caught in
the Nets of Prophecy?: The Death of King Ahab and the Character of God," *CBQ*
56 (1994) 657.

[4] See, in a similar vein, Jerome T. Walsh, *1 Kings* (Berit Olam; Collegeville, MN:
Liturgical Press, 1996) 356. The theme of looking to confound the divine decree is
seen in the very donning of the armor. Hobbs (T.R. Hobbs, *A Time for War: A Study
of Warfare in the Old Testament* [Wilmington, Delaware: M . Glazier, 1989]131-33)
notes that with the exception of 2 Chr 26:14, there is no indication in either biblical or extra-biblical sources that armor was the lot of the common Israelite/Judean
solider. He notes that the Lachish relief does not depict soldiers in armor, nor in
the booty brought Sennacherib. He concludes that it was rare in Israel, as seen that

Turning now to the characterization of Jehoshaphat, we begin by analyzing the epitaph granted him at the close of the narrative (vv. 41-51). The epitaph provides an editorial lens through which the author of Kings offers directional clues that will assist us in reading the narrative of Jehoshaphat's role in the battle of Ramoth Gilead. Following the account of the ignominious demise of Ahab in vv. 33-40, Scripture summarizes Jehoshaphat's reign (vv. 41-51) and includes a single statement (v. 45) concerning the joint venture with Ahab: "Jehoshaphat made peace with the king of Israel." [5] Qimḥi maintains that the verse is critical of Jehoshaphat's joint enterprise with Ahab, as it is juxtaposed with the note that Jehoshaphat failed to remove the high places (v. 44).

While Qimḥi contextualizes the note concerning the union vis-à-vis the content of the previous verse, an alternative context may be proposed. The epitaph pericope to Jehoshaphat's reign should be seen in comparison with and in contrast to the description of his father Asa's reign in chapter 15:11-16.[6] The opening verse of the epitaph, in fact, invites the comparison: "He followed closely the course of his father Asa and did not deviate from it, doing what was pleasing to the Lord" (v. 43). While the words "he did that which was pleasing to the Lord," are a stock phrase used with reference to several good kings (1 Kgs 15:11; 2 Kgs 12:3; 14:3; 15:3; 15:34; 18:3; 22:2) the phrase "he did not deviate," is an expression found elsewhere only in reference to Josiah (2 Kgs 22:2). The invocation of a superlative not normally found in the formulaic accolades accorded righteous kings, implies that the overall estimation of Jehoshaphat is favorable. When the epitaph section is broken down into its component parts, it becomes evident that each component bears an analogous comment in the assessment

---

only Saul wears it (1 Sam 17:5). When Ahab donned plated armor, therefore, it was an exceptional move.

[5] The translation is my own. The JPS translation here reads "submitted," which would be appropriate for the *hiphil* form of the verb, וישלים, (cf. Josh 10:1, 4; 11: 19; 2 Sam 10:19 = 1 Chr 19:19). The present form of the verb, וישלם, is therefore to be differentiated. The RSV translation, "Jehoshaphat also made peace with the king of Israel," is likewise prejudicial. The word "also," which does not appear in the text, unfairly groups this action with the clearly negative failure to eradicate the high places, reported in the previous verse.

[6] Within Phoenician epigraphic material, a son's reign is contrasted with that of his father's in the 9th century B.C.E. Kilamuwa Inscription. See translation and commentary in M. O'Connor, "The Rhetoric of the Kilamuwa Inscription," *BASOR* 226 (1977) 15-30.

offered Asa's reign. Point by point, Jehoshaphat's reign is compared
to that of his father, and in all instances Jehoshaphat either equals his
father or exceeds him. Jehoshaphat did that which was pleasing to
the Lord (v. 43) just as Asa had (1 Kgs 15:11). The high places were
not eradicated under Jehoshaphat (v. 44), just as they had not been
under Asa (15:14). Asa began the process of eradicating male prostitu-
tion (15:12); Jehoshaphat completes the process (v. 47). On one score
only do they differ sharply, and that is concerning their relationship
to the Northern Kingdom. 1 Kgs 15:16 states that, "there was war
between Asa and King Baasha of Israel all their days." The continuation of 1 Kings 15 relates an unprecedented situation: one kingdom,
Judah, forges an alliance with a foreign nation, Aram, against the
other kingdom. The contrast presented in the epitaph for Jehoshaphat
could not be stronger. Once again the trilateral relationship between
Judah, Israel and Aram is addressed. In 1 Kings 15 the rift was so
great that Asa, king of Judah, enlisted Aram against Israel. In 1 Kings
22 Jehoshaphat, king of Judah "makes peace" with the king of Israel,
allowing the two kingdoms to face Aram as a common enemy. Note
that Scripture spreads the blame evenly for the civil strife in the earlier
period: "there was war between Asa and King Baasha of Israel all their
days" (15:16). Yet, in peace, it is Jehoshaphat who is credited with
having brought about the change of affairs: "Jehoshaphat made peace
with the king of Israel." Indeed, the opening of the story attests that it
was Jehoshaphat who took the initiative to visit the court of Samaria.
The estimation of Jehoshaphat's alliance with Ahab is expressed in
wholly positive terms.[7]

We may now turn to the narrative itself, and assess the character of
Jehoshaphat. Jehoshaphat is portrayed as a good king, and stands as a
foil to the figure of Ahab. Jehoshaphat initiates the move to ascertain
God's will by calling for consultation with a prophet of God (v. 5).
He risks offending his ally by challenging the impartiality of the 400
prophets that Ahab brings (v. 7). He rebukes Ahab for speaking of the
prophet of God in an irreverent manner (v. 8). Ahab sought to circum-

---

[7] Cf. Gene Rice, *1 Kings: Nations Under God* (ITC; Grand Rapids: Eerdmans,
1990) 193; John W. Wright, "The Fight for Peace: Narrative and History in the
Battle Accounts in Chronicles," in M. Patrick Graham, Kenneth G. Hoglund and
Steven L. McKenzie (eds.), *The Chronicler as Historian* (JSOTSup 238; Sheffield: Shef-
field Academic Press, 1997) 169; Gary N. Knoppers, "Reform and Regression: The
Chronicler's Presentation of Jehoshaphat," *Biblica* 72 (1991) 503.

vent the divine decree and was nonetheless felled. Jehoshaphat appeared to the Aramean archers as Ahab and was nonetheless saved.

The Battle for Ramoth Gilead in 2 Chronicles 18: A Different Frame for a Different Characterization of Jehoshaphat

The primary changes found in the Chronicler's reworking of 1 Kings 22 are to be found in the introduction and conclusion of the story.[8] We labeled the narrative of 1 Kings 22 an Ahab narrative, observing that it is situated within an overall framework of narratives about his reign, while Jehoshaphat had previously received the attention of only a single formulaic verse. The converse is true of the framework that surrounds 2 Chronicles 18. Here, the story is cast in the middle of a four-chapter sequence detailing the reign of Jehoshaphat, King of Judah. The reign of Ahab, by contrast, is mentioned nowhere else in the Book of Chronicles.

The Chronicler is unequivocal in his criticism of Jehoshaphat, as is evidenced from the remarks that precede (18:1-2) and follow (19:1-3) the body of the account. The most explicit criticism of Jehoshaphat is the censure he receives from Jehu ben Hanani in 19:1-3, in conjunction with Jehoshaphat's brush with death on the battlefield.[9] The censure is indicative of the Chronicler's *Weltanschauung* that, as Thompson puts it, "flirtation with apostasy is flirtation with catastrophe."[10] It is no wonder that the Chronicler omits the verse, "And Jehoshaphat made peace with the king of Israel" (1 Kgs 22:45). Joint ventures with the Northern Kingdom are ultimately corrupting and are to be avoided.[11] The peace that Jehoshaphat initiated, so celebrated by the author of Kings, is seen by the Chronicler to be a blemish on Jehoshaphat's otherwise favorable record.

A close reading of the opening verses of the narrative of 2 Chronicles 18, in comparison with those of the *Vorlage*, reveals the same shift in disposition towards Jehoshaphat's initiative. Verse 1 establishes the fact

---

[8] Cf. Japhet *I & II Chronicles*, 756; Wright, "The Fight for Peace," 169.

[9] Simon J. De Vries, *Prophet Against Prophet: The Role of the Micaiah Narrative in the Early Prophetic Tradition* (Grand Rapids: Eerdmans, 1978) 316.

[10] John Arthur Thompson, *1, 2 Chronicles* (New American Commentary 9; Nashville: Broadman & Holman, 1994) 283.

[11] Cf. 2 Chr 20:35-37; 22:10-12; 23:1-21; Japhet, *Ideology*, 313-14; Raymond B. Dillard, *2 Chronicles* (WBC; Waco: Word Press, 1987) 140; Johnstone, *1 and 2 Chronicles*, 1:83).

that Jehoshaphat had "wealth and honor in abundance." Johnstone correctly observes that the statement is concessive and is to be seen in light of the identical phrase in 2 Chr 17:5; in spite of the "wealth and honor in abundance" that he had been granted by God for his proper conduct earlier, he nonetheless sought political alliance with Ahab through marriage.[12] Intermarriage with the Northern monarchy is elsewhere marked as a road to spiritual corruption, and hence to dire consequences.[13]

Verse 2 relates that Ahab slaughtered for him "sheep and oxen *in abundance*," creating an epiphora, a word that appears at the end of two clauses in order to draw a contrast between them. Rather than faithfully accepting "the wealth and honor in abundance" from the hand of God, Jehoshaphat is drawn to "the sheep and oxen in abundance," offered him by Ahab. As Japhet observes, the rationale for Ahab's campaign is spelled out in the *Vorlage*, and implicitly condoned by the text.[14] No rationale is offered for the campaign by the Chronicler. The union of Jehoshaphat and Ahab is described as an act of "enticement" on the part of Ahab (18:2).[15] The term demonstrates the rhetorical device of a global statement followed by its detailed elaboration. The enticement of Jehoshaphat has not been completed by the end of v. 2. Rather, the clause, "and he enticed him to rise to Gilead," serves as a global heading for the content of the ensuing narrative.[16] As we have established, the Chronicler's primary focus here is on the character of Jehoshaphat. While Ahab may be guilty of enticement, it is more to

---

[12] Johnstone, *1 and 2 Chronicles*, 1:82; cf. H.G.M. Williamson, *1 and 2 Chronicles* (NCBCC; Grand Rapids: Eerdmans, 1982) 285; Martin J. Selman, *2 Chronicles* (Tyndale Old Testament Commentary; Leicester: Inter-Varsity, 1994) 409.

[13] (cf. 2 Kgs 8:18, 26-27; 2 Chr 22:10-12; Japhet, *Ideology*, 312; Daniel Lee Gard, "Warfare in Chronicles," Ph.D. dissertation, University of Notre Dame, 1991, 266; Selman, *2 Chronicles*, 409.

[14] Japhet, *I & II Chronicles*, 758.

[15] The translation of ויסיתהו as "he enticed him" is preferable to the JPS translation, "persuaded." While the root .ס.ו.ת. is employed in a positive or neutral connotation in several instances (Josh 15:18 = Judg 1:14; 1 Sam 26:19; 2 Sam 24:1; Job 36:16), the great preponderance of instances are negative in connotation (Deut 13: 7, 1 Kgs 21:25; 2 Kgs 18:32; Isa 36:18; Jer 38:13; 43:3; Job 2:3; 36:18; 1 Chr 21:1; 2 Chr 32:11; 2 Chr 32:15). Note that all occurrences in Chronicles are negative. See the discussion in Thomas Willi, *Die Chronik als Auslegung* (FRLANT 106; Göttingen: Vandenhoeck & Ruprecht, 1972) 144.

[16] Kalimi, *The Book of Chronicles*, 353-59 has demonstrated that in numerous instances the Chronicler restructures the *Vorlage*, in accordance with the principle of offering a global statement followed by its detailed elaboration.

the point of the Chronicler's agenda to note that Jehoshaphat is no less guilty;[17] his alliance with Ahab is not one of union and of peace as we saw in Kings. His alliance with Ahab should signal to the reader the onset of a process of enticement; a process that witnesses capitulation and ideological yielding by the one enticed, Jehoshaphat.

The Subtle Reworking of the Deliberations and the Battle in 2 Chronicles 18

While many have noted the way in which the Chronicler changes the meaning of the *Vorlage* through framing, less attention has been paid to the highly nuanced way in which the body of the narrative has been altered to contribute to a critical portrayal of Jehoshaphat. It is in this vein that Japhet profiles the reworking of the material found in the *Vorlage*:

> Chapter 18 is one of the units in which the Chronicler adopts in its entirety from his source in 1 Kings 22, with no internal alterations of content, and only very few deviations of a linguistic, stylistic, literary and theological nature.[18]

The subtle changes introduced, however, can be seen as serving the Chronicler's aim of casting Jehoshaphat in a negative profile, as the culpable victim of enticement. Johnstone has noted that Micaiah's reproof "*hear now* the word of the Lord" in 1 Kgs 22:19 is expressed in the singular, while in 2 Chr 18:18, the same phrase appears in the plural. The adjustment, he correctly assesses, brings Jehoshaphat into the circle of the condemned, whereas in the *Vorlage*, he is absent from the stage of Ahab's insolence.[19]

We may also observe that in two other instances prior to Micaiah's reproof the Chronicler likewise substitutes plural language for singular, thus implicating Jehoshaphat together with Ahab. In the *Vorlage*, Ahab queries the prophets, "shall *I* (האלך) march upon Ramoth Gilead?" (22:6), while in the Chronicler's version Ahab asks, "shall *we* (הנלך) march..." (18:5). A similar divergence is seen in the two versions of Micaiah's initial response to Ahab. In the *Vorlage*, Micaiah replies, "go up (s., עלה) and succeed (s., והצלח) and God will grant into the king's hand" (22:15).[20] By contrast, the Chronicler renders the statement as

---

[17] Cf. Thompson, *1, 2 Chronicles*, 284.

[18] Japhet, *I & II Chronicles*, 756.

[19] Johnstone, *1 and 2 Chronicles*, 1:87.

[20] Note that in the *Vorlage*, Ahab's question in 22:15 is expressed in the plural,

follows (18:14): "go up (pl., עלו) and succeed (pl., והצליחו) and they will be given into your hands (pl., בידכם)." The battle account itself bears a fourth instance. The *Vorlage* underscores its attention on Ahab and his insolence by stating, "and *he* went (ויבוא) out to battle" (22:30). The Chronicler, by contrast, creates a sense of association, stating, "and *they* went (ויבאו) out to battle"[21] In 1 Kings 22, Jehoshaphat served as a foil by which to judge Ahab. Jehoshaphat's steadfast commitment to determining God's true will stood in sharp contrast to Ahab's disregard of God's will. In 2 Chronicles 18 Jehoshaphat emerges as "enticed," and is brought into the sphere of the morally culpable together with the wicked Ahab.[22]

Subtle changes that contribute to the negative portrayal of Jehoshaphat are evident in the battle report itself. The *Vorlage* account states that when the archers mistakenly identified Jehoshaphat as Ahab, they "turned (ויסרו) to fight against him" (22:32 RSV). The Chronicler, however, intensifies the danger to Jehoshaphat, by stating that the archers "surrounded" him,[23] ויסבו, or "compassed about" him (KJV), to fight against him. The intensification of the danger accords with the greater culpability ascribed to Jehoshaphat in the Chronicler's version.

To this we may add the note that the precise form of the word ויסבו, which, as stated, is absent from the *Vorlage*, has a precedent within

---

"shall *we* go up?" Micaiah's response in the singular foreshadows his prophecy of doom that Ahab and Jehoshaphat will endure separate fates on the battlefield.

[21] v.29; cf. a slightly different interpretation in Johnstone, *1 and 2 Chronicles*, 89. It should be noted, however, that in one instance the trend is reversed, as the Chronicler renders in the plural a term found in the singular in the *Vorlage*. In 1 Kgs 22:15 Ahab queries Micaiah, "shall we march upon Ramoth Gilead, or shall *we* desist (נחדל)?" The parallel passage in Chronicles, however (18:14), reads, "shall we march upon Ramoth Gilead, or shall *I* desist? (אחדל)." Interestingly, the LXX version—both of Chronicles and of Kings— reads אחדל, and perhaps serves as a textual witness that the *Vorlage* of Chronicles may likewise have read אחדל, in contradistinction to the MT version of Kings, נחדל. Alternatively, we may suggest that the Chronicler wished to harmonize the phrasing of the query made of Micaiah here, in v. 14, with that made of the 400 prophets, in v. 5; both instances in Chronicles read, "shall *we* march upon Ramoth Gilead, or shall *I* desist?" For more on the Chronicler's penchant for harmonization, see Kalimi, *The Book of Chronicles*, 125-62. It must be admitted, however, that the shift from singular in the *Vorlage* to the plural in Chronicles exhibited in 1 Chr 18:25-26, is not adequately explained according to this hypothesis.

[22] In spite of his culpability, however, Jehoshaphat will endure a different fate than that of Ahab. Whereas Jehoshaphat is passive, Ahab's misdeeds here are acts of commission. Ahab is, in Jehu's words, a "hater of the Lord" (19:2), whereas Jehoshaphat has other meritorious deeds to his credit (19:3) that earn him a better fate.

[23] Johnstone, *1 and 2 Chronicles*, 1:90.

the Jehoshaphat narratives of 2 Chronicles. 2 Chr 17:7-9 records the efforts Jehoshaphat made to spur a religious revival in Judah. He gathered Levites who then "made the rounds (ויסבו) of all the cities of the Lord" (17:9). A semantic field is created, then, that creates a tension between the two occurrences of the word. When Jehoshaphat follows the path of God, his influence is felt all around the cities of Judah. The tension between Jehoshaphat's good and bad behavior is underscored by the narrator's use of the same verb to describe each. When Jehoshaphat has been enticed from the path of God, he finds himself surrounded by Aramean archers, with the word ויסבו signifying divine disapproval and castigation.[24]

Criticism of Jehoshaphat is detected even in his very salvation from the archers. The *Vorlage* states simply, "and Jehoshaphat cried out and when the chariot officers became aware that he was not the king of Israel, they turned from pursuing him" (22:32-33). The Chronicler, however, adds to this: "and Jehoshaphat cried out *and the Lord helped him, and God drew them away from him*" (18:31). Of particular interest here is the verb used to denote the act of God drawing them away from him. The verb employed is ויסתם, and marks the second time in this chapter that the root ס.ו.ת. has been employed (cf. v. 2, "and he enticed him [ויסיתהו] to march upon Ramoth Gilead"). The fact that this is the only chapter in the Hebrew Bible in which the verb is found twice, is perhaps a curiosity and not more than that. Yet, it must be stressed here, that both occurrences in 2 Chronicles 18 are glosses added to the *Vorlage* version of 1 Kings 22, suggesting that the Chronicler wished to establish a semantic linkage between them.

Scholars have suggested possible meanings of this semantic association. Kalimi[25] maintains that the verb is twice employed to stress Jehoshaphat's favored status. Through the verb of ס.ו.ת., maintains Kalimi, Ahab endangered Jehoshaphat's life. His life, however, was never really in jeopardy—witness the fact that God grants him salvation through the same root. Kalimi's reading, however, is predicated on his assumption that the Chronicler views Jehoshaphat's actions favorably. In light of the censure of Jehu ben Hanani (19:1-3) and the

---

[24] One could suggest that the difference between ויסרו and ויסבו is the result of a scribal error owing to the orthographic resemblance between the letter *resh* and the letter *bet* in ancient Hebrew. I prefer to see the difference as intentional, as the word ויסבו accords with the pejorative presentation of Jehoshaphat in this chapter and resonates with the other occurrence of ויסבו at 17:9.

[25] Kalimi, *The Book of Chronicles*, 341.

interpretation offered concerning the pattern of substitution of plural
for singular language, Kalimi's assumption is open to challenge.

Alternatively, Johnstone proposes that the dual occurrence of
the root .ת.ו.ס serves to underscore the criticism of Ahab.[26] Ahab
enticed Jehoshaphat to enter into union. The second appearance
of the root, Johnstone claims, demonstrates that "human initiative
is overruled by divine." His claim, however, seems unsubstantiated.
The fact is that Ahab *succeeded* in enticing Jehoshaphat. His attempt
to persuade Jehoshaphat to join him was in no way "overruled" by
divine decree.

Instead, the double occurrence of the root .ת.ו.ס may be seen as
a rhetorical device that echoes the tone and tenor of Jehu's words to
Jehoshaphat: "Wrath is upon you from the Lord. However, there is
some good in you" (19:2-3). That is, says the seer, even though you
have assisted the wicked and have displayed love for those that hate
the Lord (19:2), you have been deemed worthy of salvation due to
your earlier good deeds (2 Chronicles 17). This message may be read
back into the lexical tension around the root .ת.ו.ס. In spite of the fact
that you allowed yourself to be enticed into alliance with Ahab (or, in
the language of Jehu, "you assisted the wicked and befriended [תאהב]
those that hate the Lord"), charges the prophet, you have nonetheless
been found worthy.[27] In spite of ויסיתהו—"he enticed" you to join
ranks with him—nonetheless, ויסתם; God has lured the archers away
from you in your hour of distress.

An identical rhetoric surrounding the verb .ע.ז.ר may also be seen
in the episode of Jehoshaphat's salvation. Again, a term that bears a
positive connotation within the rescue passage is found to be matched
in the Chronicler's glosses surrounding the battle story, but in a negative connotation. At the moment that Jehoshaphat cries out (18:31),
the Chronicler's version states, "and the Lord helped him (עזרו)."
This is the same root with which Jehu chastises Jehoshaphat (19:2):
"Should one give aid (לעזר) to the wicked?" The concessive implication that we saw surrounding the lexical field of .ת.ו.ס is reiterated;
Although Jehoshaphat aided the wicked (הלרשע לעזר), he nonetheless
was deemed meritorious and thus God aids him (ויהוה עזרו). To sum-

---

[26] Johnstone, *1 and 2 Chronicles*, 1:90.

[27] As Moran has demonstrated, the verb אהב and its Semitic analogs are used in the
context of diplomacy to convey political loyalty. See W.L. Moran, "The Ancient Near
Eastern Background to the Love of God in Deuteronomy," *CBQ* 25 (1963) 77-87.

marize, the Chronicler adds two verbs of salvation to the narrative of Jehoshaphat's deliverance in v. 31, .ת.ו.ס and .ע.ז.ר. He likewise inserts each of these verbs elsewhere in the narrative (.ת.ו.ס. in the prologue to the story, v. 2, and .ע.ז.ר in the epilogue, (19:2) bearing pejorative connotations for the figure of Jehoshaphat to underscore the complex nature of his standing in this story.

We summarize our analysis of the Chronicler's reworking of the material of the battle of Ramoth Gilead to this point. The account focuses on the figure of Jehoshaphat and is mixed in its review. Jehoshaphat grievously errs in forming an alliance with Ahab. The Chronicler, however, preserves the record of Jehoshaphat's vigilant argumentation during the deliberations at the entrance to the gate of Samaria (vv. 4-7), as evidence of Jehoshaphat's merits. The ledger of his merits and demerits is reflected on the battlefield. On the one hand, he falls into mortal danger at the hands of the Aramean archers. In the end, however, his merits outweigh his offenses, and he is granted salvation.

The Chronicler's Use of the Lacunae of 1 Kgs 22:5-35

Our analysis of 2 Chronicles 18 has, from a methodological standpoint, been in keeping with conventional approaches to the study of the Book of Chronicles. That is, we have identified textual changes of structure and language and have attempted to account for them. In some instances, we have followed the formalist school, whose approach is well represented in the work by Kalimi. The fundamental contention of this school is that in many instances the revisions adopted by the Chronicler are a reflection of preferred literary style alone and imply no ideological agenda.[28] In most instances we have interpreted the revisions as the product of an ideological agenda as posited by many scholars, such as Japhet.

Common to both these approaches to the study of Chronicles, however, is a sustained focus solely upon the explicit changes wrought by the Chronicler. Little attention has been paid, however, to the manner in which the Chronicler was capable of generating new readings even within texts that he left untouched. In this section I would like to suggest that in the present passage the Chronicler was highly sensitive to

---

[28] Kalimi, *The Book of Chronicles*, 387.

the lacunae within the narrative he had inherited; that he could leave a passage with little or no editing, and instead adumbrate new lines of reading even as he made virtually no changes to that text.

Thus far we have attended to elements of the reconstruction of 1 Kings 22. We noted the changes wrought in the prologue and epilogue of the story, as well as to subtle changes in language, all of which point to a critical portrayal of the figure of Jehoshaphat. At this juncture I would like to explore the impact that these changes have upon the reading of the narrative that remains virtually untouched by the Chronicler—that is, the account that stretches from Jehoshaphat's initiative to discern God's will (1 Kgs 22:5 = 2 Chr 18:4) through the death of Ahab (1 Kgs 22:35 = 2 Chr 18:34).

Recall that in our analysis of 1 Kings 22 we stated that the figure of Jehoshaphat stood as a foil of comparison through which to judge the wicked Ahab. The early verses of that narrative attest to Jehoshaphat's steadfast determination to act only in accordance with God's will. The latter verses attest, by contrast, to Ahab's obstinacy. The results of the battle, we suggested, reflected the contrast in characterization. Ahab, who sought to avert the divine decree, meets his death anyway. Jehoshaphat, who stood as an easy target, is the recipient of divine assistance, and is spared. This favorable reading of Jehoshaphat, we said, was suggested by the narrator's prologue concerning Jehoshaphat immediately following the battle (1 Kgs 22: 41-51). Of particular import for our understanding of the Ramoth Gilead battle story was the credit given Jehoshaphat for having made peace with the king of Israel (22:45).

The Chronicler, we saw, disapproved of this initiative and reconstructed the material to create a more critical portrayal of Jehoshaphat. The explicit revisions, however, tell only part of the story. The Chronicler also capitalizes upon lacunae within the story to generate a new impression of Jehoshaphat's conduct on the eve of the battle.

The story—both in Kings and in Chronicles—begins with every sign that Jehoshaphat is capable of maintaining his ideological resolve. He demands that the Lord's counsel be sought; he rejects the prophetic body proposed by Ahab, and, against Ahab's will, insists that Micaiah be consulted. He reproves Ahab for the manner in which he addresses the prophet of the Lord. This reproof, however, is where Jehoshaphat ceases to be heard in both versions of the story. Within 1 Kings 22, the narrative focus closes in on the confrontation between Micaiah and Ahab. Ahab, it will be recalled, is the primary character in the last chapters of 1 Kings, and it is toward his demise and the fulfillment of Elijah's prophecy that the narrative moves. Once Jehoshaphat has been set up as a foil in the early verses of the account through which to judge the wicked Ahab, he has served his part, and disappears from the narrative stage. The Chronicler, however, exploits Jehoshaphat's silences as part of the play of the discourse. Following 2 Chr 18:7, speech continues to dominate the rhetoric of the passage. Zedekiah speaks twice (vv. 10, 23); Ahab five times (vv. 8, 14, 15, 17, 25), and Micaiah six (vv. 13, 14, 16, 18, 24, 27). Although Jehoshaphat never speaks again, his ominous silences are heard at five junctures, and become a distinct presence in the text. In verse 17, Ahab reminds Jehoshaphat of his earlier prediction, that Micaiah would never offer an encouraging prophecy to him. Effectively no new information is presented here, and the repetition seems unnecessary. What is new, however, is Jehoshaphat's response. In the face of the identical charge in v. 7, Ahab is met with rebuke. Now, he is met with silence. In vv. 18-22 Micaiah offers his prophecy, much to the consternation of all present. Yet, Jehoshaphat offers neither consent nor support for the prophet of God. In verse 23 Micaiah is physically assaulted. Jehoshaphat, who is presumably still seated alongside Ahab (cf. v. 9), remains silent. In verse 24 Micaiah courageously scolds the false prophets. Once again Jehoshaphat is silent. Finally, in v. 26, Ahab, Jehoshaphat's new ally, incarcerates Micaiah under cruel conditions. Jehoshaphat remains mute.

2 Chr 18:28-34 – The Battle at Ramoth Gilead as Metaphor Plot

The observation that Jehoshaphat's identity as a champion of God dissipates with the progression of the narrative leads us to the primary aim of this investigation: the manner in which the battle account (vv. 28-34) functions as a metaphor of the preceding narrative, the court deliberations of vv. 4-27. In v. 29 Ahab declares his intention to disguise himself, while encouraging Jehoshaphat to enter the battle theater in his regalia. The ramifications of this are catastrophic for Jehoshaphat, as the Aramean archers mistake Jehoshaphat for Ahab (v. 31). On the field of battle, effectively, the two monarchs have become indistinguishable. And this, despite the stern warning issued by the King of Aram that his archers take due care and target the King of Israel alone. On one level, verse 30 serves to inform us of the Aramean strategy. The Bible, however, only rarely ventures into

the strategy sessions of the enemy camp and it would seem that the
plot could have proceeded apace without this information. The narrative could have taken us from Ahab's request to alter his dress to the
archer's identifying Jehoshaphat as Ahab. From this alone we would
have been able to deduce that their primary target was Ahab, as he is
the leader of the alliance. The narrative foray into the strategy session
of the Aramean camp is instructive, however, because of what it tells
us about how deeply misled the archers were. In spite of the king's
exhortation, the archers are wholly incapable of properly identifying
the king of Judah. Even in their discerning eyes, Jehoshaphat has
become utterly indistinguishable from the King of Israel.

It is not the archers alone, however, who are unable to distinguish between the two kings. Long before the kings arrive upon the
battlefield, their identities have become blurred and interchangeable.
Throughout the narrative of vv. 4-27, we are witness to the unfolding of this process. Indeed, in vv. 4-7, Jehoshaphat stands in pointed
opposition to Ahab, and the differentiation between them is apparent.
Yet, once Ahab accedes to Jehoshaphat's wish and sends for Micaiah
to be brought, the obfuscation begins. Verse 9 is a turning point in
the narrative. Alter has noted that the Bible in its strategies of characterization rarely elaborates on issues such as "physical appearance,
the tics and gestures, the dress and implements of the characters, the
material milieu in which they enact their destinies."[29] And yet, this
is precisely what we encounter in verse 9, which elaborately details
the setting of the court as the prophets begin their presentation. The
portrayal of the two kings here stands in sharp contrast to that of
the previous section. If in verses 4-7, Jehoshaphat and Ahab are set
apart in disputation, they now act in consonance and are described
in highly like terms. I offer my own, highly literal translation of v. 9
for the sake of close analysis:

a) And the king of Israel and Jehoshaphat king of Judah were sitting
    (יושבים) each one on his own throne (איש על כסאו)
b) dressed (מלבשים) in finery
c) sitting (ויושבים) at the threshing floor at the entrance of the gate
    of Samaria
d) while all of the prophets were prophesying before them (לפניהם).

All four clauses refer to the two kings with a single verb in the
plural form. Yet the variation in syntax is highly instructive. 9a depicts

---

[29] Alter, *The Art of Biblical Narrative*, 114.

the kings in unison, and yet distinct; they are seated together, yet are distinguishable, with each upon his own throne. The last three clauses, however, offer a higher degree of uniformity, as the two are described only in terms of that which is common to them. The verse opens, then, with a syntax that still bears a sense of the distinction that characterizes their interchange in vv. 4-7. It concludes, however, with a syntax of full uniformity, an index of the shift in Jehoshaphat's disposition from autonomy to complicity.[30]

From there until the close of the deliberations, the dissipation of Jehoshaphat's autonomous identity continues. Jehoshaphat's silence at five junctures, each more pressing than the prior one, is almost deafening. It underscores his adopted strategy of total capitulation, or, as Jehu puts it, his strategy of "loving those who hate the Lord" (19:2). In disposition, he has become indistinguishable from the king of Israel. In battle, therefore, this will become his fate as well.[31]

The theme of blurred vs. autonomous identity develops as the battle report progresses. The critical verse here is verse 31 (= 1 Kgs 22: 32). In the *Vorlage*, the manner through which Jehoshaphat survives is unstated: "Jehoshaphat cried out. And when the chariot officers became aware that he was not the king of Israel, they turned back from pursuing him." Gray, speculating on how the Aramean archers concluded that they had been mistaken, offers two suggestions. Either they saw Jehoshaphat cry toward the Judean soldiers and not those of the northern kingdom, or they perceived a dialect in his cry that they could identify as Judean.[32] His salvation, within the narrative of the *Vorlage* is the result of double causation where the narrative focus is on the human component. The verisimilitude of the depiction allows the narrative to be understood without necessarily reading God into the action. The positive portrayal of Jehoshaphat, however, both within the scene and in the epitaph section of vv. 41-51, suggests

---

[30] Interestingly, the opening phrase of 9c, "while sitting," is absent from the *Vorlage*, which reads verselets b and c together, "dressed in finery at the threshing floor," etc. The Chronicler inserts an additional verb that brings to four the total number of verbs that jointly describe the two kings.

[31] It is interesting to note in this context the rendering of the LXX (in both sources) concerning Ahab's disguise. Ahab instructs that his own apparel be worn by Jehoshaphat! Perhaps the LXX felt that this would better explain the misinterpretation of Jehoshaphat's identity by the Aramean archers. The MT, however, gives no hint of this.

[32] Gray, *I & II Kings*, 404-05.

that Jehoshaphat's rescue should be read as the product of double causation, with God's role unmentioned but implicitly present behind the scenes.

The Chronicler, however, reconstructs the episode: "And Jehoshaphat cried out *and the Lord helped him, and God diverted them from him.*" The address of Jehoshaphat's cry is altered. God delivers Jehoshaphat because he has cried to *Him* for salvation.[33] Johnstone has correctly noted that the verbs "cry" and "help," expressing unconditional reliance on the Lord, belong to the Chronicler's key vocabulary and have already been linked in 1 Chr 5:20 (cf. 2 Chr 14:11).[34] The episode brings the theme of Jehoshaphat's disguised identity full-circle. At the outset Jehoshaphat's identity was clearly established as that of the champion of God's will. Later, his identity becomes indistinguishable from that of Ahab as his sustained silence signals acquiescence. What has transpired on the interpersonal plane in the court of Samaria is then transposed onto the battlefield of Ramoth Gilead, as the archers cannot distinguish between the two kings. In Chronicles, however, the archers' perception is sharpened at precisely the moment that Jehoshaphat re-establishes his autonomous identity as a servant of God—the moment that he cries out to God (18:31-32): "And Jehoshaphat cried out and the Lord helped him, and God diverted them from him. And when the chariot officers realized that he was not the king of Israel, they gave up the pursuit."

To be sure, the two sides of double causation are at play here in Chronicles as they were in the *Vorlage*, but in different proportions. In Kings, the human element was explicit, the divine implicit. The equation is reversed in Chronicles. Explicitly, it is God who is responsible for Jehoshaphat's rescue. Secondary, and only implicit, is the recognition that the archers understood their mistake. Perhaps, as Gray had suggested, they could perceive the dialect of his cry.[35] Perhaps, as they closed in on him, they saw that he was in the company of other Judean soldiers. Perhaps some element of his regalia indicated his Judean identity. The archers, of course, are impervious to Jehoshaphat's inner spiritual vacillations, and do not perceive that he is crying to the Lord. Yet from a divine perspective, Jehoshaphat is saved because—for the first time in 24 verses—he speaks, nay cries,

---

[33] Japhet, *I & II Chronicles*, 767.
[34] Johnstone, *1 and 2 Chronicles*, 1:90.
[35] Gray, *I & II Kings*, 404-05.

to God. In so doing he restores the distinction between himself and the king of Israel.

To conclude, I would like to examine the opening statement heard from Jehoshaphat in each version, namely, his response to Ahab's call to arms. The two versions are highly similar. Nonetheless, I would suggest, each reflects a distinct perspective on Jehoshaphat's willingness to unite with Ahab:

1 Kgs 22:4	**2 Chr 18:3**
Like me, like you	Like me, like you
Like *my* people, like *your* people	Like *your* people, like *my* people
Like my horses, like your horses	And with you (s.) in battle

The significant change is in the third clause. Change, indeed, is evident already in the transition from the first to second clause, as the Chronicler opts for chiastic structure where the *Vorlage* prefers parallelism. Kalimi adduces this verse as an example of the Chronicler's tendency to employ the same terms found in the *Vorlage*, yet rearranged in chiastic order, as a preference of style.[36] The third clause, however, represents a significant departure from its parallel in Kings, both in language and, we suggest, in import, as well. The eighteenth century rabbinic exegete R. David Altschuler in his commentary *Metsudat David* claims that the third clause refers to the second; that is, the third clause may effectively be read as follows: "*my people* are with you in battle." The Targum however, translates the phrase in a fashion that implies that it is Jehoshaphat who is expressing his personal solidarity with Ahab, "*I* am with you." The Targum's understanding finds support earlier in the text of verse 3. Jehoshaphat's third clause, ועמך במלחמה, parallels the precise language of Ahab's query, "will you go with me (התלך עמי) to Ramoth Gilead?" To be sure, Ahab's query reflects his desire that the army of Judah join him, and not only its king. Yet his query is cast as a personal address to Jehoshaphat. Jehoshaphat echoes Ahab's query in his third and final clause, as an indication of personal camaraderie and esprit de corps with the king of Israel.

For the author of Kings, Jehoshaphat's response of "Like me, like you" is no different from, nor more prominent than, either of the other two clauses. Together they express the sense that the mission will be undertaken in unison—in leadership, in manpower, and in materiel.

---

[36] Kalimi, *The Book of Chronicles*, 235.

"Like me, like you," for the author of Kings, is a heroic statement, one that reverses the strategy adopted by Asa of collusion with the King of Aram against the King of Israel. As such, it is an appropriate statement with which to introduce the character of Jehoshaphat, who "made peace with the king of Israel" (22:45). For the Chronicler, however, the third clause is indicative of the dynamic about to unfold between the two monarchs. Indeed, it implies, on a surface level, that Judah is joining Israel in battle, as implied in the phrasing of the *Vorlage*. Yet the third clause stresses that underneath the surface of the joint mission is a merging of dispositions. In response to Ahab's query, "will *you* go with me?," Jehoshaphat enthusiastically responds in the affirmative, "I am with you." The words, "Like me, like you," then, for the Chronicler, are hardly the stuff of a heroic statement of unity against a common enemy. Rather the terse, two-word statement, "Like me, like you," is the appropriate opening of a narrative in which both in disposition and hence in fate, Jehoshaphat will emerge as indistinguishable from the king of Israel.[37]

This final case study, then, once again illustrates the way in which a battle scene may be seen to stand as a metaphor analogy of the narrative that precedes it. Note, however, the distinct nature of the base of the analogy in the present instance. All of the previous analogies that we investigated made use of lexical associations to form the base of the analogy, some to a greater extent, some to a lesser one. In our introduction we noted that with regard to the metaphor plot, this was to be expected. Unlike analogy of common subject matter, the metaphor plot compares inherently dissimilar spheres of endeavor. The burden of linkage, therefore, rests in such analogies more heavily upon lexical markers. Yet, not a single significant shared term may be found between the battle story of Ramoth Gilead and the court deliberations that precede it. Instead the Chronicler achieves a strong sense of analogy by utilizing highly vivid details—particularly those of Jehoshaphat's peril and rescue—to draw attention to a common theme: the loss of identity engendered through assimilation and complicity.

---

[37] Cf. Walsh, *1 Kings*, 343.

CHAPTER EIGHT

CONCLUSIONS: THE BATTLE REPORT AND NARRATIVE ANALOGY IN LIGHT OF THE PRESENT STUDY

We have identified six instances in which a biblical battle scene could be seen as a metaphor analogy for the narrative that immediately precedes it. At this juncture, it is time to examine the six as a group: do they share a common rhetorical function? Do their poetics differ? Do the six narratives examined here give us the mandate to adduce a "convention" of the biblical battle report? What do these six examples suggest about narrative analogy generally within biblical literature?

I should like to explore these issues by examining the six case-studies in light of two questions of poetics. A perspectival gulf is sometimes formed between the reader and the characters internal to the biblical story concerning the import of the events unfolding in the narrative.[1] In the case of narrative analogy the readers may become increasingly aware of the presence of this literary device within the text they are reading and draw the appropriate conclusions. Yet, what of the characters themselves?

Our first question, then, focuses upon an issue that Dällenbach described as "internal reception"—the consciousness of a character within the story that two spheres of action bear a resemblance.[2] Out of the six narratives examined it would appear that internal reception to the lessons of the analogy is present in five of them. Within the Book of Joshua, the erection of a cairn atop the corpse of a vanquished Canaanite foe is found only in the instance of the King of Ha-Ai (8: 29). Its only parallel is in the identically worded gesture following the execution of Achan (7:26). While we identified several common terms and motifs as the basis of the analogy, the erection of the cairn serves a distinct function concerning the issue of internal reception. In both narratives, for example, we saw that the Israelites "pursued," that Joshua "rose," and that the enemy was "burnt by fire." Yet, these

---

[1] Sternberg, *Poetics*, 410.
[2] Dällenbach, *Le Récit Spéculaire*, 111.

gestures are common gestures. As semantic markers they could allow us as readers to establish analogy within the written word, within the narrative of the two accounts. Yet, the Israelite soldiers in pursuit (וירוצו) of their foes at Ha-Ai (8:19) could hardly have been thinking of the act of running (וירוצו) that had been executed to retrieve the booty in 7:22. The erection of the latter cairn, however, would seem to indicate internal reception of the analogy on the part of Joshua. He could hardly have performed the identical gesture without intending to draw an analogy for himself and perhaps for all of Israel between Achan and Ha-Ai. In so doing, he demonstrated that the analogy was clear to him: in the wake of the debacle of the first encounter against Ha-Ai (7:2-5), Joshua could now visually demonstrate that Israel had overcome both her enemies—the internal and the external, respectively. The analogy may have been evident to Joshua from the start; it is only through this final common gesture, however, that it becomes clear to us as readers that this is indeed so.

Internal reception is evident as well in the civil war against the tribe of Benjamin in Judges 20. Recall that one understanding of the analogy between the assault upon the concubine in Judges 19 and the final battle against Benjamin in chapter 20 was that the victimization of the tribe of Benjamin at the hands of the tribes of Israel in chapter 20 was as vicious as the victimization of the concubine by the inhabitants of Gibeah in chapter 19. Among the elements that we noted as members of the base of the analogy was the common response by the tribes in the wake of each atrocity. The Israelites query the Benjaminites in 20:3 in response to the mutilated limbs they had received: "Tell us, how did this evil thing happen? (דברו איכה נהיתה הרעה הזאת). A similar query is expressed following the decimation of the Benjaminites, in 21:3: "O Lord God of Israel, why has this happened in Israel? (למה יהוה אלהי ישראל היתה-זאת בישראל). The ensuing offering of sacrifices (21:4) and resolve to find wives through whom to rebuild the decimated tribe, suggest that the question is asked as much of themselves as it is of God. Having judgmentally pondered the travesties committed at the hands of the Gibeans, they were now forced to ponder the travesty wrought by their own hands. As within the narrative analogy of Joshua 7-8, internal reception is demonstrated through the final common base element within the analogical structure.

Within the narrative of 2 Chronicles 18 that details the alliance and battle enjoined by Ahab and Jehoshaphat, the case is somewhat weaker. Jehoshaphat must certainly have realized that the Aramean

archers were aiming at him (2 Chr 18:31) under the presumption that
he was Ahab. Yet, even as he calls to God (18:31), it is not clear that
he had assimilated the full implication of the analogy: that through
his complicity with Ahab, he had made himself indistinguishable from
the Israelite king in the eyes of his once protective God and hence
in the eyes of the Aramean archers. Nonetheless, the argument for
internal reception may be made. Upon returning to Jerusalem from
the battlefield, Jehoshaphat is severely censured by the prophet Jehu
ben Hanani: "Should one give aid to the wicked and befriend those
who hate the Lord? For this wrath is upon you from the Lord" (2 Chr
19:2). Implicit in the prophet's censure is the lesson of the analogy: to
enter the sphere of comradeship with the wicked is to enter the sphere
of danger that ultimately awaits them.

Internal reception of the narrative analogy is manifest in the ark
narrative of 1 Chronicles 13-14. Recall that even though the battle
narrative of Baal Perazim (1 Chr 14:8-12) follows the account of Perez
Uzzah (1 Chr 13:1-14) along the text continuum, we claimed that
coherence of a synchronic reading of the ark narratives of 1 Chronicles
13-16 suggests that the battle of Baal Perazim chronologically preceded
the account of Perez Uzzah. Put differently, David renamed the site of
the debacle Perez Uzzah (1 Chr 13:11) only after he had triumphantly
called the site of his victory over the Philistines, Baal Perazim (1 Chr
14:11). We noted that the appearance of the verb and noun forms
together ("to burst a bursting") is found only in the verses under question in this study (i.e. 1 Chr 13:11 [= 2 Sam 6:8] and 1 Chr 14:11 [=
2 Sam 5:20]), and in one other instance, in the Book of Job. There
Scripture states, "he breached me, breach after breach (יפרצני פרץ);
He rushed at me like a warrior" (Job 16:14; cf. Exod 19:22; Ps 60:3).
The peculiar construct is an explicitly military reference, both in Job,
and in the etiology of Baal Perazim at 14:11. The etiology offered by
David underscored his realization that the glorious transfer of the ark
had evolved into an armed clash with God. God meets Israel at "The
Threshing Floor of Spear" (גורן כדון), and figuratively engages Israel
in violent confrontation.

Internal reception of the meaning of the analogy was also seen
within our analysis of the Book of Esther. We claimed that the narrative analogy between the second day of feasting in chapter 5 and the
second day of fighting in chapter 9 underscored Esther's maturity into
transcendence and subjectivity. On the first day of feasting the king
asked, "What is your wish? It shall be granted you. And what is your

request? Even to half the kingdom, it shall be fulfilled" (5:6). On the
first day of fighting, he asks similarly, "What is your wish now? It shall
be granted you. And what else is your request? It shall be fulfilled"
(9:12). In each instance, Esther asks that the next day (מחר) witness a
repetition of the events of the first. In chapter 5 she asks that the king
and Haman again the next day attend a drinking party that she will
make for them, and in chapter 9 she asks that again the next day the
Jews be allowed to take revenge on their enemies. We suggested that
the repetitions of form witnessed between the second day of feasting
and of fighting function as an index of change in the state of Esther's
self-concept. Her call in chapter 5 to re-stage on the morrow an event
that honors the king, demonstrates an inability to engage the king as
anything but an othered, inessential being. Yet, when Esther responds
to the king's identical query in chapter 9, she seizes the moment. The
repetition of the events of the first day will endow the Jews with an
even more heightened status of honor and dominion.

The only narrative analogy examined that does not reveal internal
reception is that of the analogy between Israel's scorning of God in
Judges 10 and Israel's scorning of Jephthah in Judges 11. This analogy may be seen, however, to be the exception that proves the rule.
The metaphor analogy between the two narratives, we suggested, was
employed to underscore God's sense of wound and injury in human
terms so that the reader could more easily relate to the sense, not only
of sin, or transgression, but indeed of betrayal and pain. In chapter 10
God's pain and Israel's disloyalty are concretized through the rhetoric
of the rebuke dialogue. In chapter 11, God's pain, sense of mistrust,
and betrayal are dramatized through the metaphoric and equivalent
experience of Jephthah with the elders. As the negotiation progresses
in chapter 11, there is no evidence that the elders, or even Jephthah,
for that matter, were aware of the equivalence that the author was
establishing with the previous episode. This is hardly by accident.
One of the main theological thrusts of the Book of Judges is that, as
Scripture states in Judges 2, Israel was unaware of the spiritual reality
of the period: "Another generation arose after them, which had not
experienced [the deliverance of] the Lord or the deeds that He had
wrought for Israel" (Judg 2:10). The very structure of the book underscores this point. The prologue of chapter 2, an unusual feature within
the corpus of biblical narrative, focuses the reader's attention on the
spiritual realities to which the Israelites of that generation had been

blind.[3] The highly cyclical structure of the book as a whole likewise underscores the point that there is a divine order at work at this time that needs to be made manifest because the people of the time were blind to it.[4] The narrative analogy between the scorning of Jephthah and the scorning of God is another way by which the author of the Book of Judges stresses this reality for his reader in the face of the blindness of the Israelites of that time. Because the absence of internal reception conforms to the didactic lesson that dictates the structure of the book as a whole, we may term it the exception that proves the rule: the analogies that we have identified tend to serve the didactic function of illuminating not only us as readers, but the protagonists of the respective stories as well.

To summarize the issue: five out of the six narrative analogies studied demonstrate that the lessons of narrative analogy are evident not only to readers sensitive to the language and imagery employed by the biblical author. Rather, they are usually evident to at least some of the characters internal to the stories as well. As mentioned in our introduction, there have been no studies to date that have thoroughly examined the phenomenon of narrative analogy across the Hebrew Bible. Such a study could investigate this point: do the characters internal to a story routinely comprehend the lessons that the reader does, as suggested by our findings here?

The second measure through which I wish to compare the narrative analogies studied is by means of the question of *vectors of illumination*. That is, in looking at the relationship of two analogous narratives, which may be said to illuminate and which may be said to be illuminated? For the purpose of this discussion, I will posit an ideal reader who has no foreknowledge beyond what he or she has read in that particular text. I am thinking, for example, of a reader who encounters the trial of Achan (Joshua 7), without any familiarity with what transpires in the conquest of Ha-Ai (Joshua 8). Readers possessing other hypothetical traits could be posited as well, as will be discussed shortly, but for the purposes of the initial discussion, I would like to limit myself to an act of reading that presupposes no foreknowledge of what is to follow. Here too, a general trend emerges from the cases studied: the second story—in our examples the battle account—tends to illuminate the parallel narrative that precedes it; illumination functions analeptically.

---

[3] Cf. Amit, *The Book of Judges: The Art of Editing*, 142-43.
[4] Cf. Amit, *Editing*, 34.

Within the Ha-Ai narrative of Joshua 7-8, chapter 8 elucidates chapter7. Chapter 8 is a battle account essentially undifferentiated from any of the other battle accounts of the Book of Joshua. Ha-Ai, its king, and its inhabitants are subsets of the familiar class of Canaanites. The reasons for the battle waged against them are well understood and require no elucidation. Yet, whereas chapter 8 is conceptually typical, chapter 7 is not. The challenge here before the author of Joshua was how to convey the full implications of an individual violation of the *ḥerem*. Israel had no prior experience with this set of circumstances and thus the situation, as it were, begged elucidation. In turning to narrative analogy, the author borrows from an existing typology: Achan is characterized in terms that can be interpreted as metaphorically analogous to the conquest of a Canaanite city. The vector of illumination then, seems to be retrospective; the details of the story of the battle for Ha-Ai elucidate facets of the struggle against the enemy within that are reported in chapter 7.

The dynamic of retrospective illumination would also seem to be at play in the relationship between the story of the ascent of Jephthah in Judges 11 and the account of God's scorning by Israel in Judges 10. The passage of 10:17-11:11 is not primarily concerned with the insult and snubbing accorded a local chieftain, Jephthah. In chapter 10, God's pain and Israel's disloyalty are concretized, rendered human, through the rhetoric of the rebuke dialogue. In chapter 11, God's pain, sense of mistrust, and betrayal are further illuminated through the equivalent experience of Jephthah with the elders.

Retrospection may likewise be seen in the relationship between the story of the battle of Baal Perazim and the debacle of Perez Uzzah in the ark narrative of 1 Chronicles 13-14. The first story along the text continuum, that of Perez Uzzah, remains enigmatic, even upon its conclusion at the end of 1 Chronicles 13: why has God "burst a bursting"? The array of military motifs in the Perez Uzzah narrative and their analogous elements in the battle narrative of Baal Perazim retrospectively served to demonstrate that, from the Chronicler's perspective, David's initiative had constituted an assault upon the ark.

The same retrospective vector of influence was manifest in the account of Ahab and Jehoshaphat in 2 Chronicles 18. The process throughout the court deliberations in which distinctions between the two protagonists became blurred, was a subtle one. The blurred distinction between the two on the battlefield, however, was concrete and visibly palpable. Once again, it was the earlier and parallel narrative, in this case the account of the court deliberations, that was construed in terms of the battle story.

While we may chronicle four cases in which the battle narrative illuminates the analog story that precedes it, the picture is less clear with regard to the other two accounts that we examined. In the Book of Esther the illumination between the analogous accounts seems to be mutual. In chapter 5 we find the king beseeching Esther to tell him her wish, and Esther demurring, almost stammering something about getting together again tomorrow to talk about it. In chapter 9 we again find the king beseeching Esther to tell him her wish. This time she assertively proposes a plan of action that underscores her emergence into transcendence. The two accounts are mutually illuminating, because they reinforce the overall effect of the index of change. Esther's otherness in chapter 5 is emphasized in light of her later flourishing in chapter 9. And her emerging subjectivity in chapter 9 is heightened in light of her otherness under similar circumstances in chapter 5. Whereas all of the other analogies probed drew lines of *similarity* between the analogous passages, the narrative analogy of Esther 5 and Esther 9 is the only one that is *contrastive* in nature. The analogy draws our attention to how *dis*similar Esther is in chapter 9 relative to her demeanor at the feasts of chapter 5.

If the analogy in Esther points to mutual illumination between the two passages, a final instance seems to suggest that the vector of illumination is from the analog narrative to the battle narrative that follows it. This is seen in the analogy between the rape of the concubine in Judges 19 and the battle against the tribe of Benjamin in Judges 20. Recall that we concluded that the meaning of the analogy could be construed in two ways. In one, we stated that the purpose of the analogy was to demonstrate the law of talion. The battle bore a resemblance to the rape to demonstrate that the Benjaminites received their just deserts. The battle is perceived in light of the rape, and thus it is the rape account that illuminates the battle. The same vector of illumination is true with regard to the second level of meaning that we ascribed to the analogy: that the tribes of Israel had behaved viciously vis-à-vis the Benjaminites even as the inhabitants of Gibeah had treated the concubine. Here again the battle account and its message are construed in light of the prior, analogous account of the rape.

These findings need to be understood within the larger context of the Bible's prospective and retrospective tendencies generally. Meir Sternberg couches the discussion within a larger question of two competing impulses within biblical narrative. On the one hand, prolepsis would seem to be a natural rhetorical vehicle for the biblical narrator as it highlights the notion of the human characters' lack of knowledge over against God's omniscience. Yet to pronounce at the outset of a tale the fate of its characters militates against the need to demonstrate that man exists as a free moral agent and further implies that God is nothing but a heavenly puppeteer.[5] On the other hand, to depict events as flowing freely with no indication of divine intervention would create a mistaken image of a God with a "laissez-faire" policy of worldly intervention.[6] Prolepsis, therefore, argues Sternberg, bears inherent theological, and hence rhetorical problems for the biblical narrator. One way in which Scripture covers all its theological bases, so to speak, is through the agency of analepsis, or retrospective comments.[7] While the action is still playing itself out, tips as to the ensuing course of events will be sparse, while explicit notices of God's intervention will be sparser still. Yet, at the close of a story, Scripture will therefore insert a retrospective allusion that helps the reader appreciate that God was an active and interested agent all along in what by all appearances were the free actions of the human agents involved.[8] Our findings in four of the narratives studied suggest that an analeptic function may lie behind the repeated occurrence of a battle report following its parallel narrative. We see now that this supposition resonates with the theological and rhetorical sweep of biblical narrative as accounted for by Sternberg.[9]

The one case in which the analog narrative illuminated the battle report that follows it (Judges 19-20), however, in no way contravenes Sternberg's thesis. Sternberg's comments spoke to the issue of *perspective*, proleptic or analeptic. Yet, perspective is only one of two issues

---

[5] Sternberg, *Poetics*, 266.

[6] Ibid., 267.

[7] Ibid., 268.

[8] On double causation and biblical narratology see Frank Polak, *Biblical Narrative: Aspects of Art and Design* (Biblical Encyclopedia Library 11; Jerusalem: Bialik, 1994) 251-53 (Hebrew); Yairah Amit, "The Dual Causality Principle and Its Effects on Biblical Literature," *VT* 37 (1987) 385-400; idem, "Dual Causality—Another Aspect," *Beit Miqra* 38:1 (1992) 41-55 (Hebrew). Cf. Edward L. Greenstein, "An Equivocal Reading of the Sale of Joseph," in Kenneth R.R. Gros Louis and James Ackerman (eds.), *Literary Interpretations of Biblical Narratives* (2 vols.; Nashville: Abingdon, 1982) 2:123.

[9] Yair Zakovitch (*Introduction to Inner Biblical Exegesis* [Even Yehuda: Rekhes, 1992] 9 [Hebrew]) has also noted that when two stories stand in analogous relationship to one another, the second is more likely to illuminate the first than vice versa.

that emerge when we discuss the illumination offered by one narrative upon its analogous partner. Indeed, in the four examples in which the battle story was construed as illuminating the story that preceded it the illumination was of a retrospective or, analeptic nature. Yet, to say that the rape account of Judges 19 illuminates the battle account of Judges 20 is not the same as saying that it offers a proleptic perspective on that later account. One can easily read the rape account with no sense of foreshadowing or inkling of what will later befall the tribe of Benjamin. The forward vector of influence at work here simply means that having read through the battle account of Judges 20, the sensitive reader is apt to apprehend the battle in light of the earlier story of the rape. The vector of influence here is forward. The perspective, however, cannot be rightly termed here "proleptic" or "prospective," in the sense of offering a foreshadowing of things to come. To summarize, in four cases we see that the battle report offers a retrospective view of its analogous narrative, which allows the earlier, parallel story to be understood anew in light of the battle that follows it. In one case, the two days of feasting and the two days of fighting in Esther, battle report and analog account, may be seen in synergistic illumination. In a final case, Judges 19-20, illumination is provided to the battle account (against Benjamin) by the narrative that precedes it (the rape of the concubine).

Once again, the implications of our findings are suggestive of avenues of inquiry concerning the study of the narrative analogy in biblical literature. Looking broadly across the Bible, and assuming an act of reading that presupposes no foreknowledge of the action to come, will one find the same pattern exhibited here? Do most narrative analogies tend to illuminate retrospectively?

Before leaving this issue, however, the present writer feels the need to air some uneasiness about the hermeneutical assumptions that are the underpinning of much of what has been said, and indeed the parameters of the discussion of the topic of prospection and retrosepction as presented by Sternberg. Issues of prospection, retrospection, suspense, reader awareness, and gradual illumination all presume a highly particular hermeneutic of reading, which assumes that the reader encounters the text with no foreknowledge of what the text says. The entire discussion of poetics here and in Sternberg's writings are based on this assumption, an axiom of new critical theory to literature. Indeed, when an unknown work is encountered by a reader for the first time, new critical tools of interpretation seem highly valid.

But may the same be said for the Bible? Whether the narratives of the Bible have their origins in oral or literary traditions, whether we assume that the final form in our possession is virtually unchanged from its original written form, or whether we assume that what we have is a final form established through a process of extensive redaction, this hermeneutic of reading emerges as highly problematic. For the biblical texts in our possession were probably originally written, and certainly canonized, with the intent that they be read and reread within a community of tradition. This means that while every reader or listener has a first, virginal encounter with a story, for the most part, the life of a narrative within a community of tradition is one in which the story is already known before the first word of it is spoken or read. Under such circumstances, can there be true "suspense" in any narrative? Can any story be read without its analogous implications for the continuation of the story already known? As mentioned, it seems reasonable to assume that these stories were set to writing and canonized with the intent of being read and reread. This means then, that the authors/redactors must have assumed a hermeneutic of reading that did not depend solely upon a virginal reader-text encounter.

It seems to this author that there are four ways of negotiating this conundrum. The first is an argument from historical speculation. My questioning of the "virginal reader-text encounter" rests upon the assumption that these works were widely read and reread (or told, and retold). Yet, not enough is known about the dissemination of these works and their place in the cultural life of ancient Israel. It may be that the familiarity that I ascribe to the reader of old, was, in fact, only the province of the learned, perhaps the Levites and Priests in an earlier period, the scribes in a later one. The books were written, or redacted, it may be claimed, for a wider, less educated audience, and hence done so with an assumption of a virginal reader-text encounter. Yet, as studies increasingly reveal the intertextual nature of biblical narrative, it appears clear that the many later books allude to earlier ones, in a fashion that assumes an intimate familiarity with the fabric of the biblical text.[10]

Assuming, then, that the biblical narratives do assume familiarity with the text, we may move on to three potential strategies with which to address the conundrum. The first is to posit a supposition that is axiomatic and cannot be proven: even as the biblical writers/redactors

---

[10] Cf. Zakovitch, *Through the Looking Glass*, 12.

fully intended these works to be read and reread, they expected a hermeneutic of reading as if for a first time. The way that such a reading is accomplished is through identification with the characters at each and every stage of the narrative. Through imaginative reliving of the experience through the eyes of the characters, the absolute foreknowledge that is possessed by the reader is overcome. In short, the new-critical hermeneutic of reading is maintained.

Jefferson, in her essay on prospection, outlines a different approach to the problem. Concerning the problem of encountering a literary composition after the initial reading, she writes, "[the reader's] reading of the play is a repetition, but it is also a reminder, for he too, is prone to forget what he once knew well."[11] Put differently, Jefferson rescues the new-critical hermeneutic of a virgin reading by asserting that no first reading grasps all aspects of a narrative even as no second reading recalls in vivid detail all aspects of that first reading. To that, we may add the hermeneutical observation of the Talmud, that "the one-hundredth reading of a text is not the same as the 101st reading of a text."[12] Here, again, the new-critical hermeneutic of reading is preserved by virtue of the inherently new process of assimilation that occurs with every reading.

A third, and radically different approach, however, may be taken. Canonicity, perhaps implicitly intended already at the time of original composition, mandates a different hermeneutic of reading. Sequentiality is not only ignored, but indeed denied. The foreknowledge with which readers encounter and re-encounter the text mandates that they contextualize each part of the work with every other part of the work, and perhaps with the other works that comprise the canon of their own age. Contemporary studies on the hermeneutics of Scriptural interpretation in the late second temple period in Palestine suggest that precisely such a hermeneutic was predominant. According to Daniel Patte, axiomatic to the hermeneutics of the day was the notion of "the continual interpretation of Scripture by Scripture (which could be interpreted to mean that Scripture was conceived as a "closed system of signs")."[13] In contemporary biblical scholarship, such

---

[11] Jefferson, "Mise en abyme," 203.

[12] *b. Hagigah* 9b.

[13] Daniel Patte, *Early Jewish Hermeneutic in Palestine* (SBLDiss 22; Missoula: Scholars Press, 1975) 47. See in a similar vein, Kugel's contention that at this time the inner harmony with which Scripture was apprehended meant that "any biblical text might illuminate any other." James Kugel, *Traditions of the Bible: A Guide to the*

a notion stands at the foundation of canonical approaches to biblical studies. Similarly, chronology is routinely denied in early rabbinic literature in accordance with the dictum, "there is no before and after in Scripture."[14] The present study has applied a new-critical hermeneutic of virginal reading to the texts examined and has embraced the questions of prospection, suspense, etc. as legitimate ones. The present author understands, however, that such a hermeneutic may not have been the regnant one at the time of composition and/or redaction, and that the adoption of a hermeneutic like the one employed at the close of the Second Temple period would yield highly different readings of the texts examined here.

Thus far we have examined the ramifications of six case-studies for the study of narrative analogy in biblical prose. It is at this point that we probe what may be learned from these six analogies toward our understanding of the biblical battle story. Is there a single rhetorical function that underlies all of these analogies? We believe that there is: by setting the battle report into narrative analogy the text essentially subverts the importance of the battlefield action. The very positioning of the battle report in an analogous relationship with a nearby text suggests that what is important in the battle may not be ascertained by a scrutiny of the battle report alone. Theoretically, what could emerge from analysis of a battle report in isolation could be lessons about tactics, about leadership, about valor, heroism, or preparations. By setting depictions of all these elements into narrative analogy, the text essentially assigns the significance of meaning to another point in the story. In most instances the significance is shifted to a lesson drawn from the parallel story: the conquest of Ha-Ai elucidates the potential danger of the enemy within, Achan. Israel's mismanagement of Jephthah's appointment to high office elucidates Israel's misapprehension of their covenantal responsibilities vis-à-vis God. The battle of Baal Perazim underscores the quasi-military nature of the failed attempt to transport the ark at Perez Uzzah. The battle at Ramoth Gilead underscores the degree to which Jehoshaphat had compromised his identity. In the analogy probed in the Book of Esther the account of the second day of fighting, we claimed, bore little, if any,

---

Bible as It Was at the Start of the Common Era (Cambridge, MA: Harvard University Press, 1998) 17.

[14] Cf. *Mekhilta Exod.* 15:9, and discussion in Patte, *Early Jewish Hermeneutic*, 68-69.

significance in terms of the overall outcome of hostilities. Its entire significance, we suggested, stemmed from its implications for Esther's development as a transcendent, subjective being. The lessons that emerge from each of these analogies all point to some lacking in the off-battlefield behavior of the dramatis personae upon the field of battle, either in their relationship with their fellow man (as in gang-raping a concubine) or, more often, in their relationship with God (stealing from the consigned booty).

The observation that lessons about tactics, leadership, valor, and heroism are subverted by the establishment of narrative analogy between the battle story and another story confirms findings by other scholars concerning the place of military valor within the Hebrew Bible. As Zimmerli notes, although the Hebrew Bible contains many stories of men of war, it never developed any kind of hero worship.[15] As he further notes, God intervenes in different manners, but in the end, we find a tendency to represent human agents of victory in the most humble possible terms.[16] A primary message of Patrick Miller's *The Divine Warrior in Early Israel* is that "at the center of Israel's warfare was the unyielding conviction that victory was the result of a fusion of divine and human activity... Yahweh was the general of both the earthly and the heavenly host."[17] The subversion of battlefield activity through narrative analogy accords with these assessments.

We may make a second observation about the significance of our findings for an enhanced understanding of the biblical battle story. The establishment of narrative analogy between the story of a battle and the account of the events that led up to that battle may reflect a historiosophic point. A battle, indeed, perhaps, any event, may be seen either as a consequence of the events that preceded it, or as the point of origin for the events that follow it, or both. Within modern Israeli history, for example, the Yom Kippur War of 1973 may be seen from either of these perspectives. The war and its devastating results may be seen as the consequence of the over-confidence that infected Israeli society in the wake of the Six Day War and a lack of preparedness for the possibility of war. Alternatively, the Yom Kippur may be viewed as a point of causation for subsequent events: the

---

[15] Walter Zimmerli, *Grundriss der alttestamentlichen Theologie* (Theologische Wissenschaft 3; Stuttgart: Verlag W. Kohlhammer, 1972) 51.

[16] Ibid., 51.

[17] Patrick D. Miller, Jr., *The Divine Warrior in Early Israel* (Cambridge: Harvard University Press, 1973) 156.

realization that resolution of the conflict would come only through negotiation, a recognition that ultimately led to the peace treaty with Egypt at Camp David. It would be artificial to expect biblical authors to view war monolithically one way or the other. Yet, in instances in which a biblical author did see a particular conflagration as the climax of events, one way in which this could be expressed rhetorically is through placing the battle at the end of a narrative sequence and integrating it into the literary fabric of a larger narrative unit.

The focus of this study has been upon performing a synchronic reading of texts and seeking to identify metaphor analogy. Yet, diachronic issues inherent in these texts suggest that metaphor analogy is not merely a rhetoric produced by an act of reading in accordance with certain guidelines, but a rhetoric that may be seen in the process of redaction as well. Recall that we surveyed the considerable debate surrounding the possible lines of influence between the account of the capture of Ha-Ai in Joshua 8 and the account of the decimation of the tribe of Benjamin in Judges 20. We established textual dependence between these passages on the basis of highly distinct terms that are common to those two stories alone, where more common alternatives were available. Our claim of textual dependence was further buttressed by the highly similar plot structure of the feigned battle retreat. The observation that both narratives also function as metaphor analogies to the accounts that precede them, we claimed, might also be part of the network of dependencies that these two accounts share. The latter redactor between the two passages (viz., the redactor of Joshua 8 or of Judges 20) saw in the earlier text a model not only of language or of plot structure, but a model for the larger macro-structure of the unit as well: the metaphor analogy between the battle account and the account that precedes it.

A similar diachronic observation could be made in light of the relationship between the two metaphor analogies identified in the Book of Chronicles and their corresponding passages in the *Vorlage*. In each instance comparison suggests that metaphor analogy is not only the product of a certain strategy of reading but inherent to the Chronicler's redaction process. In the table of common terms between the account of Perez Uzzah (1 Chronicles 13) and the account of Baal Perazim (1 Chronicles 14) (above, pp. 177-78) we noted that nearly all of the elements that formed the base of the metaphor analogy between the two passages were the Chronicler's innovations. A similar pattern was seen in our study of the Ahab-Jehoshaphat narrative in 2 Chronicles 18 and the *Vorlage* in 1 Kings 22. The changes wrought by the Chronicler were relatively minor. Yet nearly all of them could be explained, we claimed, by seeing them as elements that contributed to the analogical base between the two parts of the story, the court-deliberations and the battle scene. Metaphor analogy, then, would seem to have been a convention with which the Chronicler subtly reworked the material that he found in the *Vorlage*.

Future Avenues of Study

The findings of this work open up several avenues for future research with regard to the biblical battle report and the study of narrative analogy in biblical prose. The present study suggests that the details of the battles should be examined for semiotic layers of meaning and not solely for verisimilitude. While this study has identified battle reports that stand in well-developed analogies to accounts nearby along the text continuum, meaning of this sort could be found in less elaborate structures as well. In the introduction, we pointed to the way in which the attention to booty in the battle account of Genesis 14 integrated the story into the larger literary fabric of the Abraham accounts of Genesis 12-15.

The present study also has implications for the diachronic study of the battles examined here. We have seen underlying unity where many commentators have seen the paired accounts as the products of different sources or later additions.[18] If the arguments contained in this study are found compelling, these positions would accordingly need to be revised. The narrative analogy would suggest either unitary composition, or, alternatively, a redactional attempt to more thoroughly integrate the two narratives than has been suggested heretofore in the literature.[19]

Broadening our scope, the present study bears significance for both form and generic studies in general. The search for the components of

---

[18] Concerning the redactional relationship between Joshua 7 and 8 see Soggin, *Joshua*, 96; Butler, *Joshua*, 81. Concerning Judges 10 and 11 see Gray, *Joshua, Judges*, 230; Boling, *Judges*, 30. Concerning Esther 9 and the earlier chapters of the book, see Bush, *Ruth, Esther*, 279-82.

[19] On the prior assumptions that underlie respectively synchronic and diachronic readings of the Bible, see Edward L. Greenstein, "Theory and Argument in Biblical Criticism," in idem, *Essays on Biblical Method and Translation* (Atlanta: Scholars Press, 1989) 53-68.

a given genre are usually limited to semantic, structural, and motival elements. Yet, it may be that a given form also employs a particular rhetorical strategy on a regular basis, though to examine this any further would go well beyond the scope of this work.

Perhaps the most significant avenues opened by this study, concern the general study of narrative analogies in biblical literature. Many paths may be taken with this, but they all stem from a need to look at narrative analogies systematically across the Bible. In this study we identified a particular form of narrative analogy, the metaphor analogy, or what Richard Levin termed in his study of Renaissance drama, the equivalence plot. The metaphor analogy, we claimed, was distinct in two fashions. First, in the standard narrative analogy subtleties may abound, but the issue of what to compare is usually straightforward, as the subject matter is the same in each account. In a metaphor analogy, however, the central conceptual field of comparison is not always clear. Toward what end has the artist contrasted these two disparate areas of human endeavor? The proper drawing of the comparison, we claimed, will require a higher degree of abstraction in the metaphor analogy than in the standard narrative analogy. Second, because the establishment of the metaphor analogy rests so heavily on formal elements of comparison, and particularly semantic ones, we established the criterion of rhetorical congruence as a measure of which common terms could legitimately enter into the base of the analogy.

More questions remain, however. Are narrative analogies formed in the same way by all books across the canon? In the earlier chapters of this study, we offered charts that listed all of the common elements that served as the base of the narrative analogy. The analogies drawn from Joshua 7-8 and Judges 19-20 were much longer than similar summary accounts offered for the narrative analogies studied in the Book of Chronicles. It goes without saying that a study of six narratives cannot serve as a basis for broad conclusions on this issue. It is enough, however, to serve as a basis for a question: Are narrative analogies formed in the same way across all of biblical literature, or can we discern varying strategies from book to book? To clarify the question I am posing I would like to draw from findings demonstrated by Kalimi in his work on the formal aspects of the Book of Chronicles. Whereas others had demonstrated differences in theology and orthography between the *Vorlage* and the Book of Chronicles, Kalimi saw differences in form on the macro level as well. He notes that the presence of *inclusio* and of chiastic structure in large literary units is much more characteristic of the Chronicler than of the *Vorlage*.[20] It is not unreasonable to suspect, then, that the macro-structural tool of narrative analogy may exhibit different characteristics in pre-exilic material and in later material.

---

[20] Kalimi, *The Book of Chronicles*, 263-308. On differences in syntax between the Persian and pre-exilic period see Frank H. Polak, "The Oral and the Written: Syntax, Stylistics and the Development of Biblical Prose Narrative," *JANES* 26 (1999) 59-105.

APPENDIX: NARRATIVE ANALOGY AND THE BATTLE REPORT IN THE ANCIENT NEAR EAST

With our increasing understanding of the ancient Near East we would be remiss to conclude this study without contextualizing it within the field of scholarship of the ancient Near Eastern battle report. The battle report is, arguably, along with building records, the most common genre of annalistic or epigraphic material in the writings of the ancient Near East. The potential for fruitful comparison between the two bodies of literature is great. To what extent do we find a rhetoric of narrative analogy within the epigraphic material? And if such a rhetoric is absent, what implications does that have for an understanding of the comparative historiography at play within these two bodies of literature?

My comments on the battle report as narrative analogy in the epigraphic material of the ancient Near East could be quite brief: this writer has reviewed Luckenbill's *Ancient Records of Assyria and Babylonia* and the series *Royal Inscriptions of Mesopotamia* as well as the secondary literature concerning the ancient Near Eastern battle report and is unaware of any inscription in which a battle report is constructed as an analogy, let alone a metaphor analogy, of the type examined in this study.[1] Yet, to state categorically that no ancient Near Eastern

---

[1] Daniel David Luckenbill, *Ancient Records of Assyria and Babylonia* (2 vols.; Chicago: University of Chicago Press, 1927); A. Kirk Grayson *Assyrian Rulers* (3 vols.; Royal Inscriptions of Mesopotamia: Assyrian Periods; Toronto: University of Toronto Press, 1987-1996); Grant Frame, *Rulers of Babylonia* (Royal Inscriptions of Mesopotamia: Babylonian Periods, vol. 2; Toronto: University of Toronto Press, 1995); For secondary literature on ancient Near Eastern battle reports, see Frank Moore Cross Jr., *Canaanite Myth and Hebrew Epic: Essays in the History of the Religion of Israel* (Cambridge, MA: Harvard University Press, 1973) 91-111; Albert Ernst Glock, "Warfare in Mari and Early Israel," Ph.D. dissertation, University of Michigan, 1968; James K. Hoffmeier, "Some Egyptian Motifs Related to Enemies and Warfare and their Old Testament Counterparts," *The Ancient World* 6 (1983) 53-70; Sa-Moon Kang, *Divine War in the Old Testament and in the Ancient Near East* (Berlin/New York: de Gruyter, 1989); Moshe Weinfeld, "Divine Intervention in War in Ancient Israel and in the Ancient Near East," in Moshe Weinfeld and Hayim Tadmor (eds.), *History, Historiography and Interpretation* (Jerusalem: Magnes, 1983) 121-47; Kenneth Lawson Younger, Jr., *Ancient Conquest Accounts: A Study in Near Eastern and Biblical History Writing* (JSOTS 98; Sheffield: Sheffield Academic Press, 1990). Translations of various battle reports are also found in *ANET* 227-321, 554-66.

battle report ever formed such an analogy would lack credibility, and this for two reasons. First, the present author does not command the broad language skills necessary to assess all the extant material. Second, unlike the MT of the Hebrew Bible, the corpus of ancient Near Eastern inscriptions is not a closed body of material; tomorrow's archaeological find could revolutionize what we know today. Nonetheless, the samples of such battle reports in our possession are numerous. My comments, therefore, on this material are based upon representative samples of ancient Near Eastern battle reports that exist in translation. In assessing what would appear to be the absence of any battle report as narrative analogy in epigraphic literature, I would like to delineate the main characteristics of these battle reports and contrast them to those found in the biblical corpus.

Scholars have identified points of commonality between the battle reports of the Bible and those of the ancient Near East. It has been established that in both sets of literature one finds similar overarching themes: victory is a sign of divine assistance, while defeat is a sign of divine wrath.[2] Both bodies of literature exhibit common motifs such as the heavens and the earth shaking, or that divine assistance originates from the skies or the heavens.[3] Moreover, Van Seters has found that in both we find like terms: the mustering of the army, the engagement in battle, the routing of the enemy.[4]

Distinct differences, however, are readily discernible between the two sets of literature. Younger's study of the battle report in Assyrian, Hittite and Egyptian culture reveals several shared features that distinguish them from their biblical counterparts. The narratorial voice in the epigraphic material is almost always a first-person account by a king basking in self-glorification. The account is spoken at a close chronological proximity to the events told. The rhetoric is typically what Younger calls "stereo-typed syntagms" that produce a "high-redundancy message" for the reader.[5] One example from the Aššur prism

---

[2] H. Tadmor, "Autobiographical Apology in the Royal Assyrian Literature," in *History, Historiography and Interpretation*, 42-43; Simon B. Parker, *Stories in Scripture and Inscriptions: Comparative Studies on Narratives in Northwest Semitic Inscriptions and the Hebrew Bible* (New York: Oxford University Press, 1997) 75.

[3] Moshe Weinfeld, "Divine Intervention," 121-47.

[4] John Van Seters, "Oral Patterns or Literary Conventions in Biblical Narrative," *Semeia* 5 (1976) 143-44.

[5] Younger, *Ancient Conquest* Accounts, 122-23.

of Tiglath-Pileser I (1114-1076 B.C.E.) will serve as an example:

> I destroyed the lands of Sarauš (and) Ammauš, which from ancient
> times had not known submission, (so that they looked) like ruin hills
> (created by) the deluge.
> I fought with their extensive army in Mt. Aruma, and brought about
> their defeat.
> I laid out like grain heaps the corpses of their men-at-arms.
> I conquered their cities, took their gods, and brought out their booty,
> possessions (and) property.
> I burned, razed, (and) destroyed their cities (and) turned them into
> ruin hills.
> I imposed the heavy yoke of my dominion upon them (and) made them
> vassals of Aššur, my lord.[6]

Within these global observations, Younger does discern some local
distinctions; Hittite accounts feature slightly more narrative concerning battle details and divine involvement. Egyptian texts speak of the
king in the third-person and display heavy embellishment of hyperbole
and rhetoric.

The major differences between these battle accounts and those of
the Hebrew Bible have been identified by Parker, whose work on
Northwest Semitic inscriptions focuses mainly on battle accounts.
We note with Parker that the narratorial voice of the Bible's battle
accounts is uniformly third person, omniscient and at some chronological distance from the events narrated. Glorification of the king is
rare.[7] Most importantly for us, however, is Parker's observation that
battle reports in the Bible are set as components of larger narrative
units and that the purpose of these larger units is ultimately to convey
a moral or theological message.[8]

Thus, the absence of narrative analogy in ancient Near Eastern
annals and chronicles needs to be understood within the larger question of the absence of large literary units in which a plot unfolds over
an extended literary structure. For von Rad, the presence of larger
literary units in Israel but not elsewhere is a question of historiosophy. Historiographic writing of the type found in the Hebrew Bible
is predicated on causational thinking. To view events as woven into

---

[6] Cylinder A (III.73-87). Translated by A. Kirk Grayson, *Assyrian Royal Inscriptions*
(2 vols; Wiesbaden: Harrassowitz, 1972-76) 2:10.
[7] Parker, *Stories in Scripture*, 60, 136.
[8] Ibid., 104.

larger patterns of cause and effect presupposes a God who imposes cosmic order. God's intervention in all things became a powerful organizing principle that led to a view of the inescapable succession of historical events. In neighboring cultures divine intervention in the affairs of man was not considered as all-pervasive, and hence there was no intellectual recourse to causational thinking in historiographic materials.[9] Yet Bertil Albrektson has demonstrated that this distinction is unwarranted and that much of the historiography contained in the epigraphic material demonstrates a theology of divine intervention in a broad array of human endeavors.[10]

Rather, it would seem that the absence of large narrative composition in the ancient Near East should be explained as a function of genre, rather than of historiosophy. The epigraphic narratives in our possession are composed by agents of the kings, by people close to the events themselves. These are works whose purpose is to bring glory to the kings and to the gods that assisted them. By contrast, the biblical battle story, like all elements of biblical narrative, is embedded within the extensive narrative history of Israel, for didactic purposes that are alien to the genre of the classical royal inscription.

One ramification of the embedding of battle stories into larger narrative tapestries is reflective of a broader historiographic trend within the Bible and that is a distinct attention to human action. As Yairah Amit has recently written concerning the basic thrust of biblical historiography:

> God is displaced from the world of myth… and interest becomes focused on the connection between Him and humanity, thus giving a new significance to human events. These in turn, become means of learning and understanding God's ways.[11]

Amit's recent comments echo assertions made by Don Isaac Abarbanel concerning the purpose of the books of the Former Prophets. Abarbanel was a man of the Renaissance and attuned to historical

---

[9] Gerhard Von Rad, "Der Anfang der Geschichtsschreibung im alten Israel," in idem, *Gesammelte Studien zum Alten Testament* (München: Chr. Kaiser Verlag, 1971) 148-54; Sigmund Mowinckel, "Israelite Historiography," *Annual of the Swedish Theological Institute* 2 (1963) 8.

[10] Bertil Albrektson, *History and the Gods: An Essay on the Idea of Historical Events as Divine Manifestations in the Ancient Near East and in Israel* (Lund: Gleerup, 1967).

[11] Yairah Amit, *History and Ideology: An Introduction to Historiography in the Hebrew Bible* (Biblical Seminar 60; Sheffield: Sheffield Academic Press, 1999) 16.

and historiographical concerns unlike any rabbinic writer before
him.[12] He writes:

> The first end common to these four books is to teach us important les-
> sons pertaining to the true path of proper thought and conduct, and to
> the attainment of proper traits, as is borne out by these stories.[13]

One literary implication of this comment is that characterization will
play a major role in biblical historiography and that characters will be
richly developed. It is through a thorough probing of the characters
and their actions that the appropriate lessons, often complex in nature,
can be properly learned. This explains Gunn's comments concerning the embedded nature of battle reports within a larger narrative
tapestry.[14] The battle reports typically revolve around characters who
are developed outside of the battle narrative as well. The battle story
is but one element of the larger narrative that contributes to their
characterization.

The intimate connection between biblical historiography and the
narrative interest in human events leads us to a substantive addition
to the list of typical features of the biblical battle report. The present
author has counted approximately 70 major biblical battle reports
of four or more verses. No single plot element or thematic element
mentioned by von Rad, Niditch or by any of the other scholars whose
work we reviewed in the introduction, appears in more than one-fifth
of these. In choosing the number of four verses, it is not my intention
to state that a depiction of a battle in only three verses (or less) is not a
battle report. Indeed, no scholarship exists that defines the minimum
number of verses necessary to consider the description of a battle, as
a battle "report," as opposed to the mere mention that a battle had
transpired. My sole intention in choosing the quantity of four verses is
for the purposes of dramatization. In an account of four or more verses,
we tend to find several of the typical lexical features of the battle report
outlined in the review of the scholarship above, and ample opportunity
to employ other typical elements as well. Despite this, no single plot
element or thematic element—like those identified by von Rad and
Niditch respectively—appears in more than a fifth of them.

Yet, I would claim that even if all of those elements were to be

---

[12] See Eric Lawee, *Isaac Abarbanel's Stance Toward Tradition: Defense, Dissent, and Dialogue* (Albany: State University of New York Press, 2001).
[13] Isaac Abarbanel, *Commentary on Former Prophets* (Jerusalem: 1955) 6.
[14] See above, pp. 19-21.

assembled into a single narrative, one would still not have a "biblical battle report," for a biblical battle report *must include an element of characterization.* I define "an element of characterization," here in a precise fashion. Leaders are often named in a battle narrative in a mode that is entirely metonymic, as in, "at that time Joshua captured Makkedah" (Josh 10:28). I am discounting these as characterizations, as I am the description of actions taken by entire armies. Rather, by "an element of characterization" I mean to say that the biblical battle report will always detail at least one action of at least one sub-party within the story. It may be a leader, Israelite or otherwise, or it may be a portion of the force of either of the warring parties. The comment is significant not in terms of the Bible's poetics of narration, but in terms of comprehending the Bible's depiction of battle within its larger historiographic context of documenting the actions of individuals and the assessment of their conduct.

Narrative doubling and narrative analogy also served part of this didactic purpose. As Ackerman has pointed out, the world order in the ancient Near East was seen as a function of tension between various deities whose power and dispositions were in constant flux. Myth and ritual served to preserve the cosmic order. One way in which Israel's belief in a stable unified order manifested itself within its historiography was through the incorporation of narrative doubling, predicated upon this stability.[15]

The presence or absence of narrative doubling for Sternberg is reflective of the historiography of ancient cultures in a second way. The hermeneutics of narrative analogy imply that the reader will not fully comprehend the full message of the work until the second story of the analogy has been fully disclosed. This, says Sternberg, reinforces for the reader the perspectival gulf that exists between God and himself.[16] The epigraphic materials concerning warfare do indeed imply the divine role in victory or defeat. But the reader encountering these inscriptions does not undergo a sense of slow disclosure and illumination. The message, as Younger stated it, is a "high-redundancy message"; it is clear, and need only be internalized through repetitive emphasis.

To conclude, the findings of this study in how they relate to the epigraphic materials of the ancient Near East would seem to challenge Rowlett's claim that,

---

[15] Ackerman, "Joseph, Judah and Jacob," 112; Sternberg, *Poetics*, 114.
[16] Sternberg, *Poetics*, 92.

> [Younger's] book, along with Kang's has sounded the final death knell
> for the older belief that there is something unique about the way the
> Bible presents divine participation in 'history' through warfare.[16]

Indeed, in the epigraphic material, as in Biblical narrative, one sees
divine participation in warfare. Yet the genre through which this is
presented is indeed unique. Biblical narrative history—including divine
participation in warfare—is positioned and shaped in accordance
with didactic design and perspective. Specifically for our purposes,
the vehicle of narrative analogy allows both readers and internal
characters to reflect upon behavior off the battlefield in light of the
events that transpired upon it.

---

[16] Lori L. Rowlett, *Joshua and the Rhetoric of Violence: A New Historical Perspective*
(JSOTSup 226; Sheffield: Sheffield Academic Press, 1996) 65.

BIBLIOGRAPHY

Abramsky, S., and M. Garsiel, eds. *1 Samuel*. Olam HaTanakh. Tel-Aviv: Davidson-Eti, 1993 (Hebrew).
———. *2 Samuel*. Olam HaTanakh. Tel-Aviv: Davidson-Eti, 1993 (Hebrew).
Ackerman, J.S. "Joseph, Judah, and Jacob." *Literary Interpretations of Biblical Narratives. Vol. 2.* Edited by K.R.R. Gros Louis and J. Ackerman. Nashville: Abingdon, 1982, pp. 85-113.
Ahituv, S. *Joshua*. Miqra LeYisrael. Tel Aviv: Am Oved, 1995 (Hebrew).
Albrektson, B. *History and the Gods: An Essay on the Idea of Historical Events as Divine Manifestations in the Ancient Near East and in Israel*. Lund: Gleerup, 1967.
Allen, L.C. "Kerygmatic Units in 1 & 2 Chronicles." *JSOT* 41 (1988): 21-36.
Alter, R. *The Art of Biblical Narrative*. New York: Basic Books, 1981.
———. *The Art of Biblical Poetry*. New York: Basic Books, 1985.
Amit, Y. "The Dual Causality Principle and Its Effects on Biblical Literature." *VT* 37 (1987): 385-400.
———. "Studies in the Poetics of the Book of Chronicles." *Professor H.M. Gevaryahu Jubilee Volume: Studies in Biblical Studies and in Jewish Thought*. Edited by B.Z. Luria. Jerusalem: Kiryath Sefer, 1989 (Hebrew).
———. *The Book of Judges: The Art of Editing*. Biblical Encyclopedia Library VI. Jerusalem: Bialik Institute, 1992 (Hebrew).
———. "Dual Causality – Another Aspect." *Bet Miqra* 38 (1992): 41- 55 (Hebrew).
———. *History and Ideology: An Introduction to Historiography in the Hebrew Bible*. Translated by Y. Lotan. Biblical Seminar 60. Sheffield: Sheffield Academic Press, 1999.
———. *The Book of Judges*. Miqra LeYisrael. Tel Aviv: Am Oved, 1999 (Hebrew).
———. *Hidden Polemics in Biblical Narrative*. Translated by J. Chipman. Biblical Interpretation Series 25. Leiden: Brill, 2000.
Asis, E. "The Literary Structure of the Conquest Narrative in the Book of Joshua and its Meaning." Ph. D. diss., Bar-Ilan University, 1999.
Bach, A. *Women, Seduction, and Betrayal in Biblical Narrative*. Cambridge: Cambridge University Press, 1997.
Bahti, T. "Auerbach's Mimesis: Figural Structure and Historical Narrative." In *After Strange Texts: The Role of Theory in the Study of Literature*. Edited by G.S. Jay and D.L. Miller. University, AL: University of Alabama Press, 1985, pp. 121- 45.
Bal, M. *Narratology: Introduction to the Theory of Narrative*. Toronto: University of Toronto Press, 1985.
———. *Lethal Love: Feminist Literary Readings of Biblical Love Stories*. Bloomington: Indiana University Press, 1987.
———. *On Meaning-Making: Essays in Semiotics*. Sonoma, CA: Polebridge Press, 1994.
Bardtke, H. *Das Buch Esther*. KAT 17/5. Gütersloh: Mohn, 1963.
Barthes, R. *S/Z*. Paris: Seuil, 1970.
Bartlett, J.R. "The Use of the Word ראש as a Title in the Old Testament." *VT* 19 (1969): 1-10.
Beal, T.K. *The Book of Hiding: Gender, Ethnicity, Annihilation and Esther*. London: Routledge, 1997.
———. *Esther*. Berit Olam. Collegeville, MN: Liturgical Press, 1999.
Beauvoir, S de. *Le Deuxième Sexe*. 2 vols. Paris: Gallimard, 1976.
Bennett, R.A. "Wisdom Motifs in Psalm 14 = 53 – *nābāl* and *ʿēṣāh*." *BASOR* 220 (1975): 15-20.

Berg, S.B. *The Book of Esther*. SBLDiss 44. Missoula, Montana: Scholars Press, 1979.

Berlin, A. *Poetics and Interpretation of Biblical Narrative*. Sheffield: Almond Press, 1983.

———. *Esther*. JPS Commentary. Philadelphia: Jewish Publication Society of America, 2001.

Berman, J. "'He Who Re-enacts the Creation in His Goodness': Parallels Between Genesis 1 and Genesis 8." *Megadim* 9 (5750): 9-14 (Hebrew).

———. "Hadassah bat Abihail: From Object to Subject in the Character of Esther." *JBL* 120 (2001): 647-69.

Boling, R.B. *Judges*. AB 6A. Garden City, NY: Doubleday, 1975.

———. *Joshua*. AB 6. Garden City, NY: Doubleday, 1982.

Bradbrook, M. *Themes and Conventions of Elizabethan Tragedy*. Cambridge: The University Press, 1935.

Brenner, A. "Looking at Esther Through the Looking Glass." In *A Feminist Companion to Esther, Judith, Susanna*. Edited by A. Brenner. Sheffield: Sheffield Academic Press, 1995, pp. 71- 80.

Bush, F.W. *Ruth, Esther*. WBC 9. Dallas: Word Books, 1996.

Butler, T.C. *Joshua*. WBC. Waco, TX: Word, 1983.

Carroll, R.P. *The Book of Jeremiah*. OTL. Philadelphia: Westminster Press, 1986.

Cass, V. "Homosexual Identity Formation: A Theoretical Model." *Journal of Homosexuality* 4 (1979): 219-35.

Cassirer, E. *Individuum und Kosmos in der Philosophie der Renaissance*. Leipzig: B.G. Teubner, 1927.

Clayton, J. and E. Rothstein, eds. *Influence and Intertextuality in Literary History*. Madison: University of Wisconsin Press, 1991.

Clines, D.J.A. *The Esther Scroll*. JSOTSup 30; Sheffield: Sheffield Academic Press, 1984.

Cogan, M. "Royal City and Temple City: The History of Jerusalem From David to Josiah." in *The History of Jerusalem: The Biblical Period*. Edited by S. Ahituv and Amihai Mazar. Jerusalem: Yad Ben-Zvi Press, 2000, pp. 67-84 (Hebrew).

Coleman, E. "Developmental Stages in the Coming Out Process." *Journal of Homosexuality* 7 (1981/82): 31-43.

Conrad, E.W. *Fear Not Warrior: A Study of "al tira" Pericopes in the Hebrew Scriptures*. BJS 75. Chico: Scholars Press, 1985.

Coursen, H.R. "A Spacious Mirror: Shakespeare and The Play Within." Ph. D. diss., Univeristy of Connecticuticut, 1966.

Craghan, J. *Esther, Judith, Tobit, Jonah, Ruth*. Wilmington, DE: Michael Glazier, 1982.

Craig, Kenneth M. Jr. "Bargaining in Tov (Judges 11:4-11): The Many Directions of So-Called Direct Speech." *Biblica* 79 (1998): 76-85.

Cross, Frank M. Jr. *Canaanite Myth and Hebrew Epic: Essays in the History of the Religion of Israel*. Cambridge, MA: Harvard University Press, 1973.

Dällenbach, L. *Le Récit Spéculaire: Essai Sur La Mise en Abyme*. Paris: Seuil, 1977.

Damrosch, D. *The Narrative Covenant*. San Francisco: Harper & Row, 1987.

Dank, B.M. "Coming Out in the Gay World." *Psychiatry* 34 (1971): 180-97.

Davies, G.K. "The Ark in the Psalms." In *Promise and Fulfillment: Essays Presented to Professor S.H. Hooke*. Edited by F.F. Bruce. Edinburgh, T & T Clark, 1963, pp. 51- 61.

Davies, P. "The Role of Disclosure in Coming Out Among Gay Men." In *Modern Homosexualities: Fragments of Lesbian and Gay Experience*. Edited by K. Plummer. London: Routledge, 1992, pp. 75-83.

Day, J. "Pre-Deuteronomic Allusions to the Covenant in Hosea and Psalm LXVIII." *VT* 36 (1986): 1-12.

De Regt, L.G. *Participant Pronouns in Old Testament Texts and the Translator*. Assen: Van Gorcum, 1999.

Vaux, R. de. "Single Combat in the Old Testament." In *The Bible and the Ancient Near East*. Edited by G.E. Wright. Garden City , NY: Doubleday, 1965, pp. 122-35.

————. *Histoire Ancienne d'Israel*. 2 vols. Etudes Bibliques. Paris: J. Gabalda, 1971-73.

De Vries, Simon J. *Prophet Against Prophet: The Role of the Micaiah Narrative in the Early Prophetic Tradition*. Grand Rapids: Eerdmans, 1978.

Dillard, R.D. *2 Chronicles*. WBC. Waco: Word Press, 1987.

Dion, P.E. "The 'Fear Not' Formula and Holy War." *CBQ* 32 (1970): 565-70.

Driver, S.R. *Notes on the Hebrew Text and the Topography of the Books of Samuel*. Oxford: Clarendon Press, 1913.

Elitzur, Y. "Eben-ha-Ezer." In *Zeidel Memorial Volume: Essays in Biblical Studies*. Edited by E. Elinor, et. al. Israel Society for Biblical Studies Publications 11. Jerusalem: Kiryath Sefer, 1962, pp. 111-18 (Hebrew).

————. *The Book of Judges*. Daat Miqra. Jerusalem: Mossad Harav Kook, 1976 (Hebrew).

Empson, W. *Some Versions of Pastoral*. London: Chatto & Windus, 1935.

Eskenazi, T.C. "A Literary Approach to Chronicles' Ark Narrative." In *Fortunate the Eyes That See: Essays in Honor of David Noel Freedman*. Edited by A.B. Beck, et. al. Grand Rapids: Eerdmans, 1995, pp. 258-74.

Fearer, T.L. "War in the Wilderness: Textual Cohesion and Concept Coherence in Pentateuchal Battle Tradition." Ph. D. diss., Claremont Graduate School, 1993.

Fewell, D.N., ed. *Reading Between Texts: Intertextuality and the Hebrew Bible*. Louisville: Westminster, 1992.

Fleishman, J. "The Legality of the Expulsion of Jephthah." *Diné Israel* 18 (1995-96): 61-80.

Fokkelman, J.P. *Narrative Art and Poetry in the Books of Samuel. Vol. 3. Throne and City (2 Samuel 2-8 & 21-24)*. Assen: Van Corcum, 1990.

————. *Narrative Art and Poetry in the Books of Samuel. Vol. 4. Vow and Desire (1 Sam 1-12)*. Assen: Van Gorcum, 1993.

Fox, M.V. *Character and Ideology in the Book of Esther*. Columbia, S.C.: University of South Carolina Press, 1991.

Frame, G. *Royal Inscriptions of Mesopotamia: Babylonian Periods. Vol. 2. Rulers of Babylonia*. Toronto: University of Toronto Press, 1995.

Fuchs, E. "Status and Role of Female Heroines in the Biblical Narrative." In *Women in the Hebrew Bible*. Edited by Alice Bach. New York: Routledge, 1999, pp. 77-84.

Galil, G. ed. *Judges*. Olam HaTanakh. Tel Aviv: Davidson-Eti, 1994 (Hebrew).

Galil, G. and M. Garsiel, et. al. eds. *The Book of First Chronicles*. Olam HaTanakh. Tel-Aviv: Davidson-Eti, 1995 (Hebrew).

Galil, G. and Y. Zakovitch, eds. *Joshua*. Olam HaTanakh. Tel Aviv: Davidson-Eti, 1994 (Hebrew).

Galili, E. "The Conquest of Palestine by the Seleucian Army." *Maarachoth* 82 (1954): 64-66.

Gard, D.L. "Warfare in Chronicles." Ph. D. diss., University of Notre Dame, 1991.

Garsiel, M. *The First Book of Samuel: A Literary Study of Comparative Structures, Analogies and Parallels*. Ramat Gan: Revivim, 1985.

Gerleman, G. *Esther*. BKAT 21. Neukirchen-Vluyn: Neukirchener-Verlag, 1982.

Givan, C.F. "Thematic Doubling in Shakespeare's Plays." Ph. D. diss., Stanford University, 1970.

Glatt, D.A. *Chronological Displacement in Biblical and Related Literatures.* SBLDiss 139. Atlanta: Scholars Press, 1990.

Glock, A.E. *Warfare in Mari and Early Israel.* Ph. D. diss., University of Michigan, 1968.

Goldenberg, R. "The Problem of False Prophecy: Talmudic Interpretations of Jeremiah 28 and 1 Kings 22." In *The Biblical Mosaic: Changing Perspectives.* Edited by R. Polzin and E. Rothman. Philadelphia: Fortress Press, 1982, pp. 87-103.

Gordon, R.G. *I & II Samuel.* Grand Rapids: Zondervan, 1988.

Goslinga, C.J. *Joshua, Judges, Ruth.* Grand Rapids: Eerdmans, 1986.

Grabes, H. *The Mutable Glass: Mirror-Imagery in Titles and Texts of the Middle-Ages and English Renaissance.* Cambridge: Cambridge University Press, 1982.

Gray, J. *I & II Kings.* OTL. London: SCM Press, 1964.

———. *Joshua, Judges, Ruth.* NCBC. London: Nelson, 1967.

Grayson, A.K. *Assyrian Royal Inscriptions.* 2 Vols. Wiesbaden: Harrassowitz, 1972-76.

———. *Royal Inscriptions of Mesopotamia: Assyrian Periods. Assyrian Rulers.* 3 vols. Toronto: University of Toronto Press, 1987- 1996.

Greenberg, M. s. v. "Ḥerem." *EJ* 8:344-49.

Greenstein, E.L. "The Riddle of Samson" *Prooftexts* 1 (1981): 237-60.

———. "An Equivocal Reading of the Sale of Joseph." In *Literary Interpretations of Biblical Narratives. Vol. 2.* Edited by K.R.R. Gros Louis and J. Ackerman. Nashville: Abingdon, 1982, pp. 114-26.

———. "A Jewish Reading of Esther." In *Judaic Perspectives on Ancient Israel.* Edited by J. Neusner, et al. Philadelphia: Fortress Press, 1987, 225-43.

———. "Deconstruction and Biblical Narrative." *Prooftexts* 9 (1989): 43-72.

———. *Essays on Biblical Method and Translation.* Atlanta: Scholars Press, 1989.

———. "The Scroll of Esther: A New Translation." *Fiction* 9 (1990): 52-81.

———. "The Retelling of the Flood Story in the Gilgamesh Epic." In *Hesed Ve-Emet: Studies in Honor of Ernest S. Frerichs.* Edited by J. Magness and S. Gitin, eds. Atlanta: Scholars Press, 1998, pp. 197-204.

Gros Louis, K.R.R. "The Book of Judges." In *Literary Interpretations of Biblical Narratives. Vol. 1.* Edited by K.R.R. Gros Louis and J. Ackerman. Nashville: Abingdon, 1974, pp. 141-62.

Güdeman, M. "Tendenz und Abfassungszeit der letzten Kapitel des Buches der Richter." *MGWJ* 18 (1869): 357-68.

Gunn, D.M. "The 'Battle Report': Oral or Scribal Convention?" *JBL* 93 (1974): 513-18.

———. "Narrative Patterns and Oral Tradition in Judges and Samuel." *VT* 24 (1974): 286-317.

Gunn, D.M. and D.N. Fewell, *Narrative in the Hebrew Bible.* Oxford: Oxford University Press, 1993.

Hakham, A. *Esther.* Daat Miqra. Jerusalem: Mossad Harav Kook, 1990 (Hebrew).

Ha-Levi, R. "Micaiah ben Imlah: The Ideal Prophet." *Bet Miqra* 12 (1968): 102-06 (Hebrew).

Halliwell, S. *The Poetics of Aristotle: Translation and Commentary.* Chapel Hill: University of North Carolina Press, 1987.

Hamilton, J.M. "Caught in the Nets of Prophecy?: The Death of King Ahab and the Character of God." *CBQ* 56 (1994): 649-63.

Hamlin, E. J. *Joshua: Inheriting the Land.* ITC. Grand Rapids: Eerdmans, 1983.

———. *Judges: At Risk in the Promised Land.* Grand Rapids: Eerdmans, 1990.

Hartwig, J. *Shakespeare's Analogical Scene: Parody as Structural Syntax.* Lincoln: University of Nebraska Press, 1983.

Heninger, S.K. *Touches of Sweet Harmony: Pythagorean Cosmology and Renaissance Poetics.* San Marino: Huntington Library, 1974.

Henry, K.S. "The Shattering of Resemblance: The Mirror in Shakespeare." Ph. D. diss., Tufts University, 1989.

Hertzberg, H.W. *Die Bücher Josua, Richter, Ruth*. Göttingen: Bandenhoech & Ruprecht, 1953.

Hess, R.S. *Joshua: An Introduction & Commentary*. Tyndale Old Testament Commentaries. Leicester: Inter-Varsity Press, 1996.

Hobbs, T.R. *A Time for War: A Study of Warfare in the Old Testament*. Wilmington, Delaware: M . Glazier, 1989.

Hoffman, Y. "The Root QRB as a Legal Term." *JNSL* 10 (1983): 67-73.

Hoffmeier, J.K. "Some Egyptian Motifs Related to Enemies and Warfare and their Old Testament Counterparts." *The Ancient World* 6 (1983): 53-70.

Horbury, H. "Extirpation and Excommunication." *VT* 35 (1985): 13-38.

Horowitz, W. and V. Hurowitz, "Urim and Thummim in Light of a Psephomancy Ritual from Assur (LKA 137)." *JANES* 21 (1992): 95-114.

Humbert, P. "Etendre la Main." *VT* 12 (1962): 383-95.

Humphreys, W.L. "A Life-Style for Diaspora: A Study of the Tales of Esther and Daniel." *JBL* 92 (1973): 211-23.

Jacobs, J. "The Story of Jephthah." M.A. thesis, Bar-Ilan University, 1997 (Hebrew).

Japhet, S. *The Ideology of the Book of Chronicles and Its Place in Biblical Thought*. Frankfurt: Peter Lang, 1989.

———. *I & II Chronicles*. OTL. Louisville: Westminster, 1993.

Jefferson, A. "Mise en abyme and the Prophetic in Narrative." *Style* 17 (1983): 196-208.

Johnstone, W. *1 and 2 Chronicles. Vol. 1. 1 Chronicles 1 – 2 Chronicles 9: Israels's Place Among the Nations. Vol. 2. 2 Chronicles 10-36: Guilt and Atonement*. JSOTSup 253, 254. Sheffield: Sheffield Academic Press, 1997.

Jones, G.H. "'Holy War', or 'Yahweh War'?" *VT* 25 (1975): 642-58.

Joüon, P. *Grammaire de l'Hebreu Biblique*. Rome: Institut Biblique Pontifical, 1965.

Kalimi, I. *The Book of Chronicles: Historical Writing and Literary Devices*. Biblical Encyclopedia Library. Jerusalem: Bialik Institute, 2000 (Hebrew).

Kaminsky, J. *Corporate Responsibility in the Hebrew Bible*. JSOTSup 196. Sheffield: Sheffield Academic Press, 1995.

Kang, S. *Divine War in the Old Testament and in the Ancient Near East*. Berlin/New York: de Gruyter, 1989.

Kaufmann, Y. *Joshua*. Jerusalem: The Israel Society for the Study of the Bible, 1963 (Hebrew).

———. *The Book of Judges*. Jerusalem: Kiryath Sefer, 1968 (Hebrew).

———. *The Religion of Israel*. Translated by Moshe Greenberg. New York: Shocken Books, 1972.

———. *The Biblical Account of the Conquest of Canaan*. 2nd ed. Jerusalem: Magnes, 1985 (Hebrew).

Kiel, Y. *1 Samuel*. Jerusalem: Daat Miqra. Mossad Harav Kook, 1981 (Hebrew).

———. *2 Samuel*. Jerusalem: Daat Miqra. Mossad Harav Kook, 1981 (Hebrew).

———. *The Book of Joshua*. Daat Miqra; Jerusalem: Mossad Harav Kook, 1985 (Hebrew).

———. *1 Chronicles*. Daat Miqra; Jerusalem: Mossad Harav Kook, 1986 (Hebrew).

Klein, J.W. "Jewish Identity and Self Esteem." Ph. D. diss., The Wright School, 1977.

Klein, L. *The Triumph of Irony in the Book of Judges*. JSOTSup 68. Sheffield: Almond Press, 1988.

———. "Honor and Shame in Esther." In *A Feminist Companion to Esther, Judith,*

Susanna. Edited by Athalya Brenner. Sheffield: Sheffield Academic Press, 1991, pp. 149-75.

Knoppers, G.N. "Reform and Regression: The Chronicler's Presentation of Jehoshaphat." *Biblica* 72 (1991): 500-24.

Kugel, J.L. *The Idea of Biblical Poetry*. New Haven: Yale University Press, 1981.

———. *Traditions of the Bible: A Guide to the Bible As It Was at the Start of the Common Era*. Cambridge, MA: Harvard University Press, 1998.

Lakoff, G. and M. Johnson. *Metaphors We Live By*. Chicago: University of Chicago Press, 1980.

Lanser, S. *The Narrative Act: Point of View in Prose Fiction*. Princeton: Princeton University Press, 1981.

Lawee, E. "Don Isaac Abarbanel: Who Wrote the Books of the Bible." *Tradition* 30: (1996): 65-73.

———. *Isaac Abarbanel's Stance Toward Tradition: Defense, Dissent, and Dialogue*. Albany: State University of New York Press, 2001.

Lemaire, A. "Le Hérem Dans Le Monde Nord-Ouest Sémitique." In *Guerre et Conquête Dans Le Proche-Orient Ancien*. Edited by L. Nehmé. Antiquités Sémitiques 4. Paris: Maisonneuve, 1999, pp. 79-92.

Levenson, J.D. *Esther*. OTL: London: SCM Press, 1997.

Levin, R. *The Multiple Plot in English Renaissance Drama*. Chicago: University of Chicago Press, 1971.

Lewin, K. *Resolving Social Conflict*. New York: Harper Bros., 1948.

Lewis, L. "The Coming Out Process for Lesbians: Integrating a Stable Identity." *Social Work* 29 (1984): 464-69.

Licht, J.L. s. v. "War." *EB* 4:1061 (Hebrew).

Lindblom, J. "Lot-Casting in the Old Testament." *VT* 12 (1962): 164-78.

Liver, J., ed. *The Military History of the Land of Israel in Biblical Times*. Jerusalem: Magnes Press, 1964 (Hebrew).

Lohfink, N. s.v. "חרם." *TDOT* 5:180-99.

Long, B.O. "The Form and Significance of I Kings 22:1-38." In *Isac Leo Seeligman Memorial Volume*. Edited by Y. Zakovitch and A. Rofé. Jerusalem: A. Rubinstein, 1983, pp. 193-208.

———. "Framing Repetitions in Biblical Historiography." *JBL* 106 (1987): 385-99.

Lucas, D.W. *Aristotle – Poetics: Introduction, Commentary and Appendixes*. Oxford: Clarendon Press, 1972.

Luckenbill, D.D. *Ancient Records of Assyria and Babylonia*. 2 vols. Chicago: University of Chicago Press, 1927.

Luria, B.Z. *Saul and Benjamin*. Jerusalem: Israel Society for the Study of the Bible, 1970 (Hebrew).

Malamat, A. "Israelite Conduct of War in the Conquest of Canaan According to the Biblical Tradition." In *Symposia: Celebrating the Seventy-Fifth Anniversary of the Founding of the American School of Oriental Research (1900-1975)*. Edited by F.M. Cross. Cambridge, MA: American Schools of Oriental Research, 1979, pp. 35-55.

———. *Israel in Biblical Times*. Jerusalem: Bialik Institute, 1983.

Marcus, D. "The Bargaining Between Jephthah and the Elders (Judges 11:4-11)." *JANES* 19 (1989): 95-100.

———. "The Legal Dispute Between Jephthah and the Elders." *HAR* 12 (1990): 105-15.

Martin, J.D. *The Book of Judges*. CBC. Cambridge: Cambridge University Press, 1975.

Mazor, L. "The Account of the Victory over Ha-Ai (Joshua 8): A Textual and Literary Analysis." In *HaMiqra BeRei Mefarshav*. Edited by Sara Japhet. Jerusalem:

Magnes Press, 1994 (Hebrew), pp. 73-108.

Mazzeo, J. "Universal Analogy and the Culture of the Renaissance." *Journal of the History of Ideas* 14 (1953): 221- 34.

McCarter, P.K. *I Samuel.* AB 8. Garden City, NY: Doubleday, 1980.

———. *II Samuel.* AB 9. New York: Doubleday, 1984.

McDonald, G.J. "Individual Differences in the Coming Out Process for Gay Men: Implications for Theoretical Models." *Journal of Homosexuality* 8 (1982): 47-60.

Medan, Y and R. Medan. "Jephthah in his Time." *Megadim* 6 (1987): 22-54 (Hebrew).

Mendelsohn, I. "The Disinheritance of Jephthah in Light of Paragraph 27 of the Lipit-Ishtar Code." *IEJ* 4 (1954): 116-19.

Miller, P.D. *Divine Warrior in Early Israel.* HSM 5. Cambridge MA: Harvard University Press, 1973.

Miller, P.D. and J.J.M. Roberts. *The Hand of the Lord: A Reassessment of the "Ark Narrative" of 1 Samuel.* Baltimore: Johns Hopkins, 1977.

Miller, J.M. and G.M. Tucker. *The Book of Joshua.* CBC. Cambridge: Cambridge University Press, 1974.

Miscall, P.D. "The Jacob and Joseph Stories as Analogies." *JSOT* 6 (1978): 28-40.

Mitchell, G. *Together in the Land: A Reading of the Book of Joshua.* JSOTSup 134. Sheffield: Sheffield Academic Press, 1993.

Moore, C.A. *Esther.* AB 7B. NewYork: Doubleday, 1971.

Moore, G.F. *A Critical and Exegetical Commentary on Judges.* ICC. Edinburgh: T & T Clark, 1895.

Moran, W.L. "The Ancient Near Eastern Background to the Love of God in Deuteronomy." *CBQ* 25 (1963): 77-87.

Mosis, R. *Untersuchungen zur Theologie des Chronistischen Geschichtswerkes.* Freiburg: Heider, 1973.

Mowinckel, S. "Israelite Historiography." *Annual of the Swedish Theological Institute* 2 (1963): 4-26.

Muffs, Y. *Love & Joy: Law, Language and Religion in Ancient Israel.* New York and Jerusalem: Jewish Theological Seminary of America, 1992.

Nahkola, A. *Double Narratives in the Old Testament: The Foundation of Method in Biblical Criticism.* BZAW 290. Berlin and New York: Walter de Gruyter, 2001.

Nelson, R.D. *Joshua.* OTL. Louisville: Westminster, 1997.

Neufeld, E. *Ancient Hebrew Marriage Law.* London: Longmans, Green, 1944.

Niditch, S. *War in the Hebrew Bible.* Oxford: New York, 1993.

———. "Esther: Folklore, Wisdom, Feminism and Authority." In *A Feminist Companion to Esther, Judith and Susanna.* Edited by Athalya Brenner. Sheffield: Sheffield Academic Press, 1995,

———. *Oral World and Written Word: Ancient Israelite Literature.* Louisville, KY: Westminster John Knox Press, 1996.

Noth, M. *Das System der Zwölf Stämme Israels.* Beiträge zur Wissenschaft vom Alten und Neuen Testament. Stuttgart: W. Kohlhammer, 1930.

———. *Das Buch Josua.* HAT 7. Tubingen: Mohr, 1938.

O'Connor, M. "The Rhetoric of the Kilamuwa Inscription." *BASOR* 226 (1977): 15-30.

Ollenburger, B.C. "Introduction: Gerhard von Rad's Theory of Holy War." In *Holy War in Ancient Israel* by G. von Rad. Grand Rapids: William Eerdmans Publishing Co., 1991, pp. 1- 34.

Parker, S.B. *Stories in Scripture and Inscriptions: Comparative Studies on Narratives in Northwest Semitic Inscriptions and the Hebrew Bible.* New York: Oxford University Press, 1997.

Patte, D. *Early Jewish Hermeneutic in Palestine.* SBLDiss 22. Missoula: Scholars Press, 1975.

Peleg, Y. "Going Up and Going Down: A Key to Interpreting Jacob's Dream." Ph. D. diss., Schechter Institute of Jewish Studies, 2000.

Plöger, J.G. *Literarkritische Formgeschichliche und Stilkritische Untersuchungen zum Deutoronomium.* BBB 26. Bonn: Peter Hanstein, 1967.

Polak, F. *Biblical Narrative: Aspects of Art and Design.* Biblical Encyclopedia Library 11. Jerusalem: Bialik, 1994 (Hebrew).

―――. "The Oral and the Written: Syntax, Stylistics and the Development of Biblical Prose Narrative." *JANES* 26 (1999): 59-105.

Polzin, R. *Moses and the Deuteronomist.* New York: Seabury Press, 1980.

Porter, J. "The Legal Aspects of the Concept of 'Corporate Personality' in the Old Testament." *VT* 15 (1965): 361-80.

Propp, V.I. *Morphology of the Folktale.* Translated by Laurence Scott. Austin: University of Texas Press, 1968.

―――. *Theory and History of Folklore.* Tranalted by Ariadna Y. Martin, Richard P. Martin, et al. Manchester: University of Manchester Press, 1984.

Reich, R. "The Concubine at Gibeah: Judges 19-21 ― A Literary Analysis." M.A. thesis, Bar-Ilan University, 1985 (Hebrew).

Revell, E.J. "The Battle with Benjamin (Judges xx 29-48) and Hebrew Narrative Techniques." *VT* 35 (1985): 417-33.

Rice, G. *1 Kings: Nations Under God.* ITC. Grand Rapids: Eerdmans, 1990.

Richter, W. *Die Bearbeitungen des "Retterbuches" in der Deuteronomischen Epoche.* BBB 210. Bonn: Peter Hanstein, 1964.

―――. *Traditiongeschichtliche Untersuchungen zum Richterbuch.* 2nd ed. BBB 18. Bonn: Peter Hanstein, 1966.

Robertson, D. "Micaiah ben Imlah: A Literary View." In *The Biblical Mosaic: Changing Perspectives.* Edited by R. Polzin and E. Rothman. Philadelphia: Fortress Press, 1982, pp. 139-46.

Rösel, H. "Studien zur Topographie der Kriege in den Büchern Josua und Richter." *ZDPV* 91 (1975): 159-90; 92 (1976): 31- 46.

―――. "Jephtah und das Problem der Richter." *Biblica* 61 (1980): 251-55.

Rost, L. *Die Überlieferung von der Thronnachfolge Davids.* Stuttgart: W. Kohlhammer, 1926.

Roth, W. "NBL." *VT* 10 (1960): 394-409.

―――. "Hinterhalt und Scheinflucht: der Stammespolemische Hintergrund von Jos 8." *ZAW* 75 (1963): 296-304.

Rowlett, L.L. *Joshua and the Rhetoric of Violence: A New Historical Perspective.* JSOTSup 226. Sheffield: Sheffield Academic Press, 1996.

Rudin-Ubarsky, T. "The Appendix to the Book of Judges (Judges 17-21)." *Be'er Sheva* 2 (1985): 141-65 (Hebrew).

Rudolph, W. *Chronikbücher.* HAT. Tübingen: Mohr, 1955.

Satterthwaite, P.E. "Narrative Artistry in the Composition of Judges xx 29ff." *VT* 42 (1992): 80-89.

Scharbert, J. *Solidarität in Segen und Fluch im Alten Testament und in seiner Umwelt. I: Väterfluch und Vätersegen.* BBB 14. Bonn: Peter Hanstein, 1958.

Schwally, F. *Der Heilige Krieg im Alten Israel.* Semitische Kreigsaltertumer 1. Leipzig: Deitrich, 1901.

Seevers, B. "The Practice of Ancient Near East Warfare with Comparisons to the Bible." Ph. D. diss., Trinity Evangelical Divinity School, 1998.

Segal, M.Z. *The Books of Samuel.* Jerusalem: Kiryath Sefer, 1956 (Hebrew).

Selman, M.J. *2 Chronicles.* Tyndale Old Testament Commentary. Leicester: Inter-Varsity, 1994.

Shemesh, Y. "Measure for Measure in Biblical Literature." *Bet Miqra* 44 (1999): 261-70 (Hebrew).

Sherlock, C. "The Meaning of *hrm* in the Old Testament." *Colloquium* 14 (1982): 13-24.

Shuger, D.K. *The Renaissance Bible: Scholarship, Sacrifice and Subjectivity.* Berkeley: University of California Press, 1994.

Skinner, J. *I and II Kings.* CBC. Edinburgh: T.C. & E.C. Jack, 1904.

Smelik, K.A.D. "The Ark Narrative Reconsidered." In *New Avenues in the Study of the Old Testament.* Edited by A. S. van der Woude. Oudtestamentische Studiën 25. Leiden: Brill, 1989, pp. 128-44.

Smith, H.P. *The Books of Samuel.* ICC. Edinburgh: T & T Clark, 1961.

Soggin, J.A. *Joshua: A Commentary.* Translated by R.A. Wilson. OTL. London: SCM Press, 1972.

———. *Judges.* Translated by John Bowden. OTL. Philadelphia: Westminster, 1981.

Speiser, E.A. *Genesis.* AB 1. Garden City, NY: Doubleday, 1964.

Stern, P.D. *The Biblical Herem: A Window on Israel's Religious Experience.* BJS 22. Atlanta: Scholars Press, 1991.

Sternberg, M. "The Structure of Repetition in Biblical Narrative: Strategies of Informational Redundancy." *Hasifrut* 25 (1977): 109-50 (Hebrew).

———. *The Poetics of Biblical Narrative.* Bloomington: Indiana University Press, 1985.

Stirrup, A. "Why has Yahweh Defeated Us Today Before the Philistines? The Question of the Ark Narrative." *Tyndale Bulletin* 51 (2000): 81-100.

Stoltz, F. *Jahwes und Israels Kriege.* Zurich: Theologischer Verlag, 1972.

Tadmor, H. "Autobiographical Apology in the Royal Assyrian Literature." In *History, Historiography and Interpretation.* Edited by H. Tadmor and M. Weinfeld. Jerusalem: Magnes Press, 1983, pp. 36-57.

Talmon, S. "The Presentation of Synchroneity and Simultaneity in Biblical Narratives." In *Studies in Hebrew Narrative Art Throughout the Ages.* Edited by J. Heinemann and S. Werses. Scripta Hierosolymitana 27. Jerusalem: Magnes Press, 1978, pp. 9-26.

Thompson, A. "Who Sees Double in the Double Plot?" In *Shakesperean Tragedy.* Edited by Malcolm Bradbury and David Palmer. Stratford-Upon-Avon Studies 20. London: Edward Arnold, 1984, pp. 47-75.

Thompson, J.A. *1, 2 Chronicles.* New American Commentary 9. Nashville: Broadman & Holman, 1994.

Tidwell, N.L. "The Philistine Incursions into the Valley of Rephaim." In *Studies in the Historical Books of the Old Testament.* Edited by J.A. Emerton. Leiden: Brill, 1979, pp. 190-212.

Todorov, T. *Poetique.* Paris: Seuil, 1973.

Van Dam, C. *The Urim and Thummim.* Winona Lake: Eisenbrauns, 1997.

Van der Lingen, A. *Les Guerres de Yahvé: L'implication de YHWH dans les guerres d'Israël selon les livres historiques de l'Ancien Testament.* LD 139. Paris: Cerf, 1990.

Van Seters, J. "Oral Patterns or Literary Conventions in Biblical Narrative." *Semeia* 5 (1976): 139-54.

Rad, G. von. *Der Heilige Krieg im Alten Israel.* Zurich: Zwingli- Verlag, 1951.

———. *Gesammelte Studien zum Alten Testament.* München: Kaiser Verlag, 1971.

Walsh, J.T. *1 Kings.* Berit Olam. Collegeville, MN: Liturgical Press, 1996.

Webb, B.G. *The Book of Judges: An Integrated Reading.* Sheffield: Almond Press, 1987.

Weinberg, M.S. and C.J. Williams. *Male Homosexuals: Their Problems and Adaptations.* New York: Penguin, 1974.

Weinfeld, M. "Divine Intervention in War in Ancient Israel and in the Ancient Near East." In *History, Historiography and Interpretation.* Edited by M. Weinfeld and H. Tadmor. Jerusalem: Magnes, 1983, pp. 121-47.

Weippert, M. "'Heiliger Krieg' in Israel und Assyrien: Kritische Anmerkungen zu Gerhard von Rads Konzept des 'Heiligen Krieges im Alten Israel.'" *ZAW* 84 (1972): 460-93.

Wevers, J.W. s.v. "War, Methods of." *IDB* 4:801-05.

———. s.v. "Weapons and Implements of War." *IDB* 4:820-25.

White, S.A. "Esther: A Feminine Model for Jewish Diaspora." In *Gender and Difference in Ancient Israel*. Edited by P.L. Day. Minneapolis: Fortress Press, 1989, pp. 161-77.

Willi, T. *Die Chronik als Auslegung*. FRLANT 106. Göttingen: Vandenhoeck & Ruprecht, 1972.

Williamson, H.G.M. *1 and 2 Chronicles*. NCBC. Grand Rapids: Eerdmans, 1982.

———. "The Temple in the Book of Chronicles." In *Templum Amicitiae: Essays on the Second Temple Presented to Ernst Bammel*. Edited by W. Horbury. JSNTSup 48. Sheffield: Sheffield Academic Press, 1991, pp. 15-31.

Willis, T. "The Nature of Jephthah's Authority." *CBQ* 59 (1997): 33-44.

Wittig, S. "Theories of Formulaic Narrative." *Semeia* 5 (1976): 65- 91.

Wood, J.A. *Perspectives of War in the Bible*. Macon, GA: Mercer University Press, 1998.

Woudstra, M.H. *The Book of Joshua*. NICOT. Grand Rapids: Eerdmans, 1981.

Wright, J.W. "The Fight for Peace: Narrative and History in the Battle Accounts in Chronicles." In *The Chronicler as Historian*. Edited by M.P. Graham, K.G. Hoglund and S.L. McKenzie. JSOTSup 238 Sheffield: Sheffield Academic Press, 1997, pp. 150-77.

———. "The Founding Father: The Structure of the Chronicler's David Narrative." *JBL* 117 (1998): 45-59.

Yadin, Y. *The Art of Warfare in Biblical Lands*. New York: McGraw Hill, 1963.

Young, E.J. *An Introduction to the Old Testament*. London: Tyndale House, 1964.

Younger, Kenneth L., Jr. *Ancient Conquest Accounts: A Study in Near Eastern and Biblical History Writing*. JSOTSup 98. Sheffield: Sheffield Academic Press, 1990.

Zakovitch, Y. *"Every High Official Has a Higher One Set Over Him": A Literary Analysis of 2 Kings 5*. Tel Aviv: Am Oved, 1985 (Hebrew).

———. *Introduction to Inner Biblical Exegesis*. Even Yehuda: Rekhes, 1992 (Hebrew).

———. *Through the Looking Glass: Reflection Stories in the Bible*. Tel Aviv: Hakibbutz HaMeuchad, 1995 (Hebrew).

Zimmerli, W. *Grundriss der alttestamentlichen Theologie*. Theologische Wissenschaft 3. Stuttgart: Verlag W. Kohlhammer, 1972.

GENERAL INDEX

INDEX OF SCRIPTURAL REFERENCES

SUPPLEMENTS TO VETUS TESTAMENTUM

2. POPE, M.H. *El in the Ugaritic texts.* 1955. ISBN 90 04 04000 5
3. *Wisdom in Israel and in the Ancient Near East.* Presented to Harold Henry Rowley by the Editorial Board of Vetus Testamentum in celebration of his 65th birthday, 24 March 1955. Edited by M. NOTH and D. WINTON THOMAS. 2nd reprint of the rst (1955) ed. 1969. ISBN 90 04 02326 7
4. *Volume du Congrès* [international pour l'étude de l'Ancien Testament]. *Strasbourg 1956.* 1957. ISBN 90 04 02327 5
8. BERNHARDT, K.-H. *Das Problem der alt-orientalischen Königsideologie im Alten Testament.* Unter besonderer Berücksichtigung der Geschichte der Psalmenexegese dargestellt und kritisch gewürdigt. 1961. ISBN 90 04 02331 3
9. *Congress Volume, Bonn 1962.* 1963. ISBN 90 04 02332 1
11. DONNER, H. *Israel unter den Völkern.* Die Stellung der klassischen Propheten des 8. Jahrhunderts v. Chr. zur Aussenpolitik der Könige von Israel und Juda. 1964. ISBN 90 04 02334 8
12. REIDER, J. *An Index to Aquila.* Completed and revised by N. Turner. 1966. ISBN 90 04 02335 6
13. ROTH, W.M.W. *Numerical sayings in the Old Testament.* A form-critical study. 1965. ISBN 90 04 02336 4
14. ORLINSKY, H.M. *Studies on the second part of the Book of Isaiah.* — The so-called 'Servant of the Lord' and 'Suffering Servant' in Second Isaiah. — SNAITH, N.H. Isaiah 40-66. A study of the teaching of the Second Isaiah and its consequences. Repr. with additions and corrections. 1977. ISBN 90 04 05437 5
15. *Volume du Congrès* [International pour l'étude de l'Ancien Testament]. *Genève 1965.* 1966. ISBN 90 04 02337 2
17. *Congress Volume, Rome 1968.* 1969. ISBN 90 04 02339 9
19. THOMPSON, R.J. *Moses and the Law in a century of criticism since Graf.* 1970. ISBN 90 04 02341 0
20. REDFORD, D.B. *A Study of the Biblical Story of Joseph.* 1970. ISBN 90 04 02342 9
21. AHLSTRÖM, G.W. *Joel and the Temple Cult of Jerusalem.* 1971. ISBN 90 04 02620 7
22. *Congress Volume, Uppsala 1971.* 1972. ISBN 90 04 03521 4
23. *Studies in the Religion of Ancient Israel.* 1972. ISBN 90 04 03525 7
24. SCHOORS, A. *I am God your Saviour.* A form-critical study of the main genres in Is. xl-lv. 1973. ISBN 90 04 03792 2
25. ALLEN, L.C. *The Greek Chronicles.* The relation of the Septuagint I and II Chronicles to the Massoretic text. Part 1. The translator's craft. 1974. ISBN 90 04 03913 9
26. *Studies on prophecy.* A collection of twelve papers. 1974. ISBN 90 04 03877 9
27. ALLEN, L.C. *The Greek Chronicles.* Part 2. Textual criticism. 1974. ISBN 90 04 03933 3
28. *Congress Volume, Edinburgh 1974.* 1975. ISBN 90 04 04321 7
29. *Congress Volume, Göttingen 1977.* 1978. ISBN 90 04 05835 4
30. EMERTON, J.A. (ed.). *Studies in the historical books of the Old Testament.* 1979. ISBN 90 04 06017 0
31. MEREDINO, R.P. *Der Erste und der Letzte.* Eine Untersuchung von Jes 40-48. 1981. ISBN 90 04 06199 1
32. EMERTON, J.A. (ed.). *Congress Volume, Vienna 1980.* 1981. ISBN 90 04 06514 8
33. KOENIG, J. *L'herméneutique analogique du Judaïsme antique d'après les témoins textuels d'Isaïe.* 1982. ISBN 90 04 06762 0

34. BARSTAD, H.M. *The religious polemics of Amos*. Studies in the preachings of Amos ii 7B-8, iv 1-13, v 1-27, vi 4-7, viii 14. 1984. ISBN 90 04 07017 6

35. KRAŠOVEC, J. *Antithetic structure in Biblical Hebrew poetry*. 1984. ISBN 90 04 07244 6

36. EMERTON, J.A. (ed.). *Congress Volume, Salamanca 1983*. 1985. ISBN 90 04 07281 0

37. LEMCHE, N.P. *Early Israel*. Anthropological and historical studies on the Israelite society before the monarchy. 1985. ISBN 90 04 07853 3

38. NIELSEN, K. *Incense in Ancient Israel*. 1986. ISBN 90 04 07702 2

39. PARDEE, D. *Ugaritic and Hebrew poetic parallelism*. A trial cut. 1988. ISBN 90 04 08368 5

40. EMERTON, J.A. (ed.). *Congress Volume, Jerusalem 1986*. 1988. ISBN 90 04 08499 1

41. EMERTON, J.A. (ed.). *Studies in the Pentateuch*. 1990. ISBN 90 04 09195 5

42. McKENZIE, S.L. *The trouble with Kings*. The composition of the Book of Kings in the Deuteronomistic History. 1991. ISBN 90 04 09402 4

43. EMERTON, J.A. (ed.). *Congress Volume, Leuven 1989*. 1991. ISBN 90 04 09398 2

44. HAAK, R.D. *Habakkuk*. 1992. ISBN 90 04 09506 3

45. BEYERLIN, W. *Im Licht der Traditionen*. Psalm LXVII und CXV. Ein Entwicklungs-zusammenhang. 1992. ISBN 90 04 09635 3

46. MEIER, S.A. *Speaking of Speaking*. Marking direct discourse in the Hebrew Bible. 1992. ISBN 90 04 09602 7

47. KESSLER, R. *Staat und Gesellschaft im vorexilischen Juda*. Vom 8. Jahrhundert bis zum Exil. 1992. ISBN 90 04 09646 9

48. AUFFRET, P. *Voyez de vos yeux*. Étude structurelle de vingt psaumes, dont le psaume 119. 1993. ISBN 90 04 09707 4

49. GARCÍA MARTÍNEZ, F., A. HILHORST and C.J. LABUSCHAGNE (eds.). *The Scriptures and the Scrolls*. Studies in honour of A.S. van der Woude on the occasion of his 65th birthday. 1992. ISBN 90 04 09746 5

50. LEMAIRE, A. and B. OTZEN (eds.). *History and Traditions of Early Israel*. Studies presented to Eduard Nielsen, May 8th, 1993. 1993. ISBN 90 04 09851 8

51. GORDON, R.P. *Studies in the Targum to the Twelve Prophets*. From Nahum to Malachi. 1994. ISBN 90 04 09987 5

52. HUGENBERGER, G.P. *Marriage as a Covenant*. A Study of Biblical Law and Ethics Governing Marriage Developed from the Perspective of Malachi. 1994. ISBN 90 04 09977 8

53. GARCÍA MARTÍNEZ, F., A. HILHORST, J.T.A.G.M. VAN RUITEN, A.S. VAN DER WOUDE. *Studies in Deuteronomy*. In Honour of C.J. Labuschagne on the Occasion of His 65th Birthday. 1994. ISBN 90 04 10052 0

54. FERNÁNDEZ MARCOS, N. *Septuagint and Old Latin in the Book of Kings*. 1994. ISBN 90 04 10043 1

55. SMITH, M.S. *The Ugaritic Baal Cycle. Volume 1*. Introduction with text, translation and commentary of KTU 1.1-1.2. 1994. ISBN 90 04 09995 6

56. DUGUID, I.M. *Ezekiel and the Leaders of Israel*. 1994. ISBN 90 04 10074 1

57. MARX, A. *Les offrandes végétales dans l'Ancien Testament*. Du tribut d'hommage au repas eschatologique. 1994. ISBN 90 04 10136 5

58. SCHÄFER-LICHTENBERGER, C. *Josua und Salomo*. Eine Studie zu Autorität und Legitimität des Nachfolgers im Alten Testament. 1995. ISBN 90 04 10064 4

59. LASSERRE, G. *Synopse des lois du Pentateuque*. 1994. ISBN 90 04 10202 7

60. DOGNIEZ, C. *Bibliography of the Septuagint – Bibliographie de la Septante (1970-1993)*. Avec une préface de PIERRE-MAURICE BOGAERT. 1995. ISBN 90 04 10192 6

61. EMERTON, J.A. (ed.). *Congress Volume, Paris 1992*. 1995. ISBN 90 04 10259 0

62. SMITH, P.A. *Rhetoric and Redaction in Trito-Isaiah.* The Structure, Growth and Authorship of Isaiah 56-66. 1995. ISBN 90 04 10306 6
63. O'CONNELL, R.H. *The Rhetoric of the Book of Judges.* 1996. ISBN 90 04 10104 7
64. HARLAND, P. J. *The Value of Human Life.* A Study of the Story of the Flood (Genesis 6-9). 1996. ISBN 90 04 10534 4
65. ROLAND PAGE JR., H. *The Myth of Cosmic Rebellion.* A Study of its Reflexes in Ugaritic and Biblical Literature. 1996. ISBN 90 04 10563 8
66. EMERTON, J.A. (ed.). *Congress Volume, Cambridge 1995.* 1997.
    ISBN 90 04 106871
67. JOOSTEN, J. *People and Land in the Holiness Code.* An Exegetical Study of the Ideational Framework of the Law in Leviticus 17–26. 1996.
    ISBN 90 04 10557 3
68. BEENTJES, P.C. *The Book of Ben Sira in Hebrew.* A Text Edition of all Extant Hebrew Manuscripts and a Synopsis of all Parallel Hebrew Ben Sira Texts. 1997. ISBN 90 04 10767 3
69. COOK, J. *The Septuagint of Proverbs – Jewish and/or Hellenistic Proverbs?* Concerning the Hellenistic Colouring of LXX Proverbs. 1997. ISBN 90 04 10879 3
70,1 BROYLES, G. and C. EVANS (eds.). *Writing and Reading the Scroll of Isaiah.* Studies of an Interpretive Tradition, I. 1997. ISBN 90 04 10936 6 (*Vol.* I);
    ISBN 90 04 11027 5 (*Set*)
70,2 BROYLES, G. and C. EVANS (eds.). *Writing and Reading the Scroll of Isaiah.* Studies of an Interpretive Tradition, II. 1997. ISBN 90 04 11026 7 (*Vol.* II);
    ISBN 90 04 11027 5 (*Set*)
71. KOOIJ, A. VAN DER. *The Oracle of Tyre.* The Septuagint of Isaiah 23 as Version and Vision. 1998. ISBN 90 04 11152 2
72. TOV, E. *The Greek and Hebrew Bible.* Collected Essays on the Septuagint. 1999.
    ISBN 90 04 11309 6
73. GARCÍA MARTÍNEZ, F. and NOORT, E. (eds.). *Perspectives in the Study of the Old Testament and Early Judaism.* A Symposium in honour of Adam S. van der Woude on the occasion of his 70th birthday. 1998. ISBN 90 04 11322 3
74. KASSIS, R.A. *The Book of Proverbs and Arabic Proverbial Works.* 1999.
    ISBN 90 04 11305 3
75. RÖSEL, H.N. *Von Josua bis Jojachin.* Untersuchungen zu den deuteronomistischen Geschichtsbüchern des Alten Testaments. 1999. ISBN 90 04 11355 5
76. RENZ, Th. *The Rhetorical Function of the Book of Ezekiel.* 1999.
    ISBN 90 04 11362 2
77. HARLAND, P.J. and HAYWARD, C.T.R. (eds.). *New Heaven and New Earth Prophecy and the Millenium.* Essays in Honour of Anthony Gelston. 1999.
    ISBN 90 04 10841 6
78. KRAŠOVEC, J. *Reward, Punishment, and Forgiveness.* The Thinking and Beliefs of Ancient Israel in the Light of Greek and Modern Views. 1999.
    ISBN 90 04 11443 2.
79. KOSSMANN, R. *Die Esthernovelle – Vom Erzählten zur Erzählung.* Studien zur Traditions- und Redaktionsgeschichte des Estherbuches. 2000. ISBN 90 04 11556 0.
80. LEMAIRE, A. and M. SÆBØ (eds.). *Congress Volume, Oslo 1998.* 2000.
    ISBN 90 04 11598 6.
81. GALIL, G. and M. WEINFELD (eds.). *Studies in Historical Geography and Biblical Historiography.* Presented to Zecharia Kallai. 2000. ISBN 90 04 11608 7
82. COLLINS, N.L. *The library in Alexandria and the Bible in Greek.* 2001.
    ISBN 90 04 11866 7

83,1 COLLINS, J.J. and P.W. FLINT (eds.). *The Book of Daniel.* Composition and Reception, I. 2001. ISBN 90 04 11675 3 (*Vol.* I);
ISBN 90 04 12202 8 (*Set*)

83,2 COLLINS, J.J. and P.W. FLINT (eds.). *The Book of Daniel.* Composition and Reception, II. 2001. ISBN 90 04 12200 1 (*Vol.* II); ISBN 90 04 12202 8 (*Set*).

84. COHEN, C.H.R. *Contextual Priority in Biblical Hebrew Philology.* An Application of the Held Method for Comparative Semitic Philology. 2001. ISBN 90 04 11670 2 (In preparation).

85. WAGENAAR, J.A. *Judgement and Salvation.* The Composition and Redaction of Micah 2-5. 2001. ISBN 90 04 11936 1

86. McLAUGHLIN, J.L. *The Marzēaḥ in sthe Prophetic Literature.* References and Allusions in Light of the Extra-Biblical Evidence. 2001. ISBN 90 04 12006 8

87. WONG, K.L. *The Idea of Retribution in the Book of Ezekiel* 2001. ISBN 90 04 12256 7

88. BARRICK, W. Boyd *The King and the Cemeteries.* Toward a New Understanding of Josiah's Reform. 2002. ISBN 90 04 12171 4

89. FRANKEL, D. *The Murmuring Stories of the Priestly School.* A Retrieval of Ancient Sacerdotal Lore. 2002. ISBN 90 04 12368 7

90. FRYDRYCH, T. *Living under the Sun.* Examination of Proverbs and Qoheleth. 2002. ISBN 90 04 12315 6

91. KESSEL, J. *The Book of Haggai.* Prophecy and Society in Early Persian Yehud. 2002. ISBN 90 04 12368 7

92. LEMAIRE, A. (ed.). *Congress Volume, Basel 2001.* 2002. ISBN 90 04 12680 5

93. RENDTORFF, R. and R.A. KUGLER (eds.). *The Book of Leviticus.* Composition and Reception. 2003. ISBN 90 04 12634 1

94. PAUL, S.M., R.A. KRAFT, L.H. SCHIFFMAN and W.W. FIELDS (eds.). *Emanuel.* Studies in Hebrew Bible, Septuagint, and Dead Sea Scrolls in Honor of Emanuel Tov. 2003. ISBN 90 04 13007 1

95. VOS, J.C. DE. *Das Los Judas.* Über Entstehung und Ziele der Landbeschreibung in Josua 15. ISBN 90 04 12953 7

96. LEHNART, B. *Prophet und König im Nordreich Israel.* Studien zur sogenannten vorklassischen Prophetie im Nordreich Israel anhand der Samuel-, Elija- und Elischa-Überlieferungen. 2003. ISBN 90 04 13237 6

97. LO, A. *Job 28 as Rhetoric.* An Analysis of Job 28 in the Context of Job 22-31. 2003. ISBN 90 04 13320 8

98. TRUDINGER, P.L. *The Psalms of the Tamid Service.* A Liturgical Text from the Second Temple. 2004. ISBN 90 04 12968 5

99. FLINT, P.W. and P.D. MILLER, JR. (eds.) with the assistance of A. Brunell. *The Book of Psalms.* Composition and Reception. 2004. ISBN 90 04 13842 8

100. WEINFELD, M. *The Place of the Law in the Religion of Ancient Israel.* 2004. ISBN 90 04 13749 1

101. FLINT, P.W., J.C. VANDERKAM and E. TOV. (eds.) *Studies in the Hebrew Bible, Qumran, and the Septuagint.* Essays Presented to Eugene Ulrich on the Occasion of his Sixty-Fifth Birthday. 2004. ISBN 90 04 13738 6

102. MEER, M.N. VAN DER. *Formation and Reformulation.* The Redaction of the Book of Joshua in the Light of the Oldest Textual Witnesses. 2004. ISBN 90 04 13125 6

103. BERMAN, J.A. *Narrative Analogy in the Hebrew Bible.* Battle Stories and Their Equivalent Non-battle Narratives. 2004. ISBN 90 04 13119 1